THE SACRED TRUST

THE SACRED TRUST

Sketches of the
Southern Baptist Convention Presidents

EMIR AND ERGUN CANER

BROADMAN
& HOLMAN
PUBLISHERS

NASHVILLE, TENNESSEE

978–0–8054–2668–7

Published by Broadman & Holman Publishers,
Nashville, Tennessee

Dewey Decimal Classification: 286.092
Subject Heading: SOUTHERN BAPTIST CONVENTION—
PRESIDENTS \ SOUTHERN BAPTIST CONVENTION—HISTORY \
BAPTIST—BIOGRAPHY

3 4 5 6 7 8 9 10   12 11 10 09

Dedication

To our sons,
John Mark Caner (b. 2002) and Braxton Paige Caner (b. 1999)

Of all the titles we bear—pastor, preacher, professor, author, among others—the greatest honor our Lord has ever bestowed upon us after our salvation is the name *papa*. You will never know how much we cherish you. We will never be perfect, but in our own flawed and fallible ways, we want to spend a lifetime showing you our love and affection.

Contents

foreword

$\mathscr{T}$he president of the Southern Baptist Convention has no office in a denominational headquarters, receives no salary from his position, is given no staff for assistance, and has few unilateral powers. And yet the SBC presidency is one of the most recognized and influential offices of leadership in the Christian world. Therein lies an enigma and an incredible story.

Or, to be precise, fifty-two stories about the fifty-two men who over the course of the Convention's history have served as president. Each has contributed to the stream of Southern Baptist history, each was shaped by his times, and each was driven by a vision for the future of the Convention and its churches. The biographical vignettes in this important book make for fascinating reading, but they also serve to illuminate the role of the SBC president and to tell the story of the development of the Convention as a great body of cooperating churches.

Outsiders often assume that the president of the Southern Baptist Convention sits at the top of a denominational hierarchy, supervises a vast denominational bureaucracy, and directs the work of the Convention by a command-and-control system of authority. This is a natural assumption, for this would be the case in hierarchical systems of denominational polity. But the Southern Baptist Convention is not a hierarchical system, and no individual sits at the top of a denominational flowchart.

Of course, the SBC president is invested with limited powers of appointment. The president appoints the strategic committee on committees, the committee on resolutions, the credentials committee, and a tellers committee. But the core responsibility of the president is to serve as the Convention's presiding officer during its annual business sessions, and that is where the greatest trust is invested in the president's office.

The Southern Baptist Convention annual meeting is a marvel of the democratic process. In modern times, as many as forty-five thousand messengers have participated in the meetings; and each has an equal right to make a motion, ask a question, raise a point of procedure, or nominate an individual for office. Like the proverbial bumblebee, the SBC shouldn't fly, but it does. This is largely due to the effectiveness of the men who have served as president.

General Henry M. Robert, author of the famous *Robert's Rule of Order,* noted that all deliberative organizations "must have some system of conducting business, and some rules to govern their proceedings."[1] The SBC operates by its charter, constitution, and bylaws. At its founding session in 1845, the Convention adopted the basic pattern of officers we know today, and, constitutionally speaking, the office of SBC president has changed little over the last 158 years.

Of course, the character of the role and the course of a presidency have much to do with the unique context and challenges of the times. The first presidents helped the SBC to forge an identity and gain its organizational footing. Later presidents led the Convention through times of war, national trauma, the Great Depression, denominational controversy, and the expansion of SBC work and influence around the globe.

The Southern Baptist Convention is one of the largest bodies of cooperating churches in the history of Christianity. Its presiding officer is invested with tremendous trust and confidence. James L. Sullivan, a close observer of nearly half of the Convention's presidents, served as the thirty-ninth SBC president in 1977 and noted, "The person elected president is a person in whom the messengers feel they can put their trust at that particular time to meet the issues of that particular date." He continued: "And these issues and circumstances shift from time to time, which means that the characteristics of the people elected to this office will also vary."[2]

The variation of men is a testimony to the tapestry of Southern Baptist history and the times. Most of the presidents have been pastors. Given our concern for the primacy of the preaching office, this is natural. Baptists grow to love and respect those they hear preach and teach the Word of God, and the messengers understandably turn to these men for leadership. When leaders of denominational institutions have been elected, they have generally shared this gift and have been well established as preachers. The few laymen who have served as SBC president came to the office with a rare level of denominational experience and credibility.

Presiding over the business sessions of the Southern Baptist Convention requires tact, expertise, fairness, resolve, and a sense of humor. That last quality cannot be underrated. Baptists are committed, creative, concerned, cooperative, and sometimes contentious but never boring! Each of these fifty-two presidents has brought his own personality and gifts to this office.

Over the long term the appointments made by the president will be his longest-lasting legacy. These critical appointments, especially to the committee on committees, will shape the future of the Convention's work long after the president's term is ended. This is a tremendous responsibility and stewardship.

But if a new SBC president thinks he has been elected to an office of executive power, he will soon learn otherwise. When former five-star General Dwight D. Eisenhower was elected president of the United States, incumbent President Harry Truman commented: "He'll sit here" (tapping his desk for emphasis) "and he'll say,

'Do this! Do that!' *And nothing will happen.* Poor Ike—it won't be a bit like the army."[3] Well, Ike made the government more like the army!

The SBC president may not be invested with executive authority, but he does have something more precious—*influence.* The presidents who have made the greatest impact on the SBC have been those with the greatest influence and credibility.

Proud of our nonhierarchical polity, the SBC invests its leaders with what one Baptist historian has called "expediential authority."[4] This is the authority of the man matched to the times. Presidents of the SBC have helped to resolve conflicts, assisted other Christian leaders, advised presidents of the United States, represented Southern Baptists around the world, and given critical leadership to the total denominational program. At critical times the theological and moral credibility of the president has helped to hold the Convention together.

In the media age presidents have been called upon to articulate the Convention's convictions, explain our most cherished beliefs, and speak to issues of public debate. Given the tenor of our times, this responsibility is almost certain to grow in importance.

The fifty-two stories included in this book help us to understand the development of the Convention's self-understanding and program as well as its presidency. Each name is an honored part of our common history and heritage. Emir and Ergun Caner have given Southern Baptists a great gift and rendered us a great service by writing this book. These gifted young scholars write with verve and with respect for the men and the office. They help us to see the office of SBC president in its proper frame—as a sacred trust.

R. Albert Mohler Jr., President
The Southern Baptist Theological Seminary

Preface
The Gravity of the Gavel

*I*n the published Annual of the proceedings from the 2002 SBC Annual Meeting in St. Louis, Missouri, two brief events are noted among the 153 specific events officially recorded. On Tuesday morning, June 11,

> Morris H. Chapman (TN), president and chief executive officer of the Executive Committee, presented the Broadus gavel to President James G. Merritt (GA). Merritt called to order the one hundred forty-fifth session of the Southern Baptist Convention in the one hundred fifty-seventh year of its history at 8:20 A.M. in the America's Center, St. Louis, Missouri.[1]

Then on Wednesday afternoon the proceedings record: "President Merritt presented the Broadus gavel to president elect Jack Graham (TX)."[2]

These two events took a total of perhaps one minute, and yet the gravity of the events should not be lost on Southern Baptists. The gavel, symbolic not iconic, represents the authority conferred upon the messenger, a Southern Baptist elected from among the other messengers, to chair the proceedings. It is a symbol of our polity, of our decorum, and of our direction. There is gravity in that gavel.

The gavel itself is a historic piece of Baptist history. In 1872, Dr. John A. Broadus presented the gavel as a gift to the Convention meeting in Raleigh, North Carolina. Forged in the Holy Land, the handle is made of balsam wood grown near the River Jordan, and its head is made of olive wood from the Mount of Olives. For 131 years, it has represented the position of the president as "first among equals."

The gavel itself is a reminder of a shared history, heritage, and legacy. The venerable Herschel H. Hobbs joked that after he had been presented with the gavel upon his election in 1961, "I only held it for a few minutes. Before the final 'Amen' had ceased to be heard, the Convention secretary took it, and I did not see it again until just before the opening session the next year. . . . They guard that gavel like it was the gold in Fort Knox."[3]

More important than the simple wooden gavel are the hands that have wielded the power behind it. Southern Baptists have neither pope nor bishop. We do not send delegates; we send messengers. They are free to act, without inference of compulsion.[4]

Yet to each generation of our history, leaders are born to face each contemporary crisis. God has always had a remnant to proclaim the pure gospel on this earth, and in Southern Baptist life He has always given us leaders who have spoken prophetically to their world. These fifty-two men have been anointed by God and appointed from among us to serve, lead, speak, preach, exhort, and call Southern Baptists to our perpetual task of evangelism, discipleship, and missions.

It is perhaps best at this juncture to remind the reader of the unique distinctives of the presidency in the Southern Baptist Convention. Foremost, the president must himself be a messenger to the annual Convention.

Baptists believe deeply in the foundation of the local church, anchored to Jesus Christ. The local churches, now numbering over forty thousand, elect messengers to the annual Convention meeting each year in business meetings. These messengers attend the meeting representing their local churches and give the direction to the entities of the SBC.

Baptists are emphatically a grassroots fellowship, which determines the actions of the boards who act in our stead. It is a bottom-up distinction which must be maintained, not an ecclesiastical hierarchy or bishopric. We are autonomous and willingly cooperative.

As most Baptist theologians will heartily attest, the president does not speak *for* Southern Baptists; he speaks *to* them. Baptists believe in soul autonomy, and the core beliefs that we hold dear set the parameters for our corporate mission. We are a confessional people, not a creedal people. The president casts the vision and calls us to accountability before God.

Finally, the president is one of us. He is a messenger, not a celebrity. He sets the standard, but he is not superhuman, for we have no episcopacy. Therefore, this is not an enumeration of saints but the humanization of our heroes. Our leaders and forefathers are our heroes because they made the sacrifices and paid the price to see that Southern Baptists remain as stewards of God's remarkable blessings and perpetual witnesses around the world of the love of Christ.

This history has been designed to examine the lives and ministries of the fifty-two men who have served the Convention as president. It is an investigation of their heartbeats and the passion of their lives. It is our desire that the men herein are not seen as the pastors of megachurches but rather the young ministers, often impoverished in livelihood but not of spirit, who struggled in anonymity and obscurity before they became men of renown.

These were men who dared to believe that the task of world evangelism was not too large a task, too costly a labor, or too steep a climb. They dared to believe that we were equal to the task to which God called us, in his power alone. They have dared to inspire us to seek the face of God.

Truth is immortal!

Dr. Emir Caner
Assistant Professor
Southeastern Baptist Theological Seminary
Wake Forest, North Carolina

Dr. Ergun Caner
Assistant Professor
The Criswell College
Dallas, Texas

Acknowledgments

$\mathcal{T}$he authors would like to thank the following people for their diligent aid and labors in enabling the completion of the manuscripts and research:

Hana Caner and Jill Caner, for abiding with our horrific schedules.

Dr. Paige Patterson and the Southeastern Baptist Theological Seminary, Wake Forest, North Carolina, and Dr. C. Richard Wells and The Criswell College, Dallas, Texas, for allowing us the time to research and write.

Our institutional vice presidents, Drs. L. Russ Bush, Lamar Cooper, and James Bryant, for your constant encouragement and graciousness.

Dr. Gerald Cowen, dean of Southeastern College at Wake Forest.

Phyllis Jackson, Southeastern Seminary, for her invaluable proofreading and transcribing.

Bill Sumners, director and archivist of the Southern Baptist Historical Library and Archives, Nashville, Tennessee, for the compilation of the SBC presidential addresses.

Tammi Ledbetter, Baptist Press, for her valuable advice and research.

Patrick Bottoms and the Texas Baptist Historical Archives, Dallas, Texas.

The Alabama Baptist Historical Archives.

Deron Spoo and the First Baptist Church of Tulsa, Oklahoma.

Keith Ninomiya.

Scott Smith and the BSEA.

Dr. T. T. Crabtree and the First Baptist Church of Springfield, Missouri.

Dr. Rick Garner and the First Baptist Church of Mansfield, Texas.

Calvin Wittman and the Applewood Baptist Church of Wheat Ridge, Colorado.

1
WILLIAM BULLEIN JOHNSON

June 13, 1782–October 1, 1862
Elected: 1845, 1846, 1849

*O*n October 1, 1862, a day in the life of William Bullein Johnson had drawn to an ordinary close. In Anderson, South Carolina, Johnson had finished his daily routine and was talking with his beloved granddaughter Ella Townes. Though separated by many years, the two found a great affinity with each other. Ella intensely admired her grandfather, even reading his *Reminiscences,* an autobiographical account of Johnson's life and accomplishments. That night she told him, "How grateful you must be, Grandfather, for doing so much good!" He responded quietly, "Not unto me, not unto me—but to Thy Name, O God, be all the glory!"[1]

This one statement, then, represents the life story of the first Southern Baptist Convention president. Johnson was born at John's Island, South Carolina, on June 13, 1782, to Joseph Johnson and Mary Bullein. The sole survivor of the three children, William revered his mother for her exemplary character and dedication to teaching him the Scripture. He explained:

> She sought to imbue my mind, at an early age, with profound reverence for the Holy Scriptures as the Word of God, and for this purpose often spoke to me of the Savior. . . . She taught me also the great principles of the doctrine of Christ which were so impressed upon my mind that they were of great service to me when I began to preach.[2]

Providentially, Johnson was also influenced by other stalwarts of the Baptist faith, including Richard Furman and Charles Screven, both of whom were members of the church the family attended. Yet, of all the memories of influential men in his childhood, Johnson emphatically recalls his reception with President George Washington. In 1791, he shook the hand of the first president of the United States of America. Little did he know the irony of such an event, as he himself would become the first president of the Southern Baptist Convention.

Although Johnson was reared with strong spiritual principles, he was not known for his spiritual prowess. Indeed, Edmund Botsford, a pastor in Georgetown, South Carolina, and mentor to William, described his pupil's heart as showing "only pride, vanity, lust, anger, disrespect to God, his word, his gospel, and his ministers."[3] Strangely enough, Johnson was a member of the Antipedo Baptist Church of Georgetown. But by his own admission, he never made a public profession of faith, nor was there any evidence of a Spirit-filled life.

This rebellious attitude changed shortly after his mother's death in 1804. The family, including his father's new wife, moved to Beaufort, where William was persuaded to attend an evangelistic camp meeting. But the preaching did little to convince William of his need for Jesus Christ. Instead, William recalled two dreams he had that would forever change his life:

My attention was drawn upward to the right where I beheld the same form I had the night before. But oh, how changed! Instead of distress in [Christ's] countenance, joy beamed forth upon the attendants around him, of whom I seemed to be one, upon whom he looked with a benign smile and a moral change most happy came over my spirit. I felt as though the gates of heaven were opened before me and in this happy frame I continued some weeks.[4]

Exuberant about his newfound faith, Johnson was baptized shortly thereafter at the Beaufort Baptist Church. Furthermore, Johnson, who had attended Brown University, immediately dropped his law practice and entered the ministry. In January 1805, after months of ministering to orphans, widows, and the sick, he was licensed to preach the gospel by Beaufort Church.

In 1806, Johnson accepted his first pastorate at the Euhaw Baptist Church, a congregation where George Whitefield once preached. Johnson began organizing two mission stations around the county. Regardless of the weather conditions, he traveled each Sunday to each of the stations preaching the gospel in local households. His audience was uneducated and grossly immoral. However, many of these rabble-rousers were converted and became leaders in the newly established work.

In 1809, Johnson was called to serve as chaplain of South Carolina College (now the University of South Carolina). With new intellectual opportunities, Johnson was pleased with his new position. Here he once again demonstrated his heart for missions and established the First Baptist Church of Columbia. Yet, with only thirteen members, Johnson continuously fought financial hardships. He and his wife, formerly Henrietta Hornby, recognized that the church was "not in pecuniary means adequate to support of [our] growing family."[5]

In 1811, Johnson accepted the pastorate of Savannah Baptist Church, convinced that the church could support the family. However, he was unaware of the tribulations about to beset him. Johnson believed in strong pastoral authority and insisted on interviewing baptismal candidates before they were immersed. Furthermore, Johnson contended that ordaining elders by the laying on of hands by other elders was unbiblical. This was the sole right of the pastor. Finally, when the church clerk read an opposing letter by former pastor Henry Holcombe, Johnson claimed pastoral authority once again. When the church refused to hear their pastor's response to Holcombe, Johnson resigned in haste. Allowed to preach for three more weeks, Johnson did not miss an opportunity to castigate the congregation. The next Sunday, after pronouncing the church a "corrupt body," Johnson left angrily.[6]

This event helped shape Johnson in years to come. He learned from his harsh and abrupt attitude and became a conciliator during the tumultuous times between Northern and Southern Baptists. In fact, this disharmony of the brethren taught Johnson that Christians should work together when at all possible. While in Savannah, Georgia, in 1813, Johnson was providentially introduced to the missionary pioneer and promoter Luther Rice. Rice convinced Johnson of the great need for missionary support, detailing Adoniram Judson's significant work in India. Johnson then took up the worthy cause and heralded the message to the newly formed Triennial (Baptist) Convention, which in turn began supporting such worthy causes through its Foreign Mission Board. Ultimately, one of Johnson's eight children, Francis, became one of the first missionaries of the Southern Baptist Convention, appointed to China in 1846.

This desire for cooperation among Baptists also led to his leadership in the formation of the South Carolina Baptist Convention in December 1821. Recognizing the chasm between many churches, Johnson circulated a short paper he wrote entitled, "The Alarming Condition of the Churches." He elucidated:

> The present is a season of alarming visitation from the hand of our God. Our churches generally complain of great coldness and declension. Serious troubles exist between some of them, and even between some of their ministers and venerable fathers in the gospel. . . . Are we careful to maintain secret and close communion with our God? Are we doing for God what is in the power of our hands as instruments to do for his adorable name?[7]

In the years following, Johnson became president of the South Carolina Baptist Convention, accepted the invitation to lead the Greenville Female Academy, and was appointed as a member of the Board of Commissioners for the Triennial Convention.

In the 1840s, Johnson once again found himself embroiled in controversy; this time it was of an even greater degree. Baptists were sectionalized between the North and the South. Regional concerns overshadowed missionary fervor. Many Baptists were apathetic or anti-missionary. The Triennial Convention failed to reach budget expectations. Johnson, president of the Convention, grew ill and removed himself from consideration for another term.

Johnson's conciliatory leadership faded, and rigidity took over. After the 1844 meeting, the Alabama Baptist Convention placed before the acting board of the

Convention a hypothetical case concerning the appointment of a slaveholder. The board rejected any notion of appointing a missionary who was also a slaveholder. The schism was imminent. Now Johnson, always the mediator, had to choose sides.

Dismayed at the potential to lose all missionary enthusiasm, Johnson resigned himself to the loss of the national Convention. He recognized the inevitable split between Baptists was at hand. On May 8, 1845, the Southern Baptist Convention was formed with only two boards. The Foreign Mission Board would be located in Richmond, Virginia, while the Domestic Mission Board would be situated in Marion, Alabama. Johnson, acknowledged as the premier statesmen of Baptists in America, was elected the first president. Now Southern Baptists had the two things they needed: a respected leader and a resurgent missionary effort.

In 1851, Johnson was forced to retire due to several factors, including the poor health of his daughter, Elizabeth, as well as his own severe sickness. He remained active in missionary endeavors, and though worried about hyper-Calvinists' insistence on a creed,[8] assisted in founding the Southern Baptist Theological Seminary in 1859 in Greenville, South Carolina. In 1860, Johnson began writing the long overdue *Reminiscences*, a memoir of his life.

Two years later, on October 1, 1862, William Bullein Johnson died peacefully at his home. The *Edgefield Advertiser* memorialized the spiritual giant:

> The deceased was a soldier of the Cross who feared not man, nor turned aside from his duties for the love of man. In his pastoral life he dared not dishonor his Master's cause by a complaisant, faltering discharge of his obligations. . . . As a preacher of the Word, there are those in Heaven as well as on Earth who will bear immortal testimony to his faithfulness.[9]

2

ROBERT BOYTE CRAWFORD HOWELL

March 10, 1801—April 5, 1868
Elected: 1851, 1853, 1855, 1857

*F*ew men can withstand the squalls and furies of conflict and confrontation. Throughout Christian history certain men have risen to meet a challenge, often being drained of their life's energies as a consequence. Robert Boyte Crawford Howell, the second president of the Southern Baptist Convention, withstood the storms of not one but three major controversies in the span of his three decades of ministry. Through every conflict, Howell was a statesman, a gentleman, and a Christian of the highest caliber. He evidenced Christian grace, so much so that at the memorial service held at First Baptist Church, Nashville, following his death, Dr. J. B. McFerrin, a Presbyterian minister, said:

> I lived on most intimate terms of Christian friendship with Doctor
> Howell. At one time we were both editors of church journals, and our
> expression of opinion on doctrinal differences sometimes, as did those
> of the apostles of old, became sharp, but our warm and fraternal
> regard for each other was never broken to the last. Doctor Howell was
> a scholar, a gentleman and a Christian. He enjoyed the abiding affec-
> tion of his congregation, the high esteem of the community and, what
> was better than all, the signal favor of God, as the abundant success of
> his pastoral labors testifies. I could not, were I disposed, pronounce a
> suitable eulogy upon him.[1]

Such accolades were not foreign to the life and ministry of Dr. R. B. C. Howell.

Born on March 10, 1801, in Wayne County, North Carolina, to Ralph and Jane (Crawford) Howell, Robert Boyte Crawford Howell was baptized on February 6, 1821, into the Nanchanty Baptist Church outside of Raleigh, North Carolina. Though he came from an Episcopalian family[2] and was not quite twenty years old, Howell pursued Christian devotion and ministry with a passion. Routh notes:

The very next Sunday, the young man [Howell] was to take as his text Matthew 11:2–6 and preach on the infinite grace manifested in the gospel of Christ. By the time he left for Columbian College [in Washington, D.C.] the next fall, he had won two hundred others to Jesus as Savior.[3]

That was not to say that Howell believed he was called solely to be a minister. Even in college in 1823–1827, he struggled between surrendering to the ministry and becoming a lawyer. Homer Grice continues, "After the 1825–26 session [graduating from Columbian] he left for home to become a lawyer. However, at Portsmouth, Va., he was induced to become a missionary."[4] Thus, the 1826 law graduate saw the course of his life change, as God led him elsewhere.

In Norfolk, Virginia, the Cumberland Street Baptist Church extended the invitation for Howell to become their pastor. He refused. Believing Howell was the man God had called to their church, they initiated a second invitation, at which time Howell acquiesced. On January 7, 1827, R. B. C. Howell was ordained as pastor.

Howell served the Cumberland Street congregation for seven years. During this time he married Mary Ann Morton Toy on April 23, 1829, and began his family, which would eventually include ten children, two of whom would die in infancy.

In July 1834, Howell's surrender to mission service led him to visit Nashville, Tennessee, to accept the appointment as a "missionary to the West from the American Baptist Home Mission Society."[5] Nashville in 1834 was a town of approximately six thousand people, and First Baptist Church, Nashville, was embroiled in a controversy which would become Howell's first ministerial confrontation.

Accepting the pastorate of First Baptist, Nashville, was not a prestigious step at the time. The church, founded in 1820 and once a formidable congregation, was in disarray after a doctrinal war over Campbellism (named after leader Alexander Campbell). The Campbellite teachings insisted on baptismal regeneration and the movement's exclusive claim to salvation. On May 24, 1828, all but five members followed the pastor in leaving the church and taking the building as well. Reconstituted on October 10, 1830, the waning members of the First Baptist Church were a mere shell of their once strong existence.

Howell, however, was not dissuaded from the task. Beginning on January 1, 1835, Howell built the membership of First Baptist up to approximately five hundred, including blacks and whites in the congregation. The Baptist reputation, damaged by the Campbellite schism, was restored, as the congregation built a new house of worship in 1837.

Trouble and confrontation, however, were on the horizon. In the rapid growth of the congregation, rumblings came against the missionary fervor which was spreading throughout Tennessee and northern Alabama. Luther Rice (1783–1836) was working diligently to organize a missionary movement that would work both in

America and overseas, and Howell was facing a minority revolt in his church. Tom Nettles summarizes the conflict:

> These [antimissionary] forces responded negatively to the formation of the General Missionary Convention and the work of its most notable agent, Luther Rice, referring to him as a "modern Tetzel." In addition to the ecclesiological objections they held toward centralized organizations, they discountenanced some of the methods used by the agents, declaring them to be Arminian in methodology, thus denying their Calvinistic heritage. Eventually, however, the anti-mission society movement degenerated into pure hyper-Calvinism and denied the validity of giving a free offer of the gospel to all men, railed against theological education, and viewed Bible societies as totally unwarranted by the Word of God.[6]

On June 18, 1838, Howell led the congregation to "exclude a minority of about (one hundred) antimissionary members, who claimed they were the true church and the majority no church at all."[7]

The fifteen years Howell spent at First Baptist Nashville were also productive for the Baptist movement as a whole. Almost immediately upon arriving in January 1835, Howell published a monthly newspaper called *The Baptist*. He worked as editor of the publication until he sold it to the Tennessee Baptists in 1848. *The Baptist* served as a voice for Baptists in the burgeoning state. Howell also took over the leadership of Rice's missionary society after Rice's death in 1836; led in establishing Union University;[8] advocated the inception of a theological training school for ministers, which would eventually become the Southern Baptist Theological Seminary; and in May 1842, restructured the Baptist General Association of Tennessee and North Alabama.[9] When the Southern Baptist Convention was organized at the meeting at the First Baptist Church of Augusta in 1845, Howell was "named on the committee to obtain the charter from the state of Georgia."[10]

By 1850, the reputation, health, and missionary fervor at First Baptist Nashville was intact. In the fifteen years of his leadership, the church had baptized 392 people and seen twenty-three young men surrender to the gospel ministry. In July 1850, Howell accepted the call to the Second Baptist Church of Richmond, Virginia.

During his tenure at the growing church in Richmond, the mantle of Southern Baptist leadership fell on his shoulders. William B. Johnson had been elected twice as the Convention president, but he was in poor health. When the Convention convened in 1849, Howell was elected as president in the midst of a crisis. Originally, the Convention was going to meet in Nashville, but a cholera epidemic almost caused the meeting to disintegrate before it began. Howell, serving as vice president, called for the meeting to reconvene in Charleston, South Carolina.[11] During his time at Second Baptist Richmond, Howell would be elected to serve eight years as SBC president.

In 1857, Howell returned to the pastorate of the First Baptist Church, Nashville and was immediately immersed in the third major controversy of his ministerial career a conflict that would once again threaten the life of his congregation and the Convention. In the final years of his first pastorate at Nashville, Howell had seen a young man from Vermont named James Robinson Graves join his church. Graves, born in 1820, became the assistant editor of *The Baptist* under Howell's leadership in November 1846. By June 1848, Howell had stepped aside from the publishing duties, and Graves had become the editor.

During the seven years Howell served in Richmond, J. R. Graves had become a leader in the Landmark movement. Surrounded by Methodists and Campbellites in Tennessee, Graves began to challenge the perceived ecumenism which he viewed as a threat to Baptist distinctives. When the American Bible Society refused to publish William Carey's Bengali Bible because he translated the term *baptizein* as *immerse,* many Baptists felt the growing influence of pedobaptists was untenable.[12] The subsequent movement, however, now threatened any missionary endeavor that called for cooperation, even among other Baptist churches.

As Howell assumed the pastorate at First Baptist Nashville, the two men were set at odds. The ensuing battle even caused Howell to surrender the presidency of the Convention, as Graves was excluded from the Nashville church, only to start another church directly in conflict with First Baptist Nashville.[13] The next eleven years of his life were devoted to rebuilding the Nashville congregation and continuing his writing. His prolific pen has given us many essential works in Baptist life, including *The Deaconship, The Way of Salvation, The Evils of Infant Baptism, The Terms of Christian Communion, The Cross, The Covenants,* and *The Early Baptists of Virginia,* among others.

On April 5, 1868, Robert Boyte Crawford Howell succumbed to illness and died. His failing health had caused him to resign from the Nashville church in July 1867, and he died ten months later. Few could challenge his esteemed place in Baptist history, and the Southern Baptist Convention in particular. The Nashville newspaper reported his final days:

> His death occurred on Sunday, about noon [April 5, 1868], at the very [hour] in which, for more than forty years, he had stood up for Jesus in the pulpit. For a week he had been stricken with paralysis, speechless but not unconscious. When his pastor, Doctor Skinner, spoke of the infinite pity and compassion of the Saviour for his suffering servant, he burst into tears. When asked if he saw Jesus, he answered by pointing first to his heart and then to heaven. Of Doctor Howell's labors as a voluminous author and a vigilant pastor it is not necessary to speak, as he attained a more than national reputation. He has been long considered a standard bearer in the communion in which he was so great an ornament. He was, moreover, held in high esteem in the community at large, with respect to church relations.[14]

3

RICHARD
FULLER

April 22, 1804—October 20, 1876
Elected: 1859, 1861

As Richard Fuller was standing in the river ready to be baptized, an older woman whispered to her friend, "Didn't I tell you so, Miss Harriet? I knew the Lord would bring him." Illustrating her enthusiasm about the event, she further explained, "The river looked bright that day, and the leaves on the trees along the bank were clapping their hands for joy."[1] That day in 1831, Fuller was baptized by Pastor Wyer of the Savannah Baptist Church.

Fuller had struggled for a long while with the act of rebaptism. Having already been baptized by the Episcopal church, Fuller concluded that he was not a believer at the time of that baptism and needed to demonstrate his obedience to the command of Christ to be baptized after salvation. Furthermore, he had entered the gospel ministry and desired to exhibit his commitment to Baptist doctrine.

In 1832, Fuller was ordained to the gospel ministry. On the day of his ordination, the newly called pastor of the Beaufort Baptist Church baptized one hundred people. In the years to come, Fuller would baptize stalwarts of the Baptist faith, including Annie Armstrong, founder of the Woman's Missionary Union, and James Petigru Boyce, one of the founders of The Southern Baptist Theological Seminary. Fuller was rewarded for his bold decision to be baptized biblically.

On April 22, 1804, Richard Fuller was born in Beaufort, South Carolina. He was more interested in athletics than academics, so it was somewhat surprising that young Richard entered Harvard College at the age of sixteen. Yet, by his sophomore year, Fuller was considered the best scholar in his class. Therefore, when he became ill during his last two years of education and withdrew from many of his classes, the college faculty nevertheless recommended granting his degree in law. This illness, which caused hemorrhaging of the lungs, tormented Fuller most of his life. Constantly reminded of the pain during preaching, he explained, "I almost envy these men who can speak for hours without feeling it."[2]

In 1824, Fuller started a law practice in South Carolina. He was immediately successful, and by the age of twenty-eight, Fuller was earning more than six thousand dollars annually. Also during this time, in August 1831, Richard married Charlotte Bull. In the years following the Fullers had three daughters. Richard expounded about his firstborn Bessie:

I have become the father of a most charming little daughter. . . . My heart runs over with the fullness of its gratitude to that God who is every day making his goodness to pass before me. When I look at my heart, and see so much vileness, and then to my past life—so little done, and that little so defiled,—I stand amazed amidst perpetually renewed blessings, and can only exclaim, "Is this the manner of men, O Lord God?"

Sadly, the two older daughters, Bessie and Annie, died after a brief married life. Both devout Christians, they met their Savior long before their parents died. Fuller affirmed in a letter to the youngest daughter Florence, "I constantly praise him for such a wife and such sweet children."[3] In the final analysis, Fuller demonstrated how a humble man can honor God by his devotion to his family.

Fuller also dedicated himself to the community. In 1831, he joined the Episcopal Church. Noting the social advantages of joining the established church, Fuller was nonetheless convicted about the latitude allowed in the mode of baptism. The rector of the church accordingly baptized Fuller by immersion at the local river. Considered a "mongrel Baptist" by some in the town, his family, themselves members of a Baptist fellowship, continued to pray for their son. When the famous evangelist Daniel Baker came through Beaufort, both the Episcopal and the Baptist church asked him to preach. During one of the revival services on October 26, 1831, Fuller came forward to be saved. He wrote later in his family Bible:

My life for years was spent amidst vanity and folly and sin. Pride and evil passions prevailed. I felt satisfied I had never experienced that change without which a man cannot enter the kingdom of heaven. Glory to God! I found at last what I sought, and was filled with a joy which I can never express—"unspeakable, and full of glory." These ecstatic feelings have now passed away (they would have rendered me unfit to live in such a world); but I am still filled with the peace of God.[4]

Soon after, Fuller was baptized properly and accepted the call to the gospel ministry. Recognized for his piety and talent, Fuller himself doubted his oratory skills and was his harshest critic. The church rapidly began to grow. In fact, Fuller also set up preaching stations on plantations, led by deacons of the church as well as African-Americans.

Yet Fuller overworked himself and exacerbated his persistent illness. He sought medical help in Europe. In the summer of 1836, Fuller spent significant time in Rome, center of Catholicism. Familiar with the anti-Romanism of his fellow ministers, Fuller studied Romanism firsthand and concluded, "But the churches and cathedrals here combine all that elegance and sumptuousness and age can contribute. Never was there so magnificent a superstition as that of Rome, and the whole land of Italy is sunk beneath its influence."[5]

After six months abroad Fuller was rejuvenated both physically and spiritually and was ready to return to his flock. For the next ten years, his ministry increased evangelistically while he also found himself in the middle of an international controversy. As tensions ran high between the North and South, one of the contentious issues was, of course, slavery and the question of its biblical viability. In 1844–1845, Fuller wrote numerous letters to *The Christian Chronicle* in which he pointed out that even the great evangelist George Whitefield owned slaves and rejoiced as some of them came to faith in Christ. Furthermore, he stated that blacks were treated with respect, earning an education through the local Baptist churches. Finally, Fuller articulated that he was doing his best to care for his servants and spent his salary caring for them.

In 1847, Fuller accepted the call to the Seventh Baptist Church of Baltimore, Maryland, where he would remain until his death. The city was not known for its strong Baptist influence, so Fuller immediately went to work preaching the gospel in the predominantly Catholic city. His first order of business was to build a suitable house of worship. After this preliminary task, the church experienced remarkable growth, so much so that newspapers began attacking the once obscure Baptist movement. Fuller used this platform to speak on baptism. In his *Baptism, and the Terms of Communion*, published in 1850, Fuller heralded the Baptist position as found in the New Testament as opposed to the man-made tradition of infant baptism. In the following, he explained the corruption of infant baptism:

1. Infant baptism makes void the commandment of God by a human tradition.
2. Infant baptism has introduced and perpetuated among Christians the most glaring and mischievous confusion and inconsistency as to the Churches and Church membership.
3. It destroys entirely the significancy of baptism.
4. It reflects injuriously upon God, and tarnishes the glory of the atonement.
5. The system of infant baptism would break down the distinction between the Church and the world.
6. It perpetuates unhappy and pernicious divisions among Christians.
7. The last mischievous consequence of this practice, is the injury it does to our children.[6]

Fuller, quickly becoming one of the foremost leaders among Baptists, also rose in prominence nationally. In 1841, he preached his now famous sermon, "The Cross" (John 12:32), to the Triennial Convention in Baltimore. That sermon solidified his place as one of the premier preachers of his day. In fact, he preached at each Convention until 1862. As the Civil War neared its beginning, the Baptists had already split.

The newly formed Southern Baptist Convention secured stable leadership in the persons of W. B. Johnson and R. B. C. Howell. Yet Howell was in the midst of his own theological controversy in 1859 and therefore resigned from a fourth term as president.

Fuller was known for his leadership as a pastor, so Southern Baptists quickly turned to him. Elected to two full terms (1859–1863), Fuller assumed a difficult role during the most difficult of times. The Foreign Mission Board, located in Richmond, Virginia, was cut off from any communication with its missionaries in China and Africa. Furthermore, funds from the South became scarce due to the war. Fuller acted aggressively and set up the Provisional Board in Baltimore. Here Fuller ensured that missions would continue through the arduous times of conflict.

By 1871, Fuller had led the Seventh Baptist Church in Baltimore to its height of twelve hundred members. Led by God to begin another congregation, Fuller followed more than a hundred members in the formation of the Eutaw Place Baptist Church, also located in Baltimore. After pastoring his previous flock for twenty-four years, Fuller embarked on his final pastorate. After five years of service, the new church had increased its membership to 452. Preaching his last sermon just a few weeks before his death from cancer, Fuller spoke appropriately on the subject, "We walk by faith and not by sight" (2 Cor. 5:7).

Always desiring to be a soldier of the cross, Fuller spent his last days expressing his love of the Lord. The last words he uttered before he met his Savior were, "Who'll preach Jesus?" Richard Fuller died on October 20, 1876. Ultimately, he will be less remembered as the president of the Southern Baptist Convention and much more as a preacher of the cross of Christ. His last charge to his flock reveals the heart of this man of God: "Above all, be faithful to Christ and His truth."

4
PATRICK HUES MELL

July 19, 1814—January 26, 1888
Elected: 1863, 1866, 1867, 1868, 1869, 1870, 1871, 1880, 1881,
1882, 1883, 1884, 1885, 1886, 1887

*P*atrick Hues Mell served as president of the Southern Baptist Convention for a record seventeen years, though he was often considered the reluctant leader, more often satisfied to stay behind the scenes. He was orphaned as a young teen and left to care for his siblings, and yet by the time he was twenty-one he was a college graduate. He served as pastor of a number of small churches many of his peers would have shunned yet rose to prominence to lead convocations of thousands. He was a polemicist against the perceived growth of Arminianism among Baptists and had voracious defenders but carried himself with grace and a gentle deportment. Patrick Hues Mell was more than just a president of the Southern Baptist Convention; he served as the emblem of the grace of God and a portrait of the tenacity and faith of early Southern Baptist leaders. From the gathering at Augusta in 1845 until his death in 1888, Mell poured himself into the missionary endeavor of Southern Baptists.

Major Benjamin Mell and Cynthia (Sumner) Mell were blessed with a large family in Walthourville, Georgia, just north of Jacksonville, Florida.[1] Their oldest son, Patrick Hues, was born on July 19, 1814. Tragically, Patrick's father died when he was only fourteen, and his mother passed away when he was not yet seventeen.[2] As the oldest son of eight children, Patrick assumed the responsibility of raising his brothers and sisters, but he yearned to complete his education beyond high school.

Before she died, Patrick's mother attended to the spiritual condition of each of her children. In the fall of 1829, she wrote a letter to her fifteen-year-old son, noting his already evident talents, yet concerned for his spiritual progress:

> You have arrived at an age when I wish you to become my bosom
> friend and companion in all things, but above all, in those things
> which belong to your everlasting peace. I have sometimes feared that
> other subjects have occupied your thoughts, and yet I have the firmest

hope that your mind is truly sensible of the value and importance of divine things.

I cannot but hope that you sometimes lift up your heart in prayer, and that your affections are somewhat directed towards divine truth.

I cannot express to you how much the belief comforts and strengthens my mind. None but God knows what my feeling has been on that point. It must ever be kept in mind that the mere study of the ministry, however valuable in the individual, will not suffice, but consecration to God must be had before he or another for him fixes on the ministry for his profession. And I shall not hesitate to say to you that honored and happy as I should feel in being permitted to see you a faithful preacher of righteousness, adorning the gospel which you would proclaim to others, yet without this I would rather a thousand times see you in the humblest station in life. I will not conceal from you any longer my anxiety for you to become a minister, yet I dare not decide on such a plan without much more clear evidence than I have yet seen, that your actual state, feeling and conduct, temper and conversation, habitual and fixed thoughts, are such as will justify me in doing so. I say this with anxiety, and write with fear, but I say it with earnest prayers *for the real conversion of your soul to God,* and with some hope that he will hear the petition that I have endeavored to offer up for you for many years back. I will repeat: I can never consent for you to study for the ministry until I have some satisfactory proof of your heart being turned to God in holy consistency and permanency of character.[3]

Her admonitions obviously had a strong effect. "In 1832, three years after the dates of the above letters, [Patrick] was baptized at North New Port Baptist Church, in Liberty County, by the pastor, Rev. Josiah Samuel Law."[4]

In 1833, Mell borrowed money to attend Amherst College in Amherst, Massachucetts, a full one thousand miles north of their hometown. To supplement his meager living, Mell taught in various Massachusetts schools and became so adept that he was asked to continue teaching in the area after his graduation in 1835.

Returning to Georgia in the summer of 1837, Mell continued to teach in prestigious academies and preparatory schools, including a school operated by Emory College (now University) in 1839: "The Board of Trustees of Emory College . . . elected. . . . Mell to the position of principal of the 'Oxford Classical and English School' which was a preparatory school for the college."[5]

The year 1839 also saw Mell finally settle the issue of his calling, and in correspondence with Dr. Law, he finally surrendered to the Lord's calling. Upon his return:

P. H. Mell began preaching in the neighborhood of Oxford, Georgia, in the spring of 1840, under the license given him by the North Newport church. His engagements at the college were met during the weekdays; on the Sabbaths he visited the destitute places and preached to the people the message of salvation. He was not, however, an ordained minister at this time and did not have regular charge of a church.[6]

At the dawn of the 1840s, three events took place that greatly affected young Patrick Mell. On June 29, 1840, he married Lurene Howard Cooper. It was a union that would last until Lurene's death in 1860 and produced eight children.[7] Second, Mell was ordained and became pastor of Penfield Baptist Church in Greensboro, Georgia, in November 1842. He would serve the Penfield church for ten years.[8] Finally, in 1842, Mell was elected professor of ancient languages at Mercer University, after teaching there as an assistant for a year. He would remain at Mercer for thirteen years, until 1855, teaching under the leadership of President John L. Dagg.

In 1845, Mell began his long association with the newly formed Southern Baptist Convention. When he attended the organizational meeting at the First Baptist Church of Augusta, Georgia, in May 1845, Mell was attending as the clerk of both the Georgia Baptist Association and the Georgia Baptist Convention (state). It was the first of an amazing number of positions Mell would serve. In the forty-one years from the Augusta meeting until his death, Mell would serve as either moderator or clerk of the association thirty-six times, moderator or president of the state Convention thirty-two times, and as president of the national Convention for seventeen years. All told, Mell served Baptists for a combined eighty-nine years.

Mell's love of education, however, led him to his greatest influence among Baptist students, and also his greatest academic crisis. Mell was fiercely loyal to President Dagg, and when the board of trustees of Mercer asked for Dagg's resignation in 1855 and offered the presidency to Mell, he instead united with almost the entire faculty and refused. Instead of becoming president, Mell resigned from his position as professor.[9] His lack of a livelihood was brief, however, as he was almost immediately offered other positions, including the presidency of the Baptist College of Mississippi; the position of principal of the Montgomery, Alabama Female Institute; and pastorate of the First Baptist Church of Savannah, Georgia.[10]

Mell politely declined all of these offers and in 1855 accepted the position of professor at the University of Georgia, under President Alonzo Church. Beginning in 1860, Mell was elected vice chancellor of the university, and after the term of Henry H. Tucker (1874–1878), he was elected chancellor.[11] Serving as chancellor of the university until shortly before his death in 1888, Mell would eventually give thirty-three years of service to the distinguished university and its students.

While beginning his tenure at the University of Georgia, Mell began to expand his influence into the doctrinal and educational world. At the insistence of his church members and colleagues, Mell saw his first book, *Baptism and Its Mode and Subjects*, published in 1854. This would be followed by other important works such as *Corrective Church Discipline* (1860) and *The Doctrine of Prayer* (1876).

He also published small works on slavery, predestination, Calvinism, God's providential government, and the philosophy of prayer. At the time of his death he was working on several articles and on what perhaps would have been his most useful book, a volume on Baptist church polity.[12]

During the Civil War, Mell was enlisted as a soldier in the Confederacy and was promoted to colonel in his regiment. The tragedy of the period was more personal for Mell, as he lost his beloved wife of twenty years in 1860. On December 24, 1861, he was married to Elizabeth Eliza Cooper, and she bore him six more children, for a total of fourteen.[13]

His expertise in leading Southern Baptists earned him the sobriquet "The Prince of Parliamentarians." The Texas Baptist paper, with regard to a recent Southern Baptist annual meeting held in Waco in 1883, wrote:

The Southern Baptists can never cease to admire the genius of Dr. Mell as a presiding officer. He rules with the inflexible rigor of a tyrant, and yet with a spirit so genial and sympathetic that no reasonable man can ever be embarrassed by his presence.[14]

In 1867–1868, Mell wrote *A Manual for Parliamentary Practice*, which became the standard for the procedures of the SBC for decades.

In the midst of his most fruitful period of life, Mell was stricken by a malady that would incapacitate him to some degree for the rest of his life. His son writes:

In August, 1871, while filling his pulpit at Bairdstown, he was prostrated by a nervous attack which came near terminating his life. He was unable to reach his home for several weeks and his friends all over the State despaired of his life. But it pleased God, in His kind Providence, to spare him for still greater usefulness. For an entire year or more he was unable to attend to the duties of his chair in the University of Georgia, and was forced to give up all preaching and all other active work. The Board of Trustees of the University of Georgia was exceedingly kind to him during his illness, and gave him a vacation of one year, continuing his salary.[15]

The illness would also keep him from attending to his duties as president of the Southern Baptist Convention, and between 1871 and 1880, he did not attend the sessions of which he was so fond.

After the year of confinement, Mell did resume preaching at the Antioch and Bairdstown churches, where he served twenty-eight years and twenty-three years respectively. His preaching on the sovereignty of God was known throughout the

SBC, and his leadership enabled Southern Baptists to avoid the dangers of the Arminian theology that was taking hold in many parts of the country.

Returning to the annual meetings of the Southern Baptist Convention in 1879, Mell was immediately reelected as president, a position in which he served for seven more years. On January 26, 1888, Patrick Hues Mell died in his home in Athens, Georgia. At the Southern Baptist Convention session in Richmond later that year, the Foreign Mission Board presented a resolution of tribute that attempted to summarize the life and ministry of such a man of God:

> The late President of the Southern Baptist Convention will long be remembered. His erect figure, angular features, keen eye, concise speech. His incisive thoughts, cogent logic, unyielding orthodoxy, commanding address, all represented a type of manhood which impressed indelibly, even as steel makes cuts into granite not to be worn away by the waves of time.[16]

5
JAMES PETIGRU BOYCE

January 11, 1827—December 28, 1888
Elected: 1872, 1873, 1874, 1875, 1876, 1877, 1878, 1879, 1888

As the Civil War raged in 1862, J. P. Boyce's dream of theological education in the South came to a screeching halt. Boyce, who vehemently opposed the secession of the Southern states, nonetheless served the Confederacy as a chaplain. In a letter to his sister, Boyce explained his burdened soul for the nation:

The country [my grandfather] bled for, and for which [my father] himself gave his strength and means in 1852, is still dear to me. Nor do I yet despair; I believe that ere many months have gone by we shall all be safe again under the folds of the glorious Stars and Stripes of our own United States. I believe that the Southern States will yet present their ultimatum to the North, and when they do, that it will be accepted. If not, then I am ready to leave them.[1]

In spite of the times in which he lived, Boyce distinguished himself as a statesman, a politician, and most of all, a theologian.

James Petigru Boyce was born on January 11, 1827, in historic Charleston, South Carolina. Though both his father and his mother were reared in strict Presbyterian homes, the family began to attend the services of the First Baptist Church of Charleston, which was under the leadership of Basil Manly. In November 1830, the Manly family suffered the loss of their young son John. Sadly, Basil had decided to attend the Baptist State Convention and missed the burial of his son. With a sense of duty to God, Manly preached the next Sunday a sermon entitled, "If I be bereaved of my children, I am bereaved" (Gen. 13:14). After this message Mrs. Boyce was converted. The two families became close friends, and when Manly died, J. P. Boyce, preached the funeral. He was about the same age as Manly's deceased son.

In 1845, Boyce matriculated at Brown University. The president of the university, Francis Wayland, was immersed in a theological debate with South

Carolina pastor Richard Fuller over the issue of slavery as a scriptural institution. Boyce, considered a budding scholar by many of his professors, was introduced to many issues during his education, including that of missionary endeavor when Adoniram Judson, a pioneer Baptist missionary to Burma, visited the campus in 1845.

The most important event that occurred during his formative years was Boyce's own conversion. The Second Great Awakening, begun on the campus of Yale University, was sweeping through the states. Boyce, who had returned home to Charleston for the spring vacation in 1846, was under deep conviction of his sin. On April 22, 1846, after hearing a powerful sermon by Richard Fuller, Boyce was born again and baptized. One professor remarked on the instantaneous change of young Boyce: "He returned to college a changed man. He at once joined the religious society, and with characteristic energy and zeal engaged in efforts to promote a revival, of which his conversion may be regarded as the beginning."[2]

In 1847, Boyce graduated from Brown. Though his father was hopeful that James would become a reputable lawyer, God had other plans for the young man. In 1849, Boyce entered Princeton Theological Seminary with the purpose of training for the ministry. While the professors at Brown University had played an integral role in leading Boyce to salvation in Jesus Christ, the Princeton theologians solidified Boyce's stance in Reformed doctrines as taught to him from his childhood. Indeed Boyce later used the same textbooks as a professor at the newly formed Southern Seminary in Greenville, South Carolina. Furthermore, Boyce's magnum opus, *Abstract of Systematic Theology*, is modeled after *Systematic Theology*, written by his theological mentor at Princeton, Charles Hodge.

In October 1851, satisfied with his theological training, Boyce accepted the call as pastor of the Baptist church in Columbia, South Carolina. Patiently shepherding the flock, Boyce saw steady growth during his four years of service. He implemented a ministry to the slaves in the city, winning many to Christ and discipling the new believers.

In 1854, Boyce's father died from heart trouble. Boyce, recognizing his need to take a leave of absence, was granted a sabbatical of six months.

In 1855, a year after his father's death, Boyce offered his resignation to the church in Columbia. Boyce had always desired to teach theology, and he was finally given the opportunity at Furman University in South Carolina. However, Boyce once again displayed his love for the struggling church, pledging to contribute $10,000 toward a new house of worship. The newly elected professor, only twenty-nine years old, showed remarkable maturity. This would continue in the years that followed.

In 1856, Boyce delivered his monumental message, "Three Changes in Theological Institutions." In his address the theology professor proposed three changes in Baptist education:

1. A Baptist theological school should openly accept all who want to enroll regardless of their educational background.
2. A Baptist theological school should excel in its academics, offering specialized courses to those of advanced standing. This would make American Baptists less reliant on foreign scholarship while producing preeminent theologians among Southern Baptists.
3. A Baptist theological school ought to adopt a confession of faith, an abstract of principles, to which every professor must sign and adhere.

Without knowing it at the time, Boyce had laid the groundwork for Southern Baptist education for generations to come. Indeed, Southern Baptist seminaries still use his three principles without much modification.

In 1859, Boyce's dream of a theological seminary culminated with the establishment of The Southern Baptist Theological Seminary in Greenville, South Carolina. The seminary began its inaugural year with four professors and twenty-six students. Unfortunately, the political situation overshadowed the success of the young seminary as the United States was on the brink of civil war. After three short years in existence, enrollment declined as many students enlisted in the Confederate army, some as chaplains and some as soldiers. In 1862, the seminary made the grave decision to close down temporarily, while still financially retaining the four professors. While two professors took pastorates, Boyce and his good friend John Broadus enlisted as chaplains for the Confederacy.

Though the war ravaged much of the nation, Boyce and his colleagues never abandoned the idea of reopening the seminary. At the end of the Civil War, the four professors met at Boyce's home in Greenville, South Carolina. Here they resolved in their hearts "that the seminary may die, but we will die first."[3] While the passion of the other three professors was evident, Boyce clearly held the seminary together with his leadership and his financial generosity. In fact, while his estate diminished substantially, Boyce continually turned down lucrative offers to assume the presidency of institutions such as Brown and Mercer.

Through the tireless efforts of Boyce and his contemporaries, the seminary's situation gradually stabilized and improved. In 1869, the board of trustees hired a fifth faculty member, Crawford H. Toy, appointing him professor of Old Testament and oriental languages. The student body stagnated during the 1870s, and the financial situation faltered. In 1872, in the midst of this hectic time at the seminary, Boyce was elected president of the Southern Baptist Convention. He was annually reelected to the office until 1879. As in his leadership at the seminary, Boyce mastered his position, convincing the Convention of the need to move the institution. In 1877, the board resolved to move the seminary to Louisville, Kentucky.

In his inaugural address, Boyce justified the move:

> Suffice it to say that the calamities of the war forced us to remove from South Carolina. The first endowment having been lost, it was necessary to secure another. In seeking a home elsewhere, we have

been fortunately brought to this city. Its vast extent and large population, with the thousands here who need the instruction which Sunday schools and small preaching places can afford, furnish every facility for exercising our pupils in the practical work of pastor and preacher.
With its extensive railroad facilities we are put in immediate connection with all portions of the South.[4]

On September 1, 1877, the relocated seminary opened with eighty-nine students, twenty-one more than the largest number in Greenville.

However, theological trouble loomed on the horizon due to the Darwinian historical reconstruction of the Old Testament by the newly hired professor, Crawford Toy. Dr. Toy, who had studied first at Southern Seminary before going to Europe to complete his work, rejected the full inspiration and accuracy of the Old Testament. After much discussion, Boyce eventually clashed with Toy, rejecting the notion of errancy in the Bible. In his pamphlet, *A Brief Catechism of Bible Doctrine* (1867), Boyce expounds his view on the Scripture: "God inspired holy men to write it. Did they write it exactly as God wished? Yes; as much so as if He had written every word Himself."[5]

In the end the board accepted Toy's resignation. Saddened by the unavoidable conclusion, Boyce walked with Toy to the railroad station and said his final goodbye. In a passionate gesture he explained to Toy, "Oh, Toy, I would freely give [my right] arm to be cut off if you could be where you were five years ago, and stay there."[6] Toy, by the end of his life, was an avowed Unitarian who discarded the supernatural in the Scripture.

In 1888, Boyce culminated his lifelong contribution to Southern Baptists by being reelected as president by the Convention after the death of President P. H. Mell. Working diligently for Southern Baptists to the end, Boyce's health deteriorated considerably. In the summer of 1888, Boyce traveled to Europe to attempt to relieve his ailments. Though his health seemed to rejuvenate, Boyce's condition became critical while he was visiting France. On December 28, 1888, Boyce fell asleep after a lifetime of arduous labor for the Lord.

Only sixty-one years old, Boyce was laid to rest at the Cave Hill Cemetery in Louisville. Innumerable people commemorated the life and character of Boyce, but perhaps none was as appropriate as the first brief editorial notice found in the *Seminary Magazine*:

No word from us can express what Dr. Boyce was to his students.
It was one of those sweet and tender relations that cannot be
described, and can be understood only as felt. In behalf of those who
studied under him, we have tried hard to say just what we feel, but all
in vain; for, try as we may, we unconsciously penned the words, "He
loved us, *we loved him!*" The hundreds of old students who read this
will understand it without comment. They are as unable to explain the
matter as we are; they can only say, *"We loved him!"*[7]

6
JONATHAN HARALSON

October 18, 1830—July 11, 1912
Elected: 1889, 1890, 1891, 1892, 1894, 1895, 1896, 1897, 1898

𝒪ne humorous pulpit legend notes that God created the sport of boxing as an outlet for local Baptist church business meetings. When tempers flare and issues become divisive, one common element for fanning the flames is a disagreement over parliamentary procedure. One member seated for business "calls the question," while another begins yelling, "Point of order!" Another member rises to ask for a "point of personal privilege," and the meeting reaches a fever pitch while the moderator struggles to gain some semblance of decorum. If one multiplies this fracas exponentially, the end result can often resemble the business sessions of the annual meeting of the Southern Baptist Convention. Since 1902 in Asheville, North Carolina, when the annual meeting first topped a thousand messengers (1,093), the volume of discussion has occasionally become heated.

When the Southern Baptist Convention needed a steady and firm voice as moderator of the annual Convention meetings, the messengers turned to the first layman ever to hold the post of president. Judge Jonathan Haralson was not only a respected Christian, lawyer, and judge; he was also an associate justice on the supreme court of Alabama. He was also an unrivalled expert on parliamentary procedure and a steadying influence on the denomination.

Jonathan Haralson was born in south central Alabama, in Lowndes County, on October 18, 1830.[1] As the son of prosperous farmers, Haralson had a strong Baptist influence in his parents William Browning and Temperance Martin Haralson. Saved in 1844 at the age of fourteen, Haralson was educated in country schools.

Haralson entered the University of Alabama in 1848, where Basil Manly Sr. was president.[2] Having received his bachelor of arts degree in 1851, Jonathan remained at the university to complete his master of arts (A.M.) in 1853. He also received his law degree from the University of Louisiana and, in the last half of the decade, settled into a law practice in Selma, Alabama.

In Selma, the young lawyer became quickly engaged in Baptist work. Having already been an active member and teacher in his parents' church, Haralson was ordained a deacon in 1855. His pastors in that seminal Dallas County, Alabama, ministry were nothing less than pioneers in Southern Baptist life. Abner G. McCraw was an Alabama Baptist trailblazer, preaching in various areas and starting new churches. He succeeded Charles Crow at the Ocmulgee church after Crow died. McCraw would go on to serve other churches and two terms as president of the Alabama Baptist Convention.[3]

J. B. Hawthorne, pastor of such historic churches as First Baptist Church of Atlanta, Georgia, Grove Avenue Baptist Church in Richmond, Virginia, and the First Baptist Church of Nashville, Tennessee, served as Haralson's pastor for a time. However, his closest friend and mentor was the pastor of the First Baptist Church of Selma and future founding secretary of the Baptist Sunday School Board, James Marion Frost (1848–1916).

Haralson was not only an important Baptist layman; he was also becoming a distinguished leader in the judicial world. In 1876, Haralson was "appointed to [the] city court at Selma by Governor Houston."[4] He would remain at this position for seventeen years until his appointment as an associate justice of the Alabama Supreme Court in 1892. He would serve in this capacity for another eighteen years until he retired at the age of eighty.

Judge Haralson distinguished himself with a calm and stately manner. His speech was measured and reasonable, and his methodical manner was viewed as fair, in both the secular and Baptist arenas. At the relatively young age of forty-four, Judge Haralson was elected president of the Alabama Baptist Convention and distinguished himself in that position for seventeen years, until 1891 when he was unable to attend the State Convention. He served as a trustee of Howard College, a member of the American Baptist Education Society, and a trustee of the Alabama Polytechnic Institute.[5]

In 1888, at the annual SBC meeting in Richmond, Virginia, Dr. James Boyce was elected president again, having been previously elected from 1871 to 1878. The sixty-year-old Boyce was in failing health. Though he attempted to lead the Convention in the six months following the annual meeting, it was apparent that Dr. Boyce was growing increasingly fragile. Traveling to France that fall, Boyce died on December 28, 1888.

The following summer, on May 10, 1889, the messengers of the Southern Baptist Convention gathered in the First Baptist Church of Memphis, Tennessee, with some confusion. Louis Bell Ely of Carrollton, Missouri, took the gavel and called the messengers to order.[6] The first order of business was the election of a president, and Dr. M. B. Wharton, distinguished pastor of the First Baptist Church of Eufaula, Alabama, rose to make a historic nomination. He nominated the vice president of the Southern Baptist Convention, Judge Jonathan Haralson. After a brief and perfunctory vote, the Southern Baptist Convention had elected the first layman in its forty-four-year history.

One of the most contentious issues over which President Haralson had to preside was the formation of a board that would produce materials for Sunday School classes throughout the Convention. With numerous failed attempts and questions of financial viability, the issue also hinged on local church autonomy to choose the materials without an outside structure of influence, which went against traditional Baptist polity. Southern Baptists seemed equally split on the issue, with such leaders as James B. Gambrell (against the board) and J. M. Frost (for the board) on opposite sides of the issue.

> The Baptist papers in the various states, except the *Baptist and Reflector* (Tenn.) and the *Western Recorder* (Ky.), opposed Frost's resolutions editorially. Frost's proposal was considered at the Fort Worth Convention (1890), and a Sunday school committee was set up, which served for one year with headquarters in Louisville. At the Convention in Birmingham the following year (1891), Frost made a motion that the matter be referred to yet another committee, consisting of one member from each state, and that their report be made a special order before that session of the Convention. Frost and James Bruton Gambrell, who were made subcommittee to frame the report for the larger committee, held an all-day conference harmonizing their own views concerning the best approach to the perplexing problem. Compromises were reached whereby Gambrell would write the last paragraph of the report and Frost would pen the last sentence. Gambrell stressed complete freedom of the local church in purchasing its literature, while Frost pleaded that a fair chance be given the new board to live and prosper. With President Jonathan Haralson presiding, the Convention dealt with the final resolutions [that] were read by Frost recommending a Sunday School Board. With the timely assistance of John Albert Broadus, the report was adopted without debate and with only 13 opposing votes.[7]

Judge Haralson certainly exemplified Baptist grace and statesmanship. He was evenhanded yet firm, and for the next ten years, the laconic layman served as the SBC president. His dry humor and wisdom were not lost on Southern Baptists. When once asked about the often-divisive nature of Southern Baptists, Haralson quipped, "Southern Baptists are like alley cats. They scream and holler and fight, but in a few months there are more of them."[8]

When Haralson died at the age of eighty-two, on July 11, 1912, J. M. Frost wrote of him in glowing terms:

> I have seen mighty men as presiding officers, but to my thinking and yet without disparagement to others, I never saw his superior in

wielding the gavel and directing the forces of the great assembly. He was equally great whether the Convention was in a mighty storm, as sometimes happened in those days, or was under the influence of a great surging wave of spiritual influence.[9]

7
WILLIAM JONATHAN NORTHEN

July 9, 1835—March 25, 1913
Elected: 1899, 1900, 1901

*O*n August 27, 1893, a major hurricane made landfall on Georgia's southern coast. Now known as the twentieth deadliest storm in the past five hundred years, the hurricane claimed more than two thousand lives, most of them African-Americans who lived on Georgia's barrier islands. In Charleston alone one thousand drowned in the tidal surges, while thirty thousand Georgians were left homeless. The governor of Georgia, W. J. Northen, acted swiftly to minimize the damage to human lives. He called on Clara Barton and the Red Cross, and the organization set up headquarters and, over the next ten months, brought back a sense of normalcy. Barton wrote later, "The submerged lands were drained, 300 miles of ditches made, a million feet of lumber purchased and houses built, fields and gardens planted with the best seed in the United States, and the work all done by the people themselves."[1]

Though much of Georgia was devastated, the people would once again rebuild as they had many times before due to war, disasters, and depressions. William Jonathan Northen, a layman in a Southern Baptist church and future president of the Southern Baptist Convention, led the way to recovery. A man of genuine character, Northen had the unique ability to be both a secular statesman and a Christian statesman. At his funeral one of his friends described his disposition:

> The secret of his success as a pronounced Christian in political
> action was not in the skillful manipulation of either the religionist or
> the politician. It was in himself. He never divided himself between
> them. He was not one and then the other—a religious man in religion
> and a political man in politics. His religion was his life, not a phase of
> his life. His political devotion was a genuine expression of his life, not
> an incidental engagement. His identity as a Christian was as personal
> in the Capitol as it was in the church. And his consciousness of public

obligation was as positive in the prayer meeting as on the political hustlings.[2]

As demonstrated in the disaster, Northen believed the best witness of inner faith was illustrated in his outward action.

William Jonathan Northen was born on July 9, 1835, in Jones County, Georgia. One of eleven children, William grew up in the shadow of Mercer University where his father supervised Steward's Hall. Furthermore, his father was a prominent lay leader in the Georgia Baptist Convention.

In 1853, Northen graduated from Mercer University. Demonstrating his appreciation for the education given to him, nineteen-year-old William began teaching at Mt. Zion Academy, his sole profession for the next twenty years with the one exception of serving in the Confederate army during the Civil War.

From 1861 to 1865, William served as a private under the command of his father, who was captain of his unit. William experienced firsthand the devastation the war had caused Georgia and the other Southern states. Returning from the conflict, he devoted himself to improving the dismal situation through education.

However, it was not long before Northen desired to increase his influence through politics. Forced to resign his teaching position due to ill health, Northen returned to his farm in Hancock County. Providentially, Northen exhibited an unusual talent in this field. The major industry in the South, the farming profession was in dire need of improvement and greater productivity in the rural communities of the South.

Northen set his sights on the Georgia House of Representatives, a place where he could propose changes in the farming situation. As one of his contemporaries stated, "He was among the first of its modern apostles to exalt the farm as the fortress from poverty and illiteracy for the people of Georgia."[3] Northen uplifted the spirits of his fellow Georgians, earning him two terms in the state legislature, one term in the state senate (1884–1885), and a term as president of the Georgia Agricultural Society (1886–1888).

In spite of his demanding political schedule, Northen never lost touch with his passion for God and his desire to uplift the situation of Georgia Baptists. In the area of education, he served as a trustee of Mercer University for forty-four years (1869–1913). Politically, he served as president of the Georgia Baptist Convention for twelve years (1896–1908), while concurrently serving as the president of the Southern Baptist Convention for three years (1899–1901).

Perhaps his greatest contribution to the faith was on a local level. Northen was a charter member of the Ponce de Leon Baptist Church in Atlanta, Georgia, where he taught an adult Bible study while chairing the board of deacons.

In 1890, Northen rose to national prominence when he was elected governor of the state of Georgia. Concerned for the welfare of the black community, Northen enacted a law in 1893 making "mobbing" or "lynching" a felony. Indeed, if a person was killed during the act, the criminal was put on trial for murder.

Though discrimination continued to be rampant, this symbolic gesture was the beginning of legal justice in Georgia for African-Americans.

This concern for African-Americans bled over into his Baptist life. In 1894, Northen attended a meeting in Monroe, Virginia, which decided that the Southern Baptist Convention would assume a greater burden for the education of blacks in the South, relieving Northern Baptists from this difficult endeavor. The committee agreed to the following:

> The Southern Baptist Convention, through its Home Mission Board, shall appeal to the Baptists of the South for the moral and financial support of these schools, and that these local committees shall encourage promising young colored people to attend these institutions. . . . It is unanimously voted by the joint committee to . . . cooperate in the mission work among the colored people of the South, in connection with the Baptist State bodies, white and colored, in the joint appointment of general missionaries, in holding ministers' and deacons' institutes, and in the better organization of the missionary work of the colored Baptists.[4]

Northen had a genuine concern for the common man, regardless of color. Elected into public and religious office, Northen believed his job was sacred. Therefore, when injustices were approved or neglected, he believed that part of the sovereignty and dignity of the state had surrendered to the hands of cowards.

In 1899, Northen was elected president of the Southern Baptist Convention because of respect for his character and integrity. He presided over the Convention during a time of steady growth and expansion into the West. Indeed, the Convention illustrated this shift while meeting in Hot Springs, Arkansas, in 1900, and New Orleans, Louisiana, in 1901. The Convention was growing under the steady hand of a lay leader.

Even when Northen was increasing in years, he continued to crusade for worthy and eternal causes. In 1907, when the Southern Baptist Convention met in Richmond, Virginia, Northen and his good friend from Maryland, Joshua Levering, organized the Layman's Missionary Movement, an association dedicated to educating men of the need to spread the gospel to all parts of the world. It seems that his last endeavor was his greatest: reaching the world for the cause of Christ.

Northen never slowed down even in his final years. Attending almost every Mercer commencement, traveling to most of the Southern Baptist Conventions, and leading Georgia Baptists until three years before his death, Northen desired to help the common man while uplifting the name of Christ. In the end his friends remembered him as a tireless proponent of great principles. He was selfless and passionate for causes most dear to him. In a written eulogy published in the Georgia Baptist paper, *The Christian Index*, one pastor wrote on the passing of his friend:

At a time when old age makes for retreat and composure, and under circumstances of financial comfort which withdraw men to ease and rest, he kept at the front of the battle. More than any man I ever knew at his age and under his circumstances his life rang true to the clarion of the poet: "Bring me my bow of burning gold, bring me my arrows of desire, bring me my spear—O, clouds unfold! Bring me my chariot of fire. I will not rest from mortal fight, nor shall my sword sleep in my hands, 'till we have wrought Jerusalem in Georgia's green and pleasant land."[5]

On March 25, 1913, Northen died. The concerns of this world faded as eternity became his home.

8
JAMES PHILLIP EAGLE

August 10, 1837—December 20, 1904
Elected: 1902, 1903, 1904

In the history of the Southern Baptist Convention, four public officials served as president: Georgia Governor W. J. Northen, Arkansas Governor James Phillip Eagle, Texas Governor Pat Neff, and Arkansas Congressman Brooks Hays. However, for Governor James Phillip Eagle, most observers of historical biographies would deduce that serving small local churches as pastor was a greater pleasure and higher calling. He was a soldier, politician, statesman, governor, farmer, and Southern Baptist president; yet in small rural churches throughout Arkansas, he was simply Brother James. This was his legacy.

Born on August 10, 1837 in Maury County, Tennessee, James Phillip Eagle was the son of pioneer farmers in the developing West.[1] His father, James Eagle (1813–1863) was born in Rowan County, North Carolina. In 1829, he moved to Maury County, Tennessee, and five years later, he married Charity Swaim (d. 1881). The marriage produced James Phillip three years later; and when James Phillip was five years old, the family moved to Lonoke County, Arkansas, to begin farming a new parcel of land.

At the beginning of the Civil War in 1861, twenty-four-year-old Eagle enlisted in the Fifth Arkansas Regiment of the Confederate army of America as a private. Shortly thereafter he was promoted to major and transferred to the Second Arkansas Mounted Riflemen Brigade as a member of the cavalry. This unit, called Reynolds' Brigade, was under the direction of Brigadier General Daniel H. Reynolds in the Army of Tennessee. Serving under General John B. Hood, the Reynolds' Brigade distinguished itself as one of the most capable in the Confederate army, and they saw much action. Eventually becoming a lieutenant colonel,[2] Eagle participated in the bloody battles of Hominy Creek, Elk Horn, Farmersville, Richmond, Murfreesboro, Chickamauga, and Dug Gap. Once the regiment traveled into Georgia, Eagle's division fought in all the battles that stretched from Dalton to Peach Tree Creek. At the Peach Tree Creek battle, near Atlanta, Eagle was wounded, and by January 23, 1865, he returned home to Lonoke County.

The period following the Civil War was profoundly important in the life of James Phillip Eagle. Though already 28, he began undergraduate studies at both Lonoke and Mississippi College in Clinton, Mississippi.

Eagle did not become a Christian until 1867 at the age of 30.[3] That year he was baptized by Elder Moses Green at the New Hope Baptist Church and began to court Mary Kavanaugh Oldham. The courtship would last fourteen years, until their marriage in Little Rock in 1882. Eagle was 45 years old when he was finally married.

In the interim years before Eagle entered the political arena, he set about establishing his farm and deepening his walk with Christ. By 1869, he had built a cabin on his family farm and was ordained as a minister by the New Hope Church.

In 1873, Eagle was elected to the Arkansas State Legislature, where his service was characterized by a firm belief in representing his constituents. Quickly rising to leadership, Eagle was a delegate to the state constitutional Convention in 1874 and became speaker of the house in 1885.[4] During his tenure in the state legislature, Eagle was elected president of the Arkansas Baptist Convention. For the next twenty-five years, from 1880 to 1905, Eagle would hold that position, unparalleled in our time.

In 1888, Eagle was nominated as the Democratic candidate for governor. The period of Reconstruction had set emotions on edge, and the campaign was a particularly heated one. The opposing candidate was Dr. C. M. Norwood, a one-legged Confederate soldier. He was a passionate speaker and populist. Eagle defeated Norwood for governor in 1888 by a narrow margin of less than twenty thousand votes. He served two terms as governor, the second term being marred by illness.

At the 1901 annual meeting of the Southern Baptist Convention in New Orleans, Louisiana, the almost eight hundred messengers elected Governor Eagle as president. He would serve three complete terms as president of the Southern Baptist Convention while simultaneously serving as governor of his state and president of the Arkansas Baptist Convention. During this period of time, the Eagles were certainly a family of distinction, traveling easily in the upper levels of political and denominational life. At the World's Columbian Exposition of 1893, Mrs. Eagle was listed in the *Prominent Portraits* book, along with Henry Drummond, Frederick Douglass, and Thomas A. Edison.[5] She was also a leader in the growth of the Women's Missionary Union work in Arkansas.[6] As a final testimony of his leadership abilities, Eagle helped establish Ouachita College and was fervent in his support of the Arkansas school.

Yet for all of the accolades and acclaim, James Phillip Eagle remained a simple preacher of the gospel. Following his ordination in 1869, Eagle began a pattern of church planting and pastoring which he continued until his death on December

20, 1904. The New Hope Baptist Church wanted to begin a new work farther from the center of the county, and Eagle was part of the work:

> During the summer of 1868, Elder A. M. Russell, Missionary of Caroline Association, who lived at Jacksonport, Arkansas, preached in the section south of here and assisted by . . . James P. Eagle, J. M. King and Moses Green, organized and built the Richwoods Baptist Church. . . . These faithful men of God through their untiring efforts brought about a large church organization and great ingathering of souls. Lonoke Baptist Church was organized by Missionary A. M. Russell, our first pastor, assisted by Bros. James P. Eagle (our second pastor) and J. M. King in the school house upon the ground where our present school building is located, in the year 1869 or 1870.[7]

In his recollections, recorded some fifty years after the founding of the Lonoke Baptist Church, W. P. Fletcher spoke fondly of the man who traveled with presidents and kings yet was most comfortable with the members of small rural churches: "His influence was felt for good by reason of his great character and the Lonoke Baptist Church was known far and wide by reason of her two Governors of the State of Arkansas, James P. Eagle and W. K. Oldham."[8]

9
EDWIN WILLIAM STEPHENS

January 21, 1849—May 22, 1931
Elected: 1905, 1906, 1907

In 1776, the United States of America declared independence from Great Britain. In the years that followed, Americans won the right to be free from the tyranny imposed by the British crown. But the battle won on the east coast had not yet been fought west of the Mississippi River. In the latter half of the eighteenth century, the Louisiana Territory was ruled by Spain. Known to many as one of the most intolerant countries in the world at that time, Spain imposed strict religious barriers on its territory, forbidding and expelling any religious meeting that was not Catholic and vehemently opposing any religious organization outside the Roman Church.

Nevertheless Baptists courageously entered the territory, risking both imprisonment and fines. By the end of the century, Baptists could be found in many towns, though the law forbade their existence. Politically, Spain had sold the territory to France in lieu of other property. When President Thomas Jefferson purchased Louisiana from Spain, the territory was open to new missionary advances. By 1806, the Bethel Baptist Church became the first permanent non-Catholic religious organization west of the Mississippi River. Exactly one hundred years later, E. W. Stephens, long-time leader of Missouri Baptists, commemorated this historical event:

> Baptists were the pioneers of religious liberty west of the
> Mississippi as they had been east of it one hundred and sixty years
> before. As they had given this precious boon to the America of the
> East they were destined under the guidance and the blessing of God to
> give it to the America of the West. . . . If, as has been justly said, it
> was the raising of an American flag west of the Mississippi River that
> made a Baptist church possible in what is now Missouri, let it also not

be forgotten that it was the raising first of the Baptist standard of soul liberty that made it possible for an American flag to be raised at all.[1] Stephens, recognizing the heritage given to him by his Baptist forefathers, gave those of the next hundred years a legacy worthy of the first hundred years.

Edwin William Stephens was born in Columbia, Missouri, on January 21, 1849. James L. Stephens, his father, came to Missouri as a young boy and established himself in Columbia as a successful businessman as well as a generous Christian. James was president of the executive board of the General Association (now the Missouri Baptist Convention), an organization in which his son also served as moderator for many years. In 1870, James Stephens also played an integral part in the founding of Stephens College, an institute dedicated to the education of women. He donated $20,000 toward the endowment of this venture.

Edwin made the most of his upbringing, graduating from Missouri State University in 1867 with his bachelor of arts and later his master's degrees. Desiring to establish a premier weekly paper, Stephens began the *Columbia Missouri Herald*. The paper quickly rose to national prominence, known for its editorial and stylistic excellence. Stephens bought other publication agencies while also becoming president of the Missouri Press Association and the National Editorial Association. Stephens had established himself as an accomplished entrepreneur.

On September 26, 1871, during his emergence in the community, Stephens married the love of his life, Laura Moss. Only four of their ten children survived to adulthood. For years their home served as a center for entertainment, demonstrating the crucial part the Stephens played in the Columbia community. As one author noted, "Their home has ever been the center of social enjoyment of the refined and unostentatious—a place where many men and women of prominence have been entertained upon their visits to Columbia but still where the less prominent were always given as cordial and just as warm-hearted a welcome."[2] This graciousness was reciprocated later in the Stephens's life when more than a thousand guests attended their golden anniversary celebration.

Honored in his life for his love of family and community, Stephens is revered today for his legacy in Baptist life. First and foremost Stephens loved his local church, the First Baptist Church of Columbia, where he taught the same Sunday school class for thirty-one years. Here he also served in the office of deacon. Regionally Stephens was elected moderator of his Baptist association while also functioning as the moderator of the Missouri Baptist Convention for twenty years.

In 1905, before the Southern Baptist Convention was held in Kansas City, then President James P. Eagle died after being in ill health for some time. Immediately, Stephens was nominated for president by Virginia messenger W. E. Hatcher, who explained, "In the field of business and also in the field of Christian fellowship, [Stephens] has shown himself to be a man of great power."[3] The other candidate, Professor T. T. Eaton of Southern Seminary, at once removed his name from nomination, signifying his respect for the Missouri

Baptist layman. Stephens was unanimously elected president, a position he held for three terms.

Stephens went to work for Southern Baptists, availing himself of national and international opportunities. While meeting in Chattanooga in 1906, Stephens passionately addressed the Convention with a message that was published and circulated throughout the Convention because of its significance and vision. Stephens explained his desire to spread the Baptist faith globally:

> It will not be until the world shall have reached the state of political freedom set forth in the Declaration of Independence, that all men are born free and equal, and until the Bible is read, free of all prejudice or dictation, ecclesiastical, political, or social, that Baptists will be recognized and valued, and will value themselves for what they really are.[4]

In humble explanation Stephens believed that the greatest legacy of Baptists is the religious liberty it afforded to all citizens. Indeed, he believed the Baptist faith would grow fastest in a society that was most free.

When the Baptist World Alliance was organized in London, England, in 1905, Stephens was called upon to speak to the crowd of more than twelve thousand. As part of his world tour as the Convention president, Stephens was promptly recognized for his passion and vision and later elected as the American treasurer of the Alliance. In fact, it seems that all who knew Stephens coveted his leadership. By the end of his life, Stephens had served in the presidency of thirty-five institutions, including the Baptist General Convention of America, the Northern Baptist Convention, and the Missouri Home and Foreign Mission Board.

Culminating his days as a lifelong resident of Missouri, Stephan was appointed by Governor Hadley as chairman of the State Capital Commission. This committee was responsible for planning the construction of the state capital building. In the end the committee earned the highest marks from the community. As one author elucidated, "He was the guiding spirit, and to this board Missouri owes the magnificent capital building which graces the grandest capitol site."[5]

Stephens never ran for any political office and was never ordained to the ministry, yet his labor affected the lives of countless citizens of Missouri as well as innumerable Baptists across the world. Ironically, he lived his entire life within the city of Columbia, Missouri, while influencing so many outside that community. On May 22, 1931, Stephens died at the age of eighty-three. He was quietly honored by his fellow Missouri Baptists:

> E. W. Stephens . . . had perhaps the longest connection in official capacity with the General Association [Missouri Baptist Convention] of all the distinguished and able men that have served that body. . . .
> All in all Missouri Baptists have had few men like E. W. Stephens, the son of a distinguished and able father who rendered, in many capacities, great services; and the father of a distinguished son, Hugh

Stephens, who has served the association as clerk and assistant moderator and a member of the executive board. The record of E. W. Stephens is a glorious one.[6]

It is appropriate that Stephens be commemorated by the Missouri Baptist Convention, for that is where his heart remained steadfast and loyal. Stephens, believing that the modern rebirth of missions through William Carey with the beginnings of Baptists in Missouri was providential, saw his state as strategic to reaching the rest of the nation for Christ. In a speech to fellow Missouri Baptists, he shared his heart and, indeed, what would become his legacy:

> Let us go forward to fields white for the harvest. Holding as we do to the truth, so simple and yet so broad that no one, Pagan, Infidel, or Christian, questions its orthodoxy. There is no reason why we should not take Missouri for Jesus Christ. We need but the faith and courage of Caleb and Joshua to possess the land.[7]

10

JOSHUA LEVERING

September 12, 1845—October 5, 1935
Elected: 1908, 1909, 1910

*F*ew historians would ever suggest that Southern Baptist presidents are nationally beloved or popular figures. At best they have been considered noble and notable leaders of a subset within the national tapestry. At worst they are viewed as spokesmen for a quaint reminder of bygone days.

With our historical stance on the exclusive claim of Jesus Christ as Lord and strong belief in the moral code of Scripture, most Southern Baptists fall outside the pale of popularity on a national or cultural scale. Yet in 1896, Joshua Levering accomplished the seemingly impossible. As the Prohibition Party candidate for president of the United States, Levering received an astonishing 132,007 votes.[1] In fact, running against the incumbent, William McKinley, and Democrat William Jennings Bryan, Levering received more than sixteen thousand votes in New York, nineteen thousand votes in Pennsylvania, and mounted one of the most successful minor party campaigns in American history. Twelve years later he became the first and only presidential candidate ever to become the president of the Southern Baptist Convention.

Born on September 12, 1845, in Baltimore, Maryland, Joshua Levering was one of twelve children born into one of the truly historic Baptist families in America. Eugene Levering Sr. was a strong Baptist layman and a successful businessman. Running a coffee importing business on Thames Street in Baltimore, Eugene Levering Sr. often hosted Baptist ministers in his home, most notably Baptist preacher and missionary Richard Fuller.[2] The senior Levering's Christian ethics were evident in his business dealings. In deep debt in the face of the impending Civil War in 1861, Levering Sr. settled his debt of $100,000 for about half of the amount. Though he was under no legal obligation to do so, the elder Levering paid back every creditor following the end of the Civil War.[3]

Joshua was trained in private schools along with his twin brother, Eugene Levering Jr. Junior was also a Baptist leader. Eugene Jr. married Mary Armstrong, the sister of Annie W. Armstrong, and served as a trustee of Johns Hopkins University and who also served as a Baptist deacon and Sunday school teacher for more than fifty years at the Eutaw Place Baptist Church.[4] Saved in 1857 at the age of twelve, Joshua Levering was baptized by Richard Fuller in the Eutaw Place Baptist Church.[5] In 1866, at the age of twenty-one, he became a partner in the family business, and became the sole owner after his father's death in June 1870 and his brother's ascent to the presidency of the Maryland National Bank.

From the beginning of his adult life, Levering was active in political and denominational affairs. In 1888, Joshua was one of the charter founders of the American Baptist Educational Society and served as treasurer of the group for decades. Dedicated to the original intentions of the organization, he served on the International Committee of the Young Men's Christian Association of the United States and Canada and as president of the Baltimore YMCA for seventeen years.[6]

Originally an independent Democrat, Levering became a Prohibitionist in 1884, when he declared his vote for and loyalty to John St. John, the Prohibition candidate. The Prohibition Party had been formed in 1869, the culmination of years of work by the Women's Christian Temperance Union (WCTU). An amalgemation of disenfranchised Republicans, Populists, and Democrats, the Prohibition Party advocated a repudiation of the manufacture, exportation, and sale of alcohol on social, moral, and ethical grounds.

Levering was passionately committed to the belief that alcohol was a societal evil that birthed poverty and economic slavery. He became chairman of the Maryland State Prohibition Convention in 1887 and again in 1893. He served as a delegate to the national Prohibition Conventions in 1888 and 1892. By the time he became the presidential candidate in the 1896 campaign, Levering had a network of Christians and social activists throughout the nation. His fourth-place showing in the election was proof of the resonance of the subject. In 1919, a federal constitutional amendment was passed prohibiting liquor.[7]

One of the major platform beliefs in the Prohibition Party was women's suffrage, the right to vote as equal citizens with men. Levering was committed to women's leadership, even in the world of the local church and denominational leadership. In 1884, the annual Southern Baptist Convention met in Baltimore, Maryland, and Levering was a messenger from his church. As one of the 637 messengers seated, Levering brought a resolution asking the Convention to appoint a woman to serve as director over women's missionary work. Though the resolution failed, Levering was able to move the discussion forward as a substantial issue in Southern Baptist life.[8]

His philanthropy and energies were not limited to the political and social arenas. In 1880, he was elected as a trustee of the Southern Baptist Theological Seminary in Louisville, Kentucky, and fifteen years later became chairman of the board of trustees. For the next forty years, from 1895 to 1935, Levering served as chairman, setting a record for service.[9] In addition, he served as a trustee of the Foreign Mission Board for forty-eight years and served for sixty-five years on the Maryland state mission board.[10]

Few men were ever as faithful, consistent, or dedicated to Southern Baptist service as Joshua Levering. By the time of the annual SBC meeting in Richmond, Virginia, in 1907, Levering had already dedicated decades of service to mission causes. At the age of sixty-two, Levering was elected president by the 1,411 messengers. His reelection in 1908 in Hot Springs, Arkansas, and in 1909 in Louisville, Kentucky, were simple formalities. Southern Baptists trusted Joshua Levering. He presided over his last annual meeting in 1910 in Baltimore, where he witnessed the election of Edwin Dargan.

By the time of his death on October 5, 1935, Joshua Levering had seen many of his dreams and aspirations for his country and his denomination come true. He had witnessed women receive the constitutional right to vote in 1920. He had seen prohibition become a federal law in 1919. He had even seen laymen in the Southern Baptist Convention take a new and more prominent position. As the fourth of only six laymen to serve as president of America's largest Protestant denomination, Levering had a deep and abiding belief that laymen should serve in substantial roles in local churches and the denomination.[11] Many call Joshua Levering the father of the Baptist men's movement. His heart for missions, sparked by the work of his sister-in-law Annie Armstrong, was ever present. His service in the Southern Baptist Convention, unmatched in Convention life, is an abiding legacy.

11
EDWIN CHARLES DARGAN

November 17, 1852—October 26, 1930
Elected: 1911, 1912, 1913

*N*earing the time of his retirement, E. C. Dargan was known throughout the Baptist world for his monumental work, *A History of Preaching,* an unprecedented attempt at tracing renowned homileticians from the early church to the twentieth century. As editorial secretary for the Sunday School Board of the Southern Baptist Convention, Dargan also desired to help the laymen of the pew "to a deeper appreciation of our priceless heritage in the Word of God." In 1924, Dargan wrote *The Bible Our Heritage,* a straightforward introduction to the Holy Scriptures and their "fadeless" value to Christians. Always focusing on the person of Christ, Dargan explained the importance of the Word of God to fallen men and women:

> Does the modern man need the plan of salvation presented in the gospel? Where is there any other? Every system of human thought, ancient or modern, leaves man where it finds him. There is no gospel outside the Bible. The heart of the Bible is the atonement. It tells of man's finding God by the way of the cross of Jesus Christ. It presents the supreme sacrifice of love. It emphasizes the need of redemption through suffering. We have here the eternal and perfect way of salvation for man.[1]

Able to blend his love for the Bible with the ability to preach the unsearchable riches of Christ, Dargan is honored today as one of the premier preaching professors ever to have taught at a Southern Baptist seminary.

Edwin Charles Dargan was born on November 17, 1852, in Darlington County, South Carolina. The product of a prominent Baptist family, Edwin was privileged to receive the best Christian education in the South. At the age of twenty-one, he earned his master of arts from Furman University. Four years later he graduated from The Southern Baptist Theological Seminary, then located in Greenville, South Carolina.

For the first time in his young life, Dargan moved away from his family and home, accepting a pastorate in Hollins, Virginia. However, he was never at ease in his early ministry and moved around for several years. In 1887, he even moved to Dixon, California, where he briefly pastored a Baptist congregation.

By 1888, Dargan had established a successful pulpit ministry and was recognized as an emerging homiletical scholar. Indeed, that year he received an honorary doctorate from Washington University while also being called to the influential Citadel Square Baptist Church in Charleston, South Carolina. Also during this time the editors of the American Commentary asked Dargan to write a commentary on the Epistle to the Colossians, which was published in 1890.

The Southern Baptist Theological Seminary quickly realized Dargan's rare combination of biblical preaching and ecclesiological expertise. In 1892, he was elected professor of homiletics and ecclesiology at the seminary, a position he would hold for fifteen years. Though he had left the pastorate, Dargan cared deeply for the local church. Five years after arriving in Louisville, he published *Ecclesiology*, a thorough examination of the life of the church. Noted for its diligent scholarship, it was immediately implemented into the curriculum of the school. Dargan expounded on the importance of the church in God's plan:

> It is desirable to consider afresh the significance of the local
> church. It is a body of believers in Christ, baptized into his name, and
> consecrated to his service; independent of earthly authority, but closely
> related with others of like mind in promoting the great purposes of
> God in this world. Each local assembly of God's people is "the church
> of the living God, the pillar and ground of the truth." As such it is in
> duty bound to comprehend the divine revelation, and to hold forth
> through darkness and trial, through weariness and even persecution,
> the sacred light of God's blessed gospel.[2]

Dargan, now a shepherd to potential shepherds, used his experience to remind his students of "how holy a privilege [it is] to be the pastor and guide of a flock of Christ!"[3]

In 1907, after helping lead in the substantial growth within the seminary, Dargan's passion for preaching surpassed his desire to teach. Dargan accepted the call to pastor the First Baptist Church of Macon, Georgia. The church acknowledged the scholarly ability of their pastor and allowed him extensive time to write. In 1912, Dargan published his most famous work, *A History of Preaching*. Like his previous publication on the church, this volume also became widely circulated among many seminaries, influencing the next three generations of preachers. Dargan used his unusual ability of surveying preaching chronologically in church history while illustrating proper homiletical method. Indeed, it is still considered by many scholars as the preeminent source on historical homiletics today.

In 1911, while the Convention was meeting in Jacksonville, Florida, evidence of the honor Southern Baptists gave to Dargan culminated as he was elected president of the Convention. Many messengers were shocked when Henry Seay, an unassuming businessman from Virginia, placed into consideration the name of Edwin Dargan. In fact, Dargan was actually the second choice of Seay, only nominating him after his first choice, Dr. S. C. Mitchell, was noticeably absent from the Convention floor. Seay asserted that Southern Baptists were in great need of a minister to lead them and not a layman such as was the case with the current president, Joshua Levering. The messengers agreed and quickly took notice of Dargan's sharp leadership skills. George Truett, pastor of the historic First Baptist Church of Dallas, Texas, testified, "Dr. E. C. Dargan . . . is making a superb president. He allowed not a minute to be lost."[4]

Southern Baptists appreciated his guidance as president so much that they called on his leadership skill and biblical exposition in 1917, asking Dargan to assume the role as editor of publications for the emerging Sunday School Board of the Convention. Baptist leaders unanimously agreed that Dargan could continue to shepherd countless Southern Baptists by publishing his expositions of Scripture passages both in periodicals and in books. This fact was well illustrated in his work *The Changeless Christ,* a collection of his sermons over the years. This book exhibits the central theme of Dargan's life and ministry, glorifying the person of Jesus Christ while recognizing the limitations of sinful man. Dargan proclaimed of his Savior:

O incomparable Teacher, we would think thy high and holy thoughts after thee! O matchless Guide, we would follow thy strong and confident leadership in pursuit of purity and righteousness! O divine Saviour, perfected through thy human suffering, we would trust thee alone for salvation and immortality! To thee we bring our baffled yet eager minds for truth on things beyond our ken, to thee we bring our wayward and oft bewildered hearts for help in daily duty, to thee we bring our hurt and sorrowing souls for healing from sin and for hope of life evermore! Here at thy pierced and hallowed feet we rest until the day dawn and the shadows flee away![5]

Until 1927, Dargan gave example of great Bible exposition, while focusing all interpretation on the Christ and the cross. All the while, he also emulated to all those around him what it was to be a humble servant of the Lord.

Upon retirement Dargan donated his extensive library to the Sunday School Board. In the years that followed, his collection created the nucleus for the Southern Baptist Historical Society. A man so enamored with history and its importance gave Southern Baptists a history of which they could be proud. On October 26, 1930, at the age of seventy-seven, Dargan died in Chicago at his son's home. The man born with so rich a Baptist heritage gave future Baptists the wealth of his wisdom and an inheritance far greater than the one he had received.

Just a few years before his death, Dargan expounded on the biblical view of the afterlife. His explanation serves as an appropriate reminder of the promises of God and the comfort found in the doctrine of the resurrection:

After the disruption of death there will be the restoration of the whole personality in body and soul, and the immortal life of both. The raised body will be free from all the ills to which this "earthly tent-house" is painfully subject; it will be glorified and ennobled, perfectly fitted to the eternal spiritual life. . . . "Death is swallowed up in victory."[6]

12

JOHN LANSING BURROWS

April 10, 1843—October 17, 1917
Elected: 1914, 1915, 1916

*F*or most men to be elected to the presidency of the Southern Baptist Convention would be the pinnacle of their denominational ministry. For Lansing Burrows it was a gracious gesture by the people he served. It was also, however, a distraction from his life ministry to the people he served. While Dr. Burrows served three terms as president of the Convention, he was also concurrently serving in the ministry in which he would invest thirty-three years. Dr. Lansing Burrows established the legacy of being the longest serving recording secretary of the SBC and gave thirty-eight years as the denomination's statistician.

Lansing Burrows was born into a rich Baptist heritage. His father, John Lansing Burrows (1814–1893) was the son of an American ship captain in the War of 1812.[1] Ordained in 1835, John Lansing Burrows served as a pastor and church planter in the Philadelphia, Pennsylvania, area. During this period of service, John Lansing Burrows attended the first meeting for the formation of the Southern Baptist Convention in Augusta, Georgia, in 1845. In 1854, he became the pastor of the First Baptist Church in Richmond, Virginia. First Baptist Richmond was a historic church, with roots deep in American history. Beginning as a prayer meeting in the home of John Franklin in 1780, one year before the British surrendered at Yorktown, the First Baptist Church was the first church to be constituted in the city of Richmond. For nearly a century beginning in 1836, the roster of pastors at the church reads like a history of the Southern Baptist Convention.

1836–1849 Jeremiah Bell Jeter
1850–1854 Basil Manly Jr.
1854–1874 John Lansing Burrows
1876–1879 Ebenezer W. Warren
1879–1884 James B. Hawthorne
1885–1903 George Cooper
1905–1927 George W. McDaniel

John Lansing Burrows not only served as president of the Foreign Mission Board for six years; he was also elected as vice president of the Southern Baptist Convention three times.[2]

While John Lansing Burrows was the pastor of the Sansom Street Baptist Church in Philadelphia, his wife Adeline gave birth to the first of three children. They named the son Lansing Burrows. The son would be raised in the glaring spotlight of a prominent ministry and would thrive in the devout Christian home.

The young Lansing moved with his family to Richmond when he was eleven years old and his father assumed the pastorate of First Richmond. Here, in May 1858, Lansing was saved and baptized; and though he was not yet sixteen, he entered Richmond College. His abilities in academia were remarkable. In 1859, his grades were sufficient to transfer to Wake Forest College in North Carolina.

Lansing's studies were interrupted by the outbreak of the Civil War. On April 25, 1861, eighteen-year-old Lansing enlisted in the Confederate army and served as a sergeant in the Fayette Artillery. For three years, Burrows distinguished himself as a soldier, until the fall of 1864: "He was captured at Winchester, Virginia (on) September 19, 1864 and was imprisoned at Ft. Delaware until near the close of the war; then he was exchanged as an incurable prisoner and returned to Richmond."[3]

Following the end of the war in 1865, Burrows received his degree after Wake Forest College reopened. He would later receive his master's degree from Princeton University in 1871 and would later have three doctoral degrees conferred upon him.[4] In 1867, Burrows surrendered to the gospel ministry and was ordained in July of that year in Stanford, Kentucky, where he was teaching. The same summer he would marry Lulie Rochester and take his first pastorate there in Stanford.

Following a brief pastorate in Lexington, Missouri (1867–1869), Burrows was called to First Baptist Church of Bordertown, New Jersey. The church, in existence since 1752, has stood on the corner of Prince and Church Streets for more than 250 years in the west central part of the state. Due to growth, the church had built the third sanctuary on their property in 1861, and Burrows saw the church grow in mission and outreach.[5]

While serving as a pastor in Lexington, Kentucky (1879–1883), Burrows attended the Southern Baptist Convention annual meeting in Columbus, Mississippi, in 1881. That year Dr. James P. Boyce nominated him as assistant recording secretary, a position for which he was imminently qualified. The following year he brought his first statistical report to the Convention and was elected recording secretary for the first time. A special committee, studying the methods and necessity of such reporting, noted:

> We regard the Report as perhaps the most valuable contribution
> which has been made to the history of Southern Baptists in many
> years. . . . We recommend that the thanks of this body be returned to

brother Lansing Burrows, for the laborious task which he has so cheerfully and faithfully performed, and that he be requested to continue in the good work.[6]

It was the beginning of a service to the denomination that would span three decades. Each year Burrows would painstakingly record by hand the statistics, decisions, baptisms, and budgets of every single Southern Baptist church. The large ledgers, now held in the Southern Baptist Historical Archives, demonstrated Burrows's excruciating attention to detail and are silent testimony to the tens of thousands of hours he labored to ensure an accurate record of the Lord's work through Southern Baptists.[7]

For sixteen years Burrows served as pastor of the First Baptist Church of Augusta, Georgia, the site of the formation of the Southern Baptist Convention in May 1845. Burrows immediately began working to ignite the mission emphasis and revival in the church, and they saw remarkable growth:

> With the call of Lansing Burrows in 1883, the church began a rapid growth. He began with a 6-week revival! He then organized the City Mission Board and also organized the women of the church into the Woman's Foreign Missionary Society. Mrs. W. M. Jordan and Mrs. Smith Irvine immediately began to invite the Chinese of the city to a Sunday afternoon Sunday School. This is still in operation today although most of the Chinese are assimilated into the congregation. The emphasis is continued on Wednesday morning and evening with the WMU's Conversational English classes for foreign students in the area.[8]

In 1899, Burrows accepted the call to become the pastor of the First Baptist Church of Nashville, Tennessee. This venerable church has had a deep and lasting impact on Southern Baptists, with three pastors having served as president of the Convention, a record matched only by Bellevue Baptist Church in Memphis. In 1998, the First Baptist Church Nashville Historical Committee reflected on their contributions through the years:

> Two FBC pastors have served as SBC president: R. B. C. Howell in 1851–59 (overlapping the early years of his second FBC pastorate in 1857–59) and H. Franklin Paschall in 1966–68. A third pastor served as president after leaving FBC: Lansing Burrows in 1913–16. Other members have held many SBC offices. Several FBC members have served as executive secretary-treasurer/president of the SBC Executive Committee, including Duke K. McCall, 1946–51; Porter W. Routh, 1951–79; and Harold C. Bennett, 1979–92. . . . FBC members have provided major leadership for the Sunday School Board (now LifeWay Christian Resources). James Marion Frost served as the agency's first chief executive in 1891–93, prior to his FBC pastorate, and then again in 1896–1916, following his FBC pastorate. Pastor William Francis

Powell served as trustee president for thirty-three years. . . . James L.
Sullivan, Grady Cothen, and Lloyd Elder, successive SSB chief execu-
tives from 1953 to 1991, were FBC members.[9]
Tragically Burrows's beloved wife Lulie died in 1901 of a protracted illness while
he was pastor in Nashville. After ten successful years at First Nashville, Burrows
became the pastor of his final church, the First Baptist Church of Americus,
Georgia. Certainly in our current culture, one would speculate on the effectiveness
of a church calling a sixty-six-year-old man as senior pastor, but First Americus and
Lansing Burrows were a tremendous match. The Sumter County church grew during his tenure, and Burrows was elected president of the Southern Baptist
Convention while serving there.

After Burrows presided over his first sessions as president in the 1914
Convention at Nashville, Tennessee, the editor of the *Alabama Baptist* wrote the
following of his deportment:

He was standing like a bull at bay with hair pointed outward, ready
to throw over the fence all who failed to get into the field in any other
way than through the parliamentary gate. On Sunday, he was trans-
formed into an angel of sweetness.[10]

Dr. Lansing Burrows was a man at peace with his Lord and at peace with his calling. In 1892, while Burrows was serving as pastor at First Baptist Augusta, the
newly formed Sunday School Board brought a report at the Southern Baptist
Convention meeting in Atlanta, Georgia. They noted: "At its first meeting after the
adjournment of the [previous] Convention, the Board unanimously and cordially
elected Rev. Lansing Burrows . . . to be its Corresponding Secretary, . . . But he
declined to accept the call."[11] Burrows's refusal paved the way for Dr. James
Marion Frost to become the first Sunday School Board secretary, a position he
would hold twice until his death in 1916. Burrows was a man who knew exactly
what he was called to do. Until his death following his final term as president of
the Southern Baptist Convention on October 17, 1917, he was a stalwart and an
exemplary leader among Southern Baptists.

13

JAMES BRUTON GAMBRELL

August 21, 1841—June 10, 1921
Elected: 1917, 1918, 1919, 1920

*H*e was a plain-spoken, often-quoted, nationally known leader. He was a fiery evangelist, a Civil War hero, a Baptist newspaper editor, a seminary professor, a college president, an author, a mission secretary, executive secretary of the Baptist General Convention of Texas, and the president of the Southern Baptist Convention. He was fondly called a prophet with a pen by denominational leaders and a defender of the faith by Baptists around the world. Yet for the hundreds of thousands of Christians who read his editorials, heard him speak, and watched his life, he was simply and affectionately called "Uncle Gideon." With his insightful wisdom, warm humor, buoyant spirit, and determined faith in God, J. B. Gambrell served in more capacities than anyone in Southern Baptist history and in so doing helped steer the denomination through murky waters for generations.

James Bruton Gambrell was born August 21, 1841, in Anderson County, South Carolina. James's parents were strong Christians, as attested by the records of his mother's baptism in the fellowship of the Big Creek Baptist Church in Williamsburg, South Carolina, in 1831,[1] and his father's almost unbroken record of twenty-five years perfect attendance at the Pleasant Ridge Baptist Church in Mississippi.[2] When James was four years old, the family moved to Union County, Mississippi, to farm the fertile ground of the northeastern part of that state. His father actually built a wooden structure on the church grounds so the family would not have to travel the great distance to and from home during protracted tent revivals. In 1856, at the age of fifteen, James, along with his brother Ira, was converted during one of those monthlong meetings.

Five years later the Civil War broke out. James was at that time studying under Professor R. M. Leavell at the Cherry Creek school, a short distance from his family home, and was torn between his belief in the rights of individual states to self-governance and his distaste for slavery. He wrote:

There were thousands of men in the South who were Abolitionists.
They would have changed the situation if it could have been done, or
if they could have seen any way of doing it without imperiling the
social order of the South. . . . I, myself, was an Abolitionist.[3]

Early in the summer of 1861, Gambrell enlisted in the company organized by his professor and was used as a scout for General Lee.[4] In the Confederate army, "Gambrell fought at Gettysburg, was commissioned a captain, and was ordered to the Memphis territory. Before the close of the war he married Mary T. Corbell of Nansemond County, Virginia on January 13, 1864."[5]

The period of time following the war, the Reconstruction, was a difficult period for most of the country. For the Gambrells it was a period of transition. The first inclination James had that God was calling him to preach came, following the war, when he and his wife were living in Virginia. Listening to a sermon by a poorly prepared preacher, Gambrell reflected:

He made an awful mess of the whole thing, belittling the subject
in a way that stirred me to the depths. . . . There came to me then a
desire and an impulse to get up and tell the people what the text
really did mean. In short, to preach, and I never got away from that
impression.[6]

Moving back to Mississippi, Gambrell was licensed by his home church, Pleasant Ridge, in December 1866; and in November 1867, the Cherry Creek Baptist Church, where he had been preaching, ordained him. The next year Gambrell accepted the call to pastor the Midway Baptist Church, some eighteen miles outside of Oxford. In 1870, Gambrell became the pastor of West Point Baptist Church in Mississippi, his first full-time church, where he also began his daily regimen of writing. His determination to discipline himself to write constantly and consistently began to bear fruit, and he became a regular contributor to the *Tennessee Baptist*, under editor J. R. Graves.

In 1872, Gambrell accepted the call to First Baptist Church of Oxford, which was in the heart of the University of Mississippi. Convinced that he needed to pursue his education, Gambrell enrolled in the university and continued to help the struggling church. The church minutes record the 1873 membership of thirty-six members and quarter-time services. In 1874, the minutes recorded sixty-eight members with full-time services.

Graduating in 1877, Gambrell was asked to become the editor of the *Baptist Record*, Mississippi's state Baptist paper. His writing had raised his prominence in the state, and he dedicated the next fifteen years to communicating the work of God to the Baptist people of the state. In 1881, Gambrell moved the headquarters of the paper to Clinton, Mississippi, near Mississippi College, and became pastor of First Baptist Church of Clinton.

As Gambrell spoke to Southern Baptists in Mississippi through the *Baptist Record*, his voice began to be heard around the nation as well. He was active in temperance and education causes throughout the nation, but Gambrell made his first mark of legacy on the SBC in the field of Bible study. Though Southern Baptists had tried and failed on numerous occasions to establish a separate Sunday School board, in February 1890, James Marion Frost began to write editorials to all of the state Baptist papers, advocating such a board. All the Southern Baptist papers, with the exception of the *Western Recorder* and the *Baptist and Reflector,* opposed the formation of the board on theological and practical grounds.

At the Convention meeting in Fort Worth in 1890, a committee was formed to report at that meeting. Though a recommendation came for the formation of a Sunday School Committee (not board), the situation was not resolved. At the 1891 SBC meeting in Birmingham, Frost and Gambrell were appointed to present a report. They held vastly different views on the issue. Gambrell felt that such a board would usurp the autonomy of the local church to teach as it felt led from the Bible. Frost saw the board as an aid to the educational endeavor of many struggling churches. A great fight was expected.

The 913 other registered messengers anxiously awaited word if denominational war had been averted. Gambrell and Frost were locked in Frost's room at the Florence Hotel. The report that was born from the negotiations contained the final paragraph:

> In conclusion, your committee in its long and earnest considera-
> tion of this whole matter . . . have been compelled to take account of
> the well-known fact that there are widely divergent views held among
> us. . . . It is therefore recommended that the fullest freedom of choice
> be accorded to every one as to what literature he will use or support,
> and that no brother be disparaged in the slightest degree on account
> of what he may do in the exercise of his right as Christ's freeman. But
> we would earnestly urge all brothers to give to this Board a fair consid-
> eration and in no case obstruct it in the great work assigned by this
> Convention.[7]

In June 1893, the trustees of Mercer University unanimously called Gambrell as president, following such Baptist luminaries as John L. Dagg and H. H. Tucker. He would serve in this capacity for three years, until 1896, when the Baptist General Convention of Texas selected him as the superintendent of state missions. Heading west at the age of fifty-four, Gambrell was to face "the greatest work of his life."[8]

The situation in Texas was tumultuous. The state had merged two competing state papers, and Gambrell had four predecessors in the seven years prior to his coming. In fact, when Jim Gaddy asked Gambrell if he wanted to come to Texas, he said, "I want to go to heaven, and I did not see any good road through Texas."[9] Yet the challenge invigorated Gambrell. He multiplied the mission and evangelistic endeavors of the Texas Baptist churches. The churches flourished and the mission work in Texas led the nation. Gambrell operated with a laser precision to extract the fervor for souls from every Baptist meeting. Reflecting on the period later, Gambrell remained intense:

> Every church is expected to be a soul-winning station. . . . A great many are trying to grow trees, roots up. All the diluted evangelism is an abomination and wicked. The time is here for an evangelism that goes out from the churches and draws back into churches. Many churches are dry and unprofitable because they have neglected the main thing, the saving of the lost. Nothing will so bless a church as the evangelistic spirit in it.[10]

It is no surprise that by 1910, Gambrell's voice was so needed among Southern Baptists, he was elected editor of the *Baptist Standard,* and in 1912, he was elected to the faculty of the Southwestern Baptist Theological Seminary. For two years Gambrell would carry on a vigorous schedule, teaching four days a week at the seminary, and then spend Saturday and Monday in the *Baptist Standard* offices. For a man over seventy years old, this was a remarkable feat.

In December 1914, Gambrell resigned both the seminary position and the editorship, as he became the executive secretary of the Consolidated Board of the Baptist General Convention. He would serve in this capacity until shortly before his death.

In 1917, 1,683 messengers gathered in New Orleans, Louisiana, for the annual Southern Baptist Convention meeting. America was in the throes of World War I, and Southern Baptists were at a juncture of change. At the outset of the meeting, as was the standard, the election of the president would take place, and Dr. J. J. Hurt nominated Gambrell for the position.

In a period of tremendous shifting, Gambrell surprised many by his affable manner and firm leadership. In retrospect Gambrell's leadership did much to chart the course for Southern Baptists. He was afforded the honor of being elected to four terms as president, and they were four years of remarkable direction. During Gambrell's tenure women were admitted as messengers for the first time, the Executive Committee was extended new authority, the Relief and Annuity Board was created, and the Seventy-Five Million-Dollar campaign was launched.

Of all the controversies which Gambrell and the Convention faced, fewer had more far-reaching implication than the invitation for Southern Baptists to join the new Inter-Church World Movement. Following the end of the war in 1919, the Convention met in Atlanta, and outside pressure mounted to have Southern Baptists unite with all denominations worldwide in a "peace and justice" effort. At the 1919 meeting, Dr. J. Campbell White represented the Inter-Church World Movement. He was allowed a time to address the over four thousand registered messengers. After he had finished, he thanked the messengers and prepared to leave the platform. Dr. Gambrell stopped him and said these historic words:

> You must not leave the platform without my personal thanks for your address. I will give you a bit of information about Baptists:

Baptists do not have popes. They never put anybody where they can't put him down. And another thing: Baptists never ride a horse without a bridle.[11]

The statement was met with hearty amens from across the auditorium.

The fall of 1920 saw Gambrell serving his final term as president of the Convention. As a representative of the Convention, he traveled with Dr. E. Y. Mullins to Europe to fellowship with the growing number of European Baptists. Returning home in December of that year, Gambrell set out to continue his travels in 1921, planning on going to New Mexico with Dr. L. R. Scarborough in February. As he ventured to the railroad station, Gambrell experienced a heart attack. From February 24 until his death on June 10, 1921, Gambrell wavered in frail health, only traveling once to hear Dr. Truett preach in May. Dr. Truett preached his funeral at the First Baptist Church of Dallas. Baptist leaders from around the world attended.

Before Gambrell left for his European trip with Mullins, he left his family a sealed envelope with instructions to open in case he died overseas. At his death his children opened the letter and read:

[M]y deepest concern for all of you is that you may be genuine Christians. There is no greater failure than to live in this world without God, and without a sure hope of the next world. My life has not been perfect; far from it, but I leave here my testimony to the infinite value of the Christian hope in this life, and its uncertainties, storms and trials.[12]

Dr. J. B. Gambrell, the editor, president, and denominational leader, had written his final editorial, advocating Christ above all.

14
EDGAR YOUNG MULLINS

January 5, 1860—November 23, 1928
Elected: 1921, 1922, 1923

In 1888, members of the Lee Street Baptist Church in Baltimore, Maryland, were in danger of splitting their fellowship over the issue of musical preference in the worship services. Their pastor, E. Y. Mullins, quickly recognized the problem as generational, between the young people who desired contemporary music and their elders who were far more traditional. The controversy began when church services were moved to the basement lecture hall due to the renovation of the auditorium. The temporary place of worship provided one extra amenity not found in the sanctuary: a piano. Mullins's wife, Isla May, described how the dispute played out:

When the first Sunday for downstairs church services arrived, it
found the old and the young people of its membership at loggerheads.
The young folks, sensing an opportunity for relaxed and informal
meetings on Sunday nights during the summer, were very determined
to use the piano and make a more sprightly thing of the music. The
deacons, especially the senior deacon, were immediately opposed. The
organ by all means must be used for all the Sunday services to give
dignity and solemnity to the occasion, a thing difficult enough to
achieve in the downstairs quarters.[1]

Mullins, illustrating early how he would be a mediator in his ministry, carefully weaved through the situation, shepherding the flock with caution. In the end the chairman of deacons led the congregation in allowing the piano to be used exclusively on Sunday nights. This would be a precursor to the many controversies in which Mullins found himself throughout his worldwide ministry.

Edgar Young Mullins was born on January 5, 1860, in Franklin County, Mississippi, the first son of Seth and Cornelia Mullins. The son of a Baptist preacher, his father desired the same of his son. It must be remembered that Edgar grew up in the background of the Civil War. The family, therefore, attempted to move their children away from the calamity, eventually ending up in the pioneer town of Corsicana, Texas. Here Seth Mullins planted what is now the First Baptist Church of Corsicana. Though young Edgar was given great educational and spiritual training, he never made a public profession of his faith in his childhood or adolescence.

In 1880, while working as a telegrapher and ambitiously pursuing a law degree in Dallas, Edgar's life changed when he attended a revival meeting led by Major W. E. Penn. Twenty years after his mother and father had prayed by their newborn's bedside consecrating him to the Lord, Mullins was born again. He went home and was baptized by his father. Shortly thereafter Mullins felt called to the ministry and gave up his desire to become a lawyer. In 1881, he matriculated at The Southern Baptist Theological Seminary in Louisville, Kentucky. Though a new convert, Mullins manifested sensibleness beyond his twenty-one years. One author explained, "The trauma of the war, the fact that he had a strong family life, the quasimilitary discipline of Texas A&M, and his years of working as a telegrapher combined to give Mullins a maturity beyond his years."[2]

For the next four years, Mullins saturated himself in theological study and reflection. After serious consideration Mullins made it known that he felt called to be a missionary to Brazil. Yet the greatest event during his educational phase occurred outside the classroom at Walnut Street Baptist Church, where he met the love of his life, Isla May Hawley. The two spent a great deal of time together as she observed Mullins's desire and passion for the Lord and was willing to follow him wherever God led.

In 1885, Mullins graduated from the seminary and was ordained by Harrodsburg Baptist Church in Harrodsburg, Kentucky. Mullins's dream of being a missionary quickly vanished as he was rejected by the Foreign Mission Board and advised by a physician to cancel his plans. Though his missionary zeal never left him, he began his pastorate with great enthusiasm. On June 2, 1886, he married Isla May at a simple home wedding attended by close friends. In the years that followed, they were blessed with two sons. Sadly neither of the sons reached adulthood. Isla Mullins explained the pain that befell the family:

> The doctor was sent for and he pronounced the little boy better
> and gave directions for the day. His mother sat down for a moment
> after the doctor left and took up the morning paper. She had not read
> five minutes, however, when something made her look around at the
> little boy, perhaps because he had said nothing. One look and she flew
> to her feet, called to the maid to get a doctor, any doctor, and took her
> place beside the dying child, for the heart had suddenly failed and he
> was indeed beyond help. As the mother stood there a little song that
> he had learned at kindergarten, was on his lips, "I live for those who
> love me, for those who know me true." A few lines came softly and
> then trailed into eternity.[3]

Edgar admitted that this was the greatest sorrow experienced in his life. However, this episode also molded the faith of Mullins. Known for his emotional faith, he learned to place his passions in the Lord or "life was not endurable."[4] During the next decade Mullins pastored Lee Street Baptist Church in Baltimore, Maryland (1888–1895), and First Baptist Church in Newton Center, Massachusetts (1895–1899). During his tenure Mullins also advanced his education, studying at Johns Hopkins University and Newton Theological Seminary.

This combination of scholarly advancement and pastoral ability did not go unnoticed. In 1899, Dr. Mullins was elected president of Southern Seminary, a position he would retain until his death nearly thirty years later in 1928. During his tenure the seminary underwent phenomenal growth as Mullins transitioned the seminary into a new theological era. The following demonstrates the expansion in the seminary, the influence of Mullins on the entire Convention, and the theological shift involved:

- The seminary moved its campus from downtown to a fifty-eight-acre campus as the student body grew from 256 to 501.
- In 1904, the SBC accepted an invitation into the newly formed Baptist World Alliance, while rejecting the same request from the Federal Council of Churches.
- After World War I, Mullins led Baptists into helping European Baptists after the devastation of war.
- In 1917, he wrote *The Christian Religion in Its Doctrinal Expression*, a theological shift from the Calvinism of J. P. Boyce to a mediating position between Calvinism and Arminianism.

In 1921, his standing among the Baptist community was evidenced by his election as president of the Southern Baptist Convention, a position he held until 1924. Though he was always conciliatory in his attitude, Mullins addressed the Convention messengers in 1923, clarifying his conservative views and his theological stance on the fundamentals of the faith:

> Jesus Christ was born of the virgin Mary through the power of the Holy Spirit. He was the Divine and eternal Son of God. He wrought miracles, healing the sick, casting out demons, raising the dead. He died as the victorious atoning Savior of the world and was buried. He arose again from the dead. The tomb was emptied of its contents. In His risen body He appeared many times to His disciples. He ascended to the right hand of the Father. He will come again in person, the same Jesus who ascended from the Mount of Olives. We believe that adherence to the above truths and facts is a necessary condition of service for teachers in our Baptist schools.[5]

Though he defended the faith on these key issues, the most controversial issue in which Mullins found himself was over the issue of scientific evolution versus biblical creation. Mullins once again attempted to find mediating ground between the

Modernists and Fundamentalists. Many Christians demanded that politicians pass a bill negating the theory of evolution in favor of creationism. Mullins wholeheartedly disagreed with such a measure, arguing that a court has no jurisdiction in spiritual matters. Moreover Mullins refused to allow this issue to overwhelm the theological landscape, allowing Southern Baptists to forget the preeminence of the Great Commission. Mullins himself rejected the theory of evolution while accepting the legitimacy of scientists to further their study on the origins of the universe.

In 1925, Mullins chaired the committee that recommended the first national confession among Southern Baptists. The new confession addressed the emerging antisupernaturalism of the culture, defended the essential doctrines of the faith, and asserted that "man was created by the special act of God." Yet in the end, attempting to find a temperate position cost Mullins his reputation from both sides of the theological setting.

Mullins spent much of his last three years of his ministry, while still president of the seminary, sailing abroad and speaking to fellow Baptists across Europe. His purpose for the lengthy trip was twofold: encourage fellow Baptists who were suffering across Europe while defending the essential Baptist tenet of religious liberty. The journey took its toll on Dr. Mullins, putting a serious strain on his heart. Upon his return to Louisville, Mullins had no opportunity to rest, as his leadership was required during the extraordinary growth of the campus and its buildings.

Above his burdensome task as president of the seminary, the delegates to the Baptist World Alliance elected him president in 1928. Although his doctor had ordered him to rest and cancel many of his engagements, Mullins nevertheless traveled extensively to fulfill his duties. By the summer Mullins was convinced of his need to cut off all engagements. The man who had spent so much time away from his wife finally was able to spend the last months of his life, as his wife explained, "almost unbrokenly together, with daily interests, and even, at times, the old merriment."[6] Dr. Mullins suffered a final stroke, taking his final rest on November 23, 1928. At his funeral Baptist stalwarts including George Truett and A. T. Robertson paid their respects and honored Mullins. He was buried in Cave Hill Cemetery, where a final inscription reminds visitors of the motto of Mullins's life:

> *My sword I give to him who shall succeed me,*
> *My courage and skill to him that can get it,*
> *My marks and scars I carry with me*
> *To be witness for me that I have fought his battles*
> *Who will now be my rewarder.*
> *So he passed over, and all the trumpets sounded on the other side.*

—JOHN BUNYAN

15
GEORGE WHITE McDANIEL

November 30, 1875–August 12, 1927
Elected: 1924, 1925, 1926

*W*hen should a pastor resign from a church? G. W. McDaniel, who had pastored the First Baptist Church in Richmond, Virginia, for more than a decade, decided it was time to leave his congregation because of their continual apathy and indifference. He announced his decision one Sunday morning:

> Looking at the church, the prospect for enlarged and permanent usefulness is not bright. . . . You are satisfied, but I am not. Coldness and formalism chill my heart. The Sunday school is the most important department of the church, but I have been unable to enlist many of our most prominent members in this phase of the work. The prayer meeting is the spiritual thermometer of church life, and I have tried in vain to secure the attendance of many of you. Our great evangelistic opportunity is the evening service, but many men and women whose presence would be an inspiration to the pastor, and a powerful example to the unsaved, never attend this service. . . . This I say frankly, but in love, for I do love every one of you.[1]

Upon hearing the unwavering words of their soon-to-be-former pastor, the congregation unanimously assured McDaniel of their allegiance to God and renewed their commitment to the Lord. McDaniel rescinded his resignation and remained pastor until his death in 1927.

George White McDaniel was born on November 30, 1875, in Grimes County, Texas. The name of his father, Francis Asbury McDaniel, demonstrates the affinity with Methodism in his ancestry. Yet George was named after a favorite cousin who served as a deacon in the First Baptist Church of Fort Worth for many years. Ironically, these two denominations were bound to collide in young George's life.

McDaniel's mother, Letitia, often prayed for her son's salvation, with seemingly no success. In fact, just moments before her death, when George was only sixteen, she committed her son to the care of the Lord. This effectual prayer always burdened McDaniel, though he ardently fought against the conviction of the Holy Spirit. In 1892, McDaniel and his childhood sweetheart attended a Methodist revival meeting where both were converted on the same night. Since his girlfriend was Methodist, she encouraged him to join the local Methodist fellowship. McDaniel's cousin, Edna Kennard, advised the new convert to read through the New Testament before making a hasty decision on which church to join. Within a week McDaniel became convinced of believer's baptism and joined the Baptist church in Navasota, where his mother had served faithfully for many years.

The decision to join the Baptist church involved not only baptism but the whole doctrine of the church. In his work *The People Called Baptists*, McDaniel expounded on his reasoning for becoming and remaining Baptist:

> Certain characters in history are named as founders of various denominations: the disciples began with Alexander Campbell, the Methodists with John Wesley. . . . Not so with the Baptists. There is no personality this side of Jesus Christ who is a satisfactory explanation of their origin. . . . We originated, not at the Reformation, nor in the Dark Ages, nor in any century after the Apostles, but our marching orders are the Commission, and the first Baptist church was the first church at Jerusalem. Our principles are as old as Christianity.[2]

The church, then, became his sole passion, and he enrolled at Baylor University in order to study for the ministry. McDaniel not only received a top quality Baptist education, but he was also privileged to reside at the home of one of his professors, B. H. Carroll. Though McDaniel did not excel in academic life, Carroll remarked of McDaniel's preaching skill, "He was from his youth up brilliant. He enriched his discourse with vital illustrations and apt literary quotations. As age and experience came upon him his sermons and addresses were richer in mellowness and very heart-searching."[3]

Carroll was not the only professor to take note of McDaniel. Martha Douglass Scarborough, the head of the modern language department at Baylor, at first resisted the advances of her student. She believed that this relationship had "insurmountable difficulties," not the least of which was her job, along with being slightly older than her student. She ultimately laid her concerns aside, believing no one else suited her but George. On March 24, 1898, the two were married at her father's home.

McDaniel graduated from Baylor a few months later, and the newlywed couple packed their belongings and moved to Louisville, Kentucky, where George enrolled as a divinity student at Southern Seminary. In 1899, McDaniel was ordained to the gospel ministry by the Baptist church in Waco, Texas. In 1900, McDaniel finished his seminary training, earning a bachelor of theology from the seminary. The family left the seminary and went back to Texas where McDaniel accepted the call to First Baptist Church of Temple.

After a brief yet successful ministry, McDaniel accepted the call to pastor the Gaston Avenue Baptist Church in Dallas, Texas, in 1902. Here the new pastor led in the building of a new auditorium while conducting revivals across the state. But McDaniel once again felt called to another pastorate. In 1905, after less than three years of ministry to the church on Gaston Avenue, McDaniel moved his family to Richmond, Virginia. Though this was the last pastorate he would hold in his beloved home state, McDaniel frequently visited Texas to conduct revival services or assist his former churches when they were without a pastor.

Before accepting the call to First Baptist Church of Richmond, where he would serve until his death in 1927, McDaniel demanded that two highly esteemed members of the church "engaged in objectionable traffic . . . dissolve all connections with the same."[4] Whatever the business in question, the two men quickly removed the ethical barrier, and McDaniel accepted the call without reservation.

McDaniel immediately immersed himself in the study of Baptists in Virginia. He gained an unfettered appreciation for the heritage given to him by stalwart Baptists such as John Leland and his stance for religious liberty. McDaniel was rewarded for his faithfulness and denominational fidelity, and was asked to serve the Foreign Mission Board (SBC), and as a trustee for the University of Richmond, as well as being elected as the president of the Baptist General Association of Virginia.

However, his greatest contribution to Virginia Baptists may have been his political battle against the compulsory reading of the Bible in public schools. Elected president of the Southern Baptist Convention in 1924, he deemed it essential to defend the tenet of religious liberty against any form of state coercion of religion. One editorial affirmed that if not for the stance of Dr. McDaniel, the measure put forward by the legislature of the State of Virginia to require the mandatory reading of passages from the Bible in public schools would have easily passed:

> The fact that the bill was rejected because of the spirited address in opposition to it by a Protestant minister, the Rev. George W. McDaniel . . . is most extraordinary because Protestant ministers are usually the most ardent proponents of such measures. Dr. McDaniel's speech was a calm and dignified plea for fidelity to the foundation stone of American religious liberty. . . . Religion, he pointed out, is a purely voluntary and private concern of each individual, and there is nothing which works to the detriment of religion as does compulsion.

McDaniel was equated as a modern-day James Madison, and many Virginians steadfastly supported the Baptist principles of the Richmond pastor. In the end McDaniel primarily rejected the forced readings on ecclesiological grounds. To say that the church needed assistance from the state is to negate the supernatural power given to the church and corrupt it by its mixture with state support.

In the 1920s McDaniel also helped Southern Baptists work through the controversy of evolution versus creation. McDaniel worried that this issue was merely a symptom of a larger problem within the Convention. In 1926, he delivered his address before the Convention, thoroughly rejecting any form of evolution. In 1927, McDaniel gave a passionate plea to the Convention to reject a foe greater than evolution—materialism. McDaniel proclaimed:

> Scientific speculation is not the gravest menace of the age: materialism is. Where one man's spirituality is devitalized by science, falsely so called, a hundred are enervated by materialism. The world is too much with us. Money getting and pleasure seeking are hastening ills, more ancient, more numerous, more subtle, and more seductive than speculation. There is little infidelity in the churches; there is much materialism. When wealth accumulates, alas, that religious enthusiasm decays![5]

McDaniel persuaded Southern Baptists once again to give sacrificially for the cause of Christ and the expansion of the kingdom of God through missionary efforts.

Within three months of this passionate message, the voice of the prophet was silenced. Two years previous McDaniel had suffered a minor stroke while speaking to the Dover Association. McDaniel feared that the stroke would end his preaching ministry. He asked the doctor, "Will I be crippled in God's service, and unable to do a full day's work for my Saviour?"[6] On August 10, 1927, less than two years later, the pastor experienced a second stroke that proved to be fatal.

During the days following his death, the McDaniel family received many letters of condolence from leaders of all major denominations. Still the most appropriate oration came from a person who remained anonymous: "Well, Mrs. Mac, all heaven and hell is rejoicing now dat de Doctor is dead! Oh yes, de angels is happy kase he has got home, and de devils is happy dat he done lef' de yearth and can't preach no more, nor hit ole Satan another lick."[7]

16

GEORGE WASHINGTON TRUETT

May 6, 1867—July 7, 1944
Elected: 1927, 1928, 1929

*I*n the spring of 1888, the Georgia State Convention was in annual meeting in the county courthouse in Marietta, Georgia. The crowd at the Georgia state meetings had gotten so large in recent years that they had moved from the largest church sanctuaries to the more cacophonous courthouses, and a packed crowd gathered to hear the reports from various agencies and institutions. In the midst of his report on Mercer University, Rev. Fernando C. McConnell wanted to use a living illustration to drive home his point. Dramatically pausing in his plea for support for the young students from the mountains, he said, "Brethren, if you don't believe me, I'll show you. There is a lad at this Convention from up there in the mountains who ought to go to Mercer. George? George! George, come up here!"[1]

Though the room had fallen silent as McConnell scanned the crowd, finally a pale slender young man of twenty-one was pushed down the aisle. McConnell urged him to tell the thousands in attendance what the Lord was doing, and slowly the young man began to speak. George Washington Truett, the young principal of the Hiawassee Academy in Towns County, Georgia, began his first public speaking assignment before a throng.

"Ladies and gentlemen," he began, "I never saw such a great, big, fine looking body of people as this one is. The truth is, I am so scared that my knees are making war on each other and I hardly know which one of my father's sons I am." And yet he spoke. For long moments the young Truett held the crowd rapt with attention as he told of the sacrifice and work in the mountain academy and the souls being won in the labor. When he finished speaking, men wept openly, "under the mastery of that mountain lad's epic story." Years later Dr. J. B. Hawthorne, the famous pastor of the First Baptist Church of Atlanta, noted,

I have heard Henry W. Grady . . . Henry Ward Beecher and
Phillips Brooks and others of the world's famous speakers, but never in

all my life has my soul been more deeply stirred by any speaker than it was that day at Marietta by that boy out of the mountains. My heart burned within me and I could not keep back the tears.[2]

Ten years after that surprising and auspicious moment, that lad would become the pastor of First Baptist Church of Dallas, Texas, and thirty-nine years later Dr. George W. Truett would become president of the Southern Baptist Convention.

George Washington Truett was born on May 6, 1867, the seventh child born to Charles L. and Mary R. (Kimsey) Truett. Born in rural Hayesville, North Carolina, Truett was raised in a devoutly Christian home, attending Sunday school and preaching services every Sunday. Though he had sensed God's conviction at age six and again at age eleven, Truett was not converted until the annual pro-tracted meeting in 1886, when he was nineteen.[3] Under the preaching of the pastor, Rev. J. G. Mashburn, and the evangelist, Rev. J. G. Pulliam, Truett was saved and baptized in the Baptist Country Church in Clay County, North Carolina.

An exceptional student, Truett graduated from Hayesville Academy in 1885, and was given the responsibility of becoming the superintendent, teacher, and manager of the Crooked Creek school, just a few miles across the state line from his home in North Carolina. With fifty students in that one-room schoolhouse, Truett taught every subject for the entire term, which in agrarian communities lasted only three months, from late fall (after the harvest) through the winter.

Following his conversion the next year, Truett conceived the idea for Hiawassee Academy, a private school of intense learning,[4] and became the founder and principal of the school in 1887. He was greatly aided by the aforementioned Fernando C. McConnell, his cousin and a preacher ten years older than Truett. Throughout their lives McConnell and Truett rejoiced to see the other rise to leadership in the Southern Baptist Convention. McConnell (1856–1929) eventu-ally became the secretary of the Home Mission Board in 1903, succeeding pastor to Dr. B. H. Carroll at First Baptist Waco in 1909, and the pastor of Druid Hills Baptist Church in Atlanta in 1915. In 1902, McConnell preached the annual sermon at the Southern Baptist Convention.[5]

In the summer of 1889, Truett and his brother Luther followed their parents to Whitewright, Texas, after the family farm in North Carolina was sold. Working on the farm in the blistering heat, Truett questioned whether leaving the "sapphire heights of the Blue Ridge Mountains" for the sweeping plains of Texas was a good idea.[6] However, by the fall Truett was teaching regularly in the First Baptist Church of Whitewright and would occasionally preach when the pastor was absent.

Still Truett had no inclination to be a preacher. His heart was set on becom-ing a lawyer, and he was studying to that end at Grayson College along with his brother. Yet the members of the Whitewright church saw something entirely dif-ferent in young Truett. Dr. Truett later wrote of the drama:

From the time of my conversion on, everywhere I went, godly men and women would pluck me aside and say, "Oughtn't you to be preaching?" I was ambitious to be a lawyer from my earliest recollection; and therefore had that big battle to fight. . . . At Whitewright, I often conducted services, making it a point always to stand out in front of the pulpit, feeling myself utterly unfit to be in a pulpit. . . . We had there, in that village church, the old Saturday meeting.[7] On a certain Saturday in 1890, the attendance was enormous. I thought within myself, "This is singular: here is a house full of people on Saturday." [After the sermon and service had ended], the oldest deacon, then quite frail in health, rose up and began to talk, ". . . There is such a thing as a church duty when the whole church must act. . . . It is my deep conviction, as it is yours—for [the church members have] talked to one another—that this church has a church duty to perform. . . . I move therefore that this church call a presbytery to ordain Brother George W. Truett to the full work of the gospel ministry." It was promptly seconded and I immediately got the floor and implored them to desist. I said, *You have me appalled; you simply have me appalled!"* And then one after another talked, and tears ran down their cheeks. . . . I appealed to them, *"Wait six months, wait six months!"* And they said, "We won't wait six *hours.* . . . We are moved by deep conviction that this is the will of God. . . ." There I was, against the whole church, against a church profoundly moved. There was not a dry eye in the house—I was thrown into the stream, and just had to swim.[8]

Truett was ordained the next morning by the pastor of the Whitewright church, Rev. R. F. Jenkins.

In 1890, the twenty-three-year-old preacher was approached by Dr. B. H. Carroll. Dr. J. B. Cranfill had served as the financial agent for Baylor University from 1888 to 1889, but he had left the position to become the corresponding secretary of the Baptist General Convention of Texas. This left Baylor with a tremendous need, as the school was crippled with a $92,000 debt. Carroll had heard from Rev. Jenkins that Truett was a winsome and passionate speaker. Imploring Truett to lead the Baylor campaign to retire the debt, Carroll defied all the pretense of the Baptist world. Not more than six leaders in the entire state had even heard of Truett, who was not even two years into his schooling. Yet the trustees of the school acquiesced to the leadership of Carroll and elected Truett. Within twenty-three months Truett crossed the entire state, tirelessly speaking to churches great and small, and retired the debt in 1893. Exhausted by the travail, Truett sat on the curb in front of First Baptist Church of Waco and wept.

Entering Baylor University in September 1893, Truett was a twenty-six-year-old freshman. His stern yet affable demeanor and strict study habits left him little time for recreation. He had developed a friendship with Dr. Carroll's son, Harvey

Jr., and Harvey had a plan. He repeatedly tried to arrange a meeting between Truett and the daughter of Judge W. H. Jenkins, a deacon at First Baptist Waco. When the two skeptical people met, the attraction was instantaneous. On June 28, 1894, Josephine Jenkins married George Washington Truett at the church, with Dr. B. H. Carroll officiating.[9]

Having graduated from Baylor in June 1897, Truett stood at a crossroads in his life. Serving a student pastorate of East Baptist Church in Waco, Truett was content to "live and die right there,"[10] at the East Waco Church. But God was about to send the Truetts on their greatest journey, to First Baptist Church, Dallas, Texas.

In the summer of 1897, First Baptist Church heard reports from such Texas Baptist leaders as Dr. Cranfill, Dr. Buckner, and Dr. Carroll that the thirty-year-old Truett was the only candidate for pastor. The committee, led by Colonel W. L. Williams[11] and Colonel C. C. Slaughter, reported to the search committee that Truett was not interested in the position. The committee did not heed his protestations and unanimously called Truett. Meeting with the church as a courtesy, Truett discovered the church had approximately seven hundred members and a twelve-thousand-dollar debt. Despite his reservations Truett felt led to accept the call and began his ministry at First Dallas on the second Sunday of September 1897.

The growth in the church was immediate. With new converts being presented in almost every service and the debt being retired quickly, all conditions seemed idyllic. Yet a tragedy of life-altering proportions loomed in the near future.

Within the first year of becoming the pastor of First Baptist Dallas, Truett was approached by the new chief of police in Dallas, Captain J. C. Arnold. The Texas Ranger wanted to take the pastor quail hunting in Johnson County, and he provided the guns, ammunition, and bird dogs for the trip. Taking the train to Cleburne, they were met by Dr. George W. Baines, pastor of First Baptist Cleburne, and the three men traveled by horse to the hunting grounds. Late in the afternoon the three were returning to their tents along a narrow path. Captain Arnold was walking a few paces ahead of Truett, when Truett shifted the position of his gun. The gun discharged, sending a load of bird shot into the calf of Arnold's leg.

Though Baines and the Captain did not think the wound was serious, the three traveled back to Dallas. For days the doctors explained that the wound was not serious, but Truett was inconsolable. Sleepless for days, Truett paced, prayed, and wept. The church gathered for the Wednesday night prayer meeting and lifted up the wounded member and heartbroken pastor. Tragically that night Captain Arnold died of a coronary thrombosis.

The funeral was held in the sanctuary of First Baptist Church, Dallas, but Truett did not preach. In a state of blackened grief and pain, Truett told Josephine that he was leaving the ministry. All the words of consolation could not lift the burden from the young pastor's heart. He was resolved. His biographer wrote that it seemed the entire city of Dallas was praying for Truett.[12] Well into Saturday night, after an excruciating week, Truett was convinced that he was not fit for the ministry. After a dream in which Truett heard the Lord tell him to preach, Truett reluctantly entered the pulpit that Sunday morning. He was forever a changed man.

During his forty-seven-year tenure as pastor of First Baptist Church, Dallas, Truett saw the Lord do remarkable things. The membership grew from 715 members to 7,804, with a total of 19,531 new members received.[13] He served as a trustee of Baylor University, Southwestern Seminary, and Baylor Hospital. His constant speaking and writing produced ten books that were collections of his sermons, including *The Leaf and the Life,*[14] *We Would See Jesus,*[15] and *Christian Education.*[16] One of his most famous books, *A Quest for Souls,* was a compilation of sermons he preached at the Fort Worth revival on June 11–24, 1917. Almost all of Truett's books were compilations of sermons, many edited and published posthumously.[17]

By 1920, Truett had become one of America's best-known preachers. For thirty-seven years he traveled to west Texas to preach at the Cowboy Camp Meetings. He preached to the Allied Forces for six months in World War I.[18] That year President J. B. Gambrell asked Truett to present a special address concerning religious liberty.[19] On Sunday, May 16, 1920, Truett stood on the steps of the Capital and spoke on "Baptists and Religious Liberty." So masterful was the address that nationwide demand took the media by storm.[20]

Truett was first elected president of the Southern Baptist Convention in 1927 at the meeting in Louisville. He followed that tenure by his election to the Baptist World Alliance from 1934 to 1939, serving as president of the BWA from 1938 to 1939. His work for Baylor Hospital saw a tower named for him, as well as an auditorium at Southwestern Seminary.

Truett's unwavering trust in Christ and the Bible produced remarkable results at First Baptist Church and around the world. On the occasion of his seventieth birthday in 1937, Truett wrote a loving letter to his wife, which included the following:

Emotions too deep for words stir in my heart. More grateful than my poor words can say, am I, both to God and humanity; for all the mercies that have been showered upon me, through all the fast-flying years! It is all of grace, grace, God's wonderful grace! I would this day rededicate my all to Christ, to go, and to say and to do and to be . . . for all the days ahead, whatever they may be! . . . And you will be by my side, to pray for me and to help me along—you my chiefest earthly comfort and inspiration.[21]

In July 1944, the seventy-seven-year-old Truett died in his bed after a prolonged illness.

17
WILLIAM JOSEPH MCGLOTHLIN

November 29, 1867—May 28, 1933
Elected: 1930, 1931, 1932

*I*n his presidential address to the Southern Baptist Convention in Kansas City in May 1923, Dr. E. Y. Mullins addressed the looming Darwinian infiltration in the American landscape:

> We record again our unwavering adherence to the supernatural elements in the Christian religion. The Bible is God's revelation of Himself through man moved by the Holy Spirit, and is our sufficient certain and authoritative guide in religion. Jesus Christ was born of the Virgin Mary through the power of the Holy Spirit. He was the Divine and eternal Son of God. He wrought miracles, healing the sick, casting out demons, raising the dead. He died as the vicarious atoning Savior of the world and was buried. He arose again from the dead. The tomb was emptied of its contents. In His risen body He appeared many times to His disciples. He ascended to the right hand of the Father. He will come again in person, the same Jesus who ascended from the Mount of Olives.[1]

He then hastened to address the professors in SBC institutions and their willingness to acquiesce to the trends of the day:

> We believe that adherence to the above truths and facts is a necessary condition of service for teachers in our Baptist schools. . . . We do insist upon a positive content of faith in accordance with the preceding statements as a qualification for acceptable service in Baptist schools. . . . The supreme issue today is between naturalism and supernaturalism. We stand unalterably for the supernatural in Christianity. Teachers in our schools should be careful to free themselves from any suspicion of disloyalty on this point. . . . We pledge our support to all schools and teachers who are thus loyal to the facts of Christianity as revealed in the Scripture.[2]

Two years later, Mullins chaired the committee that presented the *1925 Baptist Faith and Message* (BFM). This confession, based on the New Hampshire Confession of 1833, was accepted by the Convention messengers meeting in Memphis on May 14. Mullins's committee, which had worked on the BFM for months, needed Southern Baptist scholars who understood Baptist polity, theology, and history. The historian who served on the committee not only understood Baptist history within the academic world; he had lived it. Dr. W. J. McGlothlin had served at an essential juncture of Baptist life as professor, author, and president.

William Joseph McGlothlin was born on November 29, 1867, in Gallatin, Tennessee. Converted in his teens, McGlothlin surrendered to the gospel ministry before he entered college. Receiving his bachelor of arts from Bethel College in Kentucky in 1889, he continued his studies at Bethel and received the master of arts in 1891. Moving north to Southern Seminary in Louisville, he received his master of theology degree in 1894.

Immediately following his graduation from Southern, McGlothlin joined the faculty. He regularly used his spare time to pursue his Ph.D. from the University of Berlin, which he completed in 1901. Fluent in German, McGlothlin would eventually publish a German work, *Die Berner Täufer bis 1532*.[3] This was his second book, his first being published even before the completion of his doctorate, entitled *The Baptist Church of Christ on Glen's Creek, in Woodford County, Ky*.[4]

One would imagine that this would have been a wonderful period in the life of McGlothlin. As a young professor at Southern Seminary and an author with two books, McGlothlin was married on June 8, 1897, to Mary Belle Williams. The marriage would produce five children, including a son who would follow in his father's professorial footsteps. Yet this was one of the most intensely controversial times in the young life of McGlothlin.

Dr. John A. Broadus was the president of Southern Seminary who called McGlothlin to the faculty in 1894. The following year, however, Broadus died, and his successor was the professor of ecclesiastical history, William Heth Whitsitt. Dr. Whitsitt had actually become professor at Southern in 1872, when the seminary was located in Greenville, South Carolina. In 1877, the seminary relocated to Louisville, Kentucky, and Whitsitt also made the journey. In 1895, twenty-three years after joining the faculty, Whitsitt was installed as president of the hallowed institution.

Four years into his presidency, Whitsitt became embroiled in a controversy. Though Whitsitt had written copiously on Baptist history,[5] it was discovered that he was the author of an unsigned encyclopedia article stating that Baptists "invented" immersion in 1641. The article seemed to suggest a church tradition of pedobaptism and sprinkling, and Baptists were angered by the discovery. Baptist leaders such as Dr. Benjah Harvey Carroll felt that Whitsitt was denying the biblical practice of immersion, a controversy that had embroiled the Convention fifty years earlier.

At the time of the discovery, Carroll was pastor of First Baptist Church, Waco, Texas, and a trustee of Southern Seminary.[6] When the charges were brought against Whitsitt, he protested a misunderstanding. "Whitsitt explained that he had used the word 'invent' in the old English sense of 'discover' or 'uncover'—meaning that in 1641 the Baptists had restored the primitive practice of baptism by immersion."[7] The trustees found his argument unconvincing, but the faculty supported their president. Finally in 1898, Carroll called for a severing of ties between the Southern Baptist Convention and the seminary, and in 1899, Whitsitt resigned.

Whitsitt's successor was Dr. Edgar Young Mullins (1860–1928). Mullins, a graduate of Southern Seminary (B.D. 1885), was a former associate secretary of the Foreign Mission Board, and was serving as pastor of First Baptist Church of Newton Centre, Massachusetts, at the time of his election. One of his first tasks was to find someone to fill the controversial shoes of Whitsitt. Knowing that the entire Southern Baptist Convention was watching, he chose the young McGlothlin.[8]

McGlothlin's presence at Southern was certainly seen as a blessing for orthodoxy among Southern Baptists. In later years, when J. B. Cranfill, editor of the *Baptist Standard,* was lamenting the break of the University of Chicago from its Baptist moorings, he wrote of an 1895 interview with President W. R. Harper for his column in the *Standard.* Writing of the University of Chicago's chapel services, he noted, "During the time of my stay here I have heard sermons by Dr. O. C. S. Wallace, chancellor of McMaster University; Dr. W. J. McGlothlin, . . . and Dr. H. L. Stetson, who is one of the teachers in the Chicago university divinity school."[9]

For the next twenty years, Dr. W. J. McGlothlin served Southern Baptists admirably at Southern Seminary. Along with his teaching responsibilities, McGlothlin became the foremost Southern Baptist historian. His published works set forth a belief in Baptist distinctives, including *Kentucky Baptists, the Seminary and Alien Immersion,*[10] *A Guide to the Study of Church History,*[11] and *What Hinders the Union of Baptists and Disciples.*[12]

Those who had hoped McGlothlin would continue to perpetuate the belief in a recent inception of Baptist history were disappointed in 1910 with the publication of his most famous book. *Baptist Confessions of Faith* not only included such obvious Baptist confessions as the Second London Confession (1677) and the Philadelphia Confession (1742), but it also drew Baptists back to their Anabaptist roots by including such confessions as the Schleitheim Confession (1527). Though McGlothlin was certainly not a Landmarker in seeing a Baptist successionism back to the apostles, he did believe in baptistic perpetuity.[13]

McGlothlin was not content to publish for the academic world and desired to teach church history to laity. He published consistently with the Sunday School Board in Nashville, including *Infant-Baptism: Historically Considered* (1916) and *Our Baptist Principles and Their Place in the World Today* (1917). He also wrote books offering help to pastors, including *Practical Hints on Preaching: Nine Lectures on Sermon Building*,[14] and *A Vital Ministry, the Pastor of Today in the Service of Man*.[15] This type of writing enabled McGlothlin to connect to the churches and the common men and helped raise McGlothlin's stature in the Convention. He became so beloved that in 1918, he was asked to preach the annual Convention sermon concerning the world war in which the country was entrenched.[16]

In 1919, at the age of fifty-two, McGlothlin was elected as president of Furman University in South Carolina.[17] His election after twenty-five years at Louisville was a major vortex in the life of his family, but McGlothlin instilled a sense of vision to the university. Moving the university outside the center of Greenville, he saw the university grow tremendously in its new location. He also saw the university accredited in 1924, become one of the four college benefactors to the vast Duke endowment in 1929, and assume control of the Greenville Female College in 1933.

Following his involvement in the 1925 *Baptist Faith and Message*, McGlothlin was elected as president of the Southern Baptist Convention in 1930 in New Orleans. Driving to the 1933 annual Convention meeting in Washington D.C., McGlothlin tragically died in an automobile wreck on May 28. As Southern Baptists struggled to deal with the immense loss, Z. T. Cody eulogized McGlothlin in the South Carolina *Baptist Courier*:

> As president of the Convention, he rendered a notable service, for
> he brought to the great office not only a perfect knowledge of parlia-
> mentary law, but also an understanding of the complicated official life
> of Southern Baptists and an unwearied purpose to preserve our Baptist
> polity when the pressure of denominational problems was threatening
> its integrity.[18]

18

FRED FERNANDO BROWN

November 27, 1882–August 9, 1960
Elected: 1932

*M*onday, March 25, 1929, broke as a normal day in New York City. The recent inauguration of Herbert Hoover as president of United States should have had a positive effect on the New York Stock Exchange (NYSE), but it did not. In the first of many small "crashes" in the NYSE, the day ended with substantial, albeit limited, losses. That week the Federal Reserve Board met in a closed session to discuss the possibility of a looming crisis. Though the market struggled to recover throughout the summer, by September 3, stocks were steadily losing their value. A bear market was firmly established. On Thursday, October 24, the country was shocked to learn that over twelve million shares had changed hands. This was three times the normal volume, and it did not speak well for the confidence of investors and traders.[1] Panic was setting in.

Rarely has there been a period in American history so wrought with panic and despair as the fall of 1929.

While a brief recovery on Friday gave investors a small sense of relief, nothing could prepare them for what loomed the next week. On Monday, October 28, 1929, over nine million shares were traded in a fury, and around the country Americans began to withdraw funds from their banks, in fear of losing their savings. By noon on Monday, police had to be summoned to quell the rioting investors, many of whom were operating blindly, as the phone lines were overwhelmed with calls, and the stock issues were ninety minutes behind on the ticker tape. On the infamous Black Tuesday, October 29, 1929, the stock market crashed, and few investors could gather the monies necessary to cover their losses. The panic that ensued led to bankrupt firms, depleted banks, suicidal investors and traders, and the ominous threat of a great depression. By November 1929, stock values had fallen by 62 percent.

The onset of the Great Depression in 1929 had ripple effects over the entire country. Farmers lost their estates as banks foreclosed on their assets. Banks closed and entire savings accounts were lost, as families that had previously been considered working middle class were now instantly impoverished. The entire country was thrust into the depths of the worst financial catastrophe in its history. Even the Southern Baptist Convention was horribly affected. By 1931, the Southern Baptist Convention was an astonishing six million dollars in debt.

To rescue the struggling denomination, Southern Baptists turned to a preacher from Jackson County, North Carolina. For the next two years, this pastor and leader preached, worked, and traveled to the point of fatal exhaustion to call Southern Baptists to restore the viability of the denomination. In a real sense Dr. Fred Brown almost gave his life to save Southern Baptists.

Fred Fernando Brown was born on November 27, 1882, in Glenville, North Carolina. His parents, Horatio Alonzo and Dorcas Elizabeth Brown, raised him in a Christian home, and at the age of nineteen, he entered Mars Hill College as a ministerial student. Transferring to Wake Forest College in Wake Forest, North Carolina, Brown intensified his studies, receiving his bachelor of arts degree in 1908 and his master of arts in 1909.

Even though he was a ministerial student and had many opportunities to minister in local churches, it was not until he moved to Louisville, Kentucky, in 1910, that he began to pastor. While pursuing his master of theology (1912) and his doctor of theology (1913) degrees at Southern Seminary, Brown pastored churches in Harrodsburg and Frankfort, Kentucky. Ordained in 1913, Fred married Nona Lee Dover on April 12, 1914. The marriage would produce five children, four girls and a boy.[2]

In 1916, Fred and his family moved to Sherman, Texas, where he became pastor of First Baptist Church in Sherman. While Brown was serving the growing church, the country was thrust into World War I, and the pastor from Sherman became a leader in the military chaplaincy effort. At the request of President Woodrow Wilson, Brown served as special chaplain with the American Expeditionary Force and Army of Occupation in 1918. Like so many churches during wartime, First Baptist Church, Sherman, graciously released their pastor to serve at the request of the president and held his position open for him when he returned. Years later he would recount a meaningful moment in his service in France:

It was my privilege to be in the Army of Occupation . . . after the signing of the Armistice in 1918. One Sunday morning I [received] a call from an American officer asking if I would come to a little village some thirty kilometers away and speak at the noon hour. I demurred because there were four other engagements for the day, but he added . . . "If you will come, the service will be held in a Protestant church building." That interested me because for eleven months I had held services in all kinds of places—on the ship deck, in hotel lobbies, in barns, in barrack rooms, sometimes out in the open, but I had not been in a church since leaving America, so I went. In the center of the little village that nestled there in the Moselle Mountains, I found a small stone church that was older than our Western civilization. . . . I stood [in the pulpit] and with an open Bible in my hand turned to face those American soldiers. They were in the Army of Occupation— all of them were men who had seen action. Their courage had been tested on the battlefields of northern France. Something strange had taken place as we sat there. When I arose I was unable to read until I had brushed away the mist that dimmed my eyes and had gained control of my emotions. Tears . . . were flowing down the cheeks of those strong men. I did not understand what had happened until later. . . . [In our minds] we were home again! It was Sunday morning, and we had gathered for worship. . . . The unbidden tears were a silent tribute to our home churches—to the teachings and influence of those churches that had followed us through the years.[3]

In 1921, Dr. Fred F. Brown accepted the call to pastor the First Baptist Church of Knoxville, Tennessee. It would be a joyous marriage of pastor and people. For the next twenty-five years, Brown led that historic church to some of its greatest days.

Dr. Frederick Fernando Brown became pastor of First Baptist in May 1921. In September of that year property on the corner of Walnut and Main was purchased for a new church building. This was McClung family property that had been the location of an old jail and a military prison during the Civil War. The third building was completed in 1924 at a cost of $600,000. The sanctuary richly ornamented with marble and fine woods, seats 1200. The exterior of the beautiful and stately church building is modeled after St. Martin in the Fields of London. Much of the exterior marble was quarried locally. In 1997, this building was placed on the National Register of Historical Places for its architectural features.[4]

While leading First Baptist Church of Knoxville, Brown rose to prominence in the Southern Baptist Convention. He was innovative in his leadership and preaching, and the church grew rapidly. For a number of years, Brown would preach while standing on the back of a pickup truck in the center of Market Square in Knoxville on Saturday nights, far in advance of the national evangelical trend of Saturday evening services![5]

In 1929, his book *This Is My Church* was published by Broadman Press to acclaim. In 1930, he led the devotional service for the dedication of Smoky Mountain National Park at the request of President Franklin Roosevelt.[6]

When the stock market crashed in 1929, Southern Baptist institutions were deeply affected. When the debt load of six million dollars was released, many feared that our missionaries would be stranded without support and that our colleges and institutions would be threatened with closure. The SBC called for a promotion committee to be formed in 1931, and quickly they began meeting. In July of that year, the committee met in Birmingham, Alabama, with the seemingly insurmountable task of calling Southern Baptists to give over and beyond their tithes to the local church to help retire the debt. With money already in scarce supply, Southern Baptists were not optimistic that a program could be instituted to garner the funds. They needed a point man who could pour himself into the work.[7]

On July 7, 1931, the promotion committee nominated Brown as executive secretary. Brown, however, did not feel he could do the job justice and still maintain the necessary leadership as pastor of First Baptist Knoxville. The church, recognizing the huge need and pressing urgency, "released their pastor until the next session of the Convention and continued to pay his salary."[8]

Fred Brown embarked on the most rigorous schedule of his life. Tirelessly, often lacking sleep, Brown traveled the country, preaching in associational meetings, State Conventions, local churches, and other venues, attempting to enlist one million tithers to give unselfishly. He spoke multiple times in a myriad of settings and often traveled at night to arrive at his next speaking engagements the next day. He became the most-traveled man in the Southern Baptist Convention, as the fiscal viability of the SBC and the lives of missionaries were held in the balance.

It was no surprise, then, that when the 2,178 messengers gathered for the annual meeting in St. Petersburg, Florida, Dr. Fred F. Brown was elected president of the Convention. His ubiquitous presence across the nation and tireless efforts had endeared him to his fellow Southern Baptists.

The year 1932 also marked a change in the procedures of the Southern Baptist Convention presidential election process. Since 1845, presidents were elected at the opening of the annual meeting, and began to preside immediately. This system was altered in 1932. There were two elections. William McGlothlin was elected at the beginning of the Convention and presided during that annual session. Dr. Brown was elected at the end of the Convention to become president for the 1933 annual meeting. Thus, he would be both the president-elect of the SBC and would also represent Southern Baptists as the duly elected president until the 1933 session. We have followed this method ever since.

This modification of procedure has caused some confusion in Southern Baptist history books and charts, as it appears that two men were elected as president in 1932. In fact, both were elected at the 1932 session, marking the change in Southern Baptist Convention procedures.

Immediately following the Convention, Brown returned to the full-time work of his pastorate in Knoxville and continued to travel the country extensively in the second wave of promotion committee work, called the Crucible Service Campaign.

The workload and constant activity weakened him. His health began to fail, and yet he continued the arduous schedule unabated. He became increasingly frail and often spoke in a hoarse whisper at gatherings. By the late spring Brown was in bad health and unable to travel.

When the annual meeting gathered in the Washington Auditorium in Washington, D.C., an extraordinary realization struck the messengers. The elected president, Dr. Fred F. Brown, had literally worked himself to the brink of death. As the first session convened,

at 9:30 on Friday morning, May 19, 1933, Dr. M. E. Dodd of Shreveport, Louisiana, called the Convention to order. As vice-president of the Convention, he was presiding in the absence of . . . Brown . . . who was ill. The Convention acted on a motion authorizing a message of sympathy to Dr. Brown.[9]

Thus, Brown became the only elected president of the Southern Baptist Convention never to preside over the annual meeting.

Though Brown was in a bed in Knoxville, the fruit of his efforts resonated from Washington throughout the Baptist world.

During the year, a "Special Emergency Mission Relief Campaign" had been conducted. The goal of the offering was $300,000. It was announced that $203,908.51 had been raised. The report said, "It saved the day for Home Missions and Foreign Missions." There had also been employed an organization, "Crucible Service," to conduct a campaign. They reported raising $16,297.73.[10]

The indefatigable efforts of Dr. Brown were not without reward. Because of the selfless and sacrificial giving of Southern Baptists, missionaries of the Southern Baptist Convention had been spared the horror of returning from their fields. The SBC was moving toward solvency. At the conclusion of the meeting, the Convention adopted the program Debt Free in '43, which was a fitting tribute to the man who had launched the effort some two years earlier.

Gradually Brown recovered from his illness and resumed his role as pastor of First Baptist Knoxville. On his twenty-fifth anniversary as pastor of the church, Fred F. Brown retired from the active pastorate. This did not mean, however, that he retired from service in his local church or his denomination. In the next fifteen years, Brown served as a trustee of Carson-Newman College, Southeastern Baptist Theological Seminary, East Tennessee Baptist Hospital, and the Tennessee Baptist Orphanage, and he served as a member of the executive board of the Tennessee Baptist Convention. By the time of his death in Knoxville on August 9, 1960, Fred Brown had dedicated a half century to his Lord and his denomination.

19
MONROE ELMON DODD

September 8, 1878—August 6, 1952
Elected: 1933, 1934

$\mathcal{S}$outhern Baptist missionary efforts in China were pioneered through the exemplary work of Lottie Moon. In the 1920s, Dr. C. L. Culpepper was building on that heritage when he joined with other missionaries including Bertha Smith, praying for the outpouring of the Spirit of God upon the Shantung Province where they were stationed. God honored their steadfast plea and worked mightily among them. Sharing his experience years later, C. L. Culpepper detailed how God had worked among them. He recounted:

1. In one village, at least one person from every household was saved. Thereby, the Christian community grew from 50 to 1000 within a matter of six months.
2. Church services had open, unfettered confession of sin on numerous occasions that continued for days without interruption.
3. Church services had spontaneous song services that lasted for hours without interruption.
4. In one Christian school, Culpepper was asked to preach. Service was suspended constantly, and by the end of the day, 600 boys and 900 girls were born again.[1]

In *Girding the Globe*, M. E. Dodd dedicated an entire chapter to the Shantung Revival, illustrating his desire that Southern Baptists in the West experience what Southern Baptist missionaries forged in the East. His great affinity with the happenings of the revival exemplified the purpose of his ministry from the day he was called by God.

Monroe Elmon Dodd was born in Brazil, Tennessee, on September 8, 1878, to William and Lucy Dodd, both devout Christians. Dodd observed the godliness of his parents and followed suit, accepting Christ as his Savior at an early age and following in baptism in August 1891. Dodd spent his formative years in debates, yet his spiritual life emphasized not only the rational but more so the mystical. In 1898, before graduating from Trenton High School, Dodd felt a "strong urge" to enlist in the United States army during the Spanish-American War. During this brief respite Dodd turned his life over to serious Bible study.

Dodd was discharged due to the brevity of the war and returned home. His younger brother, Allen Dodd III, had accepted the call to preach, but had grown deathly ill within the few weeks after his brother's return. Before he died, Allen encouraged his older brother to stop resisting the will of God in his life. He stated, "Brother, you know God has been calling you to preach. I am going to die. I want to ask you to preach a little for me."[2] That was enough for Dodd.

Dodd immediately enrolled at Union University, where he was awarded almost every honor in debate and literary contests. In fact, he graduated in 1904 with a double major in arts and oratory. Also during his educational years, he was ordained by his home church in Trenton, Tennessee. Though Dodd never attended seminary, he was emerging as one of the great expositors of the Scripture within the Southern Baptist Convention.

His senior year at the university was one of transition for Dodd. He accepted the call to First Baptist Church of Fulton, Kentucky, a church admittedly divided among its members. During his four-year tenure, the young pastor was able to lead the church into numerical and spiritual growth, quadrupling its membership and building a new auditorium debt-free. Yet Dodd struggled with his decision to pastor the Fulton congregation, believing that God had impressed him to be a missionary abroad. After only a few months at the church, Dodd asked the Foreign Mission Board to assign him to the task. He quietly resigned the pastorate and accepted the appointment of the board to go to Mexico.

During this divine struggle Dodd was introduced to Emma Savage, the daughter of the president of Union University. They were happily married in October 1904. The newlywed missionaries ran into problems immediately, including being involved in three train wrecks before arriving on the field. After only four months away from home, Dodd believed he had made a grave mistake and returned to the Fulton church to pastor for three more years.

In 1908, Dodd resigned from the Fulton pastorate and accepted the call to the First Baptist Church of Paducah, Kentucky. The church grew substantially while also increasing its giving to missions around the world. Dodd was especially gifted in his preaching and thereby was courted by many churches during this time. In 1911, he agreed to pastor the Twenty-Second and Walnut Street Baptist Church in Louisville, Kentucky. It was here that Dodd became recognized by many students at nearby Southern Seminary. In the years that followed, these students would call on this mentor to preach at their churches.

In 1911, Dodd addressed the Southern Baptist Convention for the first time. Messengers from First Baptist Church of Shreveport, Louisiana, were attracted to the preaching and personality of Dodd and offered him the opportunity to pastor the influential assembly. During his trial sermon Dodd preached fervently, and when the invitation came, many received Christ as their Savior. After ministering in several churches over a brief period of time, Dodd began a relationship with a church which would span four decades.

In many ways Dodd initiated a new day among twentieth-century pastors in the South. He was the first Shreveport pastor to use an automobile for his pastoral visits. He used shortwave radio to expand the ministry to the nation and then around the world. However, the greatest change Dodd implemented was in his visitation method. Southern churches expected their pastors to visit each home on a regular basis without necessary cause. Dodd did not accept this as the most basic responsibility of the pastor and wrote:

> The old time pastor who went from house to house visiting his
> people and the old time doctor who used to call upon the sick, feel
> their pulse, look at their tongue, and hold their hand, seem to be rap-
> idly departing institutions of a passing generation. So the pastor of
> today finds out that if he starts on general pastoral calling he is gener-
> ally wasting his time because he finds so few of the people at home,
> and those that are there are not prepared for the call.[3]

Dodd determined that sermon preparation took precedence over "general" visitation and thereby limited his visits to the sick, shut-ins, new members, poor and needy, and unsaved. His time was further limited by heavy involvement in denominational affairs. The following partial list demonstrates the service Dodd gave to Southern Baptists:

1909–1910	Moderator of the West Union Baptist Association (Kentucky)
1914, 1922	Preached Convention sermon for Louisiana Baptists
1923	Launched Southwide Simultaneous Revival Crusade
1924–1925	Chaired the committee that planned the Cooperative Program
1927	Elected president of Louisiana Baptist Convention
1929	Chairman of SBC Order of Business Committee
1934	Preached to Baptist World Alliance in Berlin; world tour for missions

With such devotion to the denomination, it is not surprising that in 1933 messengers elected Dodd president of the Southern Baptist Convention. His missionary zeal once again emerged as Dodd and his wife traveled the world raising awareness of reaching the world with the gospel. In his work *Missions Our Mission*, he expounded:

> The gospel of Jesus Christ is a universal remedy from a universal
> God for the universal need of humanity. The God whom Jesus Christ
> revealed to the world is not a tribal, national, or racial God. He is for

all men of all races, classes, and colors, in all nations and throughout
all ages. The gospel is so elemental and fundamental in its application
to humanity that it meets the needs of all kinds of persons in all places
and at all times.[4]

Dodd had come full circle. The belief that he was called to missions was fulfilled
in his task to raise up an army of missionaries to go and fulfill the Great
Commission.

His excitement was further enlarged through the newly formed Cooperative
Program that financed this lofty goal. As chairman of the committee that brought
the program into being, he explained the purpose of the program:

> The ultimate aim and end of all the work, whether it be the sup-
> port of chanceless children, the healing in our hospitals of humanity's
> hurt, the taking care of aged and worn-out ministers and missionaries,
> the support of Christian educational institutions, the employment of
> evangelists, teachers, editors, mission secretaries, and missionaries, the
> aim of it all is the preaching of the gospel to every creature.[5]

At the height of his ministry, Dodd had found his stride. He was leading in the
growth of his local church while expanding the kingdom through denominational
leadership. In it all, preaching was to be central and primary to the task.

The preaching of the Word of God must be the focus of Southern Baptist pul-
pits. Dodd explained that preaching was the main feature that set Baptists apart
from all other denominations: "For Baptists, preaching the Word has ever been the
highest and holiest privilege and duty. Music, writing, organization, orders of services, ordinances, there *may* be, but preaching there *must* be."[6]

Dodd, then, was the consummate example of expository preaching. In his life
he preached eighteen thousand times, or an average of nearly one sermon each day
for fifty years. After more than five decades of service, Dodd decided it was time to
retire from full-time ministry. He resigned as pastor of the First Baptist Church of
Shreveport. Fittingly, Dodd never stopped preaching even in retirement. On August
6, 1952, after supplying as preacher of Glendale Baptist Church, Dodd died of a
heart attack. His legacy, uniting evangelistic missions and expository preaching, is
summed up in an article he wrote to fellow ministers:

> O, that preaching missions—just preaching, preaching, preaching,
> might be carried on, local, city-wide, county-wide, nation-wide, world-
> wide, until every nation, tribe, family and individual should hear of
> Christ our Lord and should be brought to face and answer the ques-
> tion, "What then shall I do with Jesus who is called the Christ?"[7]

20

JOHN RICHARD SAMPEY

September 27, 1863—August 8, 1946
Elected: 1935, 1936, 1937

$\mathcal{E}$leven-year-old John came forward during a revival service at the First Baptist Church, the same church where his father was ordained to the gospel ministry. He had fallen under the conviction of sin and prostrated himself on the mourner's bench at the front of the auditorium. Yet no one bothered to speak to John, not even the pastor. He explained later:

> I took it for granted that someone would speak to me privately and help me find the light, but no one spoke a word to me. I am sure that my father and mother were glad to see my interest in salvation, but none encouraged me by a good word. . . . I might have found the light much sooner if I had been guided.[1]

Instead, John struggled with his faith for more than two years. His life was absent of change and full of sin. He doubted his faith and believed that God could not be real to him unless he had a Damascus road experience. He admitted that he was "floundering in the Slough of Despond." On March 3, 1877, after the family had finished their daily prayers and Bible study, John suffered spiritual insomnia. In the end his anguish led to finding peace with God. He recalled:

> I was in distress over my sins. In my desperation I lifted my eyes upward and began to talk in a whisper to the Saviour. I said to him: "Lord Jesus, I do not know what to do. I have prayed, but I get no relief. I have read the Bible, but my sins are still a burden to my soul. I have listened to preaching, but find no help. I do not know what to do except to turn it all over to you; and if I am lost, I will go down trusting you." Then something happened. It seemed that a great Presence filled the room and said to me almost in audible words: "My boy, I have been waiting for you to do what you have just done. You can count on me to save you. I will not fail you."[2]

Thus began the mighty work of God in a young man who would preach and teach to thousands but never forget that providential night when he was thirteen.

John Richard Sampey was born at Fort Deposit, Alabama, on September 27, 1863. His father was a devout Methodist minister who became convinced of believer's baptism after carefully reading the New Testament. The wise words of encouragement from his wife gave the elder Sampey the courage to ask the local Baptist church to ordain him as a Baptist minister after both parents were first baptized at the local pond.

John followed in the footsteps of his father, being licensed to preach by the Ramer Baptist Church in July 1879. The family farm was a lucrative business and allowed Sampey to attend Howard College (now Samford University). During his first year at the college, Sampey was able to lead a fellow student to faith in Jesus Christ. This was absolute confirmation of his ministry, and he remembered later how for thirty minutes afterward he felt the "glow of the Presence" in his dormitory.

In 1882, Sampey graduated from Howard College at the top of his class. During his commencement exercise Sampey met Annie Renfroe, his future wife. He admitted, "I lost my heart to this charming young lady."[3] The two were engaged in 1883, but because he was in seminary, they were not married for more than three years.

Sampey matriculated at Southern Seminary in the fall of 1882 and studied under such legends as J. P. Boyce, John Broadus, and Basil Manly. Professors quickly took notice of his academic prowess and diligent scholarship. Even before finishing his final courses of study in 1885, the faculty asked Sampey to consider teaching Hebrew and Old Testament at the seminary. This would begin a fifty-year relationship with Southern Seminary.

As great as Sampey would become as a professor and lecturer, the twenty-two-year-old prodigy also became famous for his pastoral abilities. In the same year he began teaching at the seminary, he also accepted a call to the Forks of Elkhorn Baptist Church in Woodford County, Kentucky, a church he pastored for the next seventeen years. The church, not known for numerical success, experienced revival in the summer of 1886. In all, forty-one people were added to the church, with thirty-five joining by baptism.

On December 12, 1889, the Sampeys announced the birth of Anita Lee Sampey, the first of five children of the family. Little Anita admired her father deeply and was fond of the nightly prayers they shared. At the age of two, Anita was overtaken with a serious illness that would shortly take her life. This experience gave the Sampeys opportunity to trust the sovereignty of God. Dr. Sampey explained their perspective of her final days:

> Toward the end all hope of her recovery left us. One day as my wife and I hovered over the wasting form of our only child, she said: "Mr. Sampey, God evidently means to take our little one; let's just *give*

her to him." We clasped hands over the crib, and I tried as best I could to tell our Heavenly Father how grateful we were that he had sent this little flower to bloom in our garden and cheer our hearts, but now that it was fading we begged him to transplant it in the heavenly garden where it could grow and flourish. Before we had finished our prayer a great Presence seemed to flood the room in which we stood praying, and we felt that the Heavenly Father would care for our dear one in his own beautiful way.[4]

Sampey believed this experience helped him understand in part the compassion and love of God through the sacrifice of his Son Jesus Christ.

The situation at Southern Seminary also became difficult during this time. The president, William Whitsitt, came under severe scrutiny because of his view that baptism by immersion was newly reintroduced in England in 1641. In 1899, Whitsitt tendered his resignation, an action that sorrowed Sampey. In writing his memoirs, Sampey explained that this chapter in the book was his most difficult since he defended Whitsitt and "[had] to place in an unfavorable light at least two persons who had befriended me, both of whom . . . still regarded me with friendly feeling."[5]

At the beginning of the twentieth century, Southern Seminary stabilized under the new leadership of Dr. E. Y. Mullins. In 1909, Sampey helped lead the Seminary Jubilee Celebration, rejoicing in fifty years of training pastors for the ministry. As Sampey began his fourth decade of teaching, the world went to war. His attention then turned toward the conflict and his ability to help the United States prevail against the enemy. He expounded, "I did what I could to enlist our people in the great struggle. I encouraged our alumni and students to volunteer as chaplains, and made patriotic speeches wherever the opportunity came to me."[6] The conflict was personal to Sampey, for his son served as second lieutenant over a machine gun battalion.

After the German surrender in 1918, the seminary once again began to flourish. Sampey's ministry also prospered as he conducted numerous revival meetings nationwide. Sampey explained one such instance where the Spirit of God was evident:

The house was filled from the beginning, and soon many had to sit on the outside steps and in vehicles so placed that they could see and hear through the open windows. . . . We had expected to close the meeting on the fifteenth day; but the interest was so deep that we decided to continue for another week. . . . As a result of our meeting I baptized thirty-five, and received by letter or statement an additional thirty-five souls.[7]

Sadly, in 1926, Annie Sampey, his wife of thirty-eight years, died after years of heart trouble. Two years later, the president of Southern Seminary, E. Y. Mullins, also passed away. Sampey's life was yet again in transition.

By 1929, Sampey was remarried to Ellen Wood and was chosen to succeed Mullins as president of the seminary. However, in the same year, America was submerged in the Great Depression. Enrollment fell to under four hundred and would not rise to that number again until 1936. The salaries of the professors were drastically cut, though Sampey was able to prevent dismissal of any of his faculty.

In 1935, prosperous days returned to the seminary in time to celebrate Dr. Sampey's fifty years as professor at Southern Seminary. But the esteem for Sampey went far beyond the seminary campus. While the Convention was meeting in Memphis that same year, the professor was nominated from the floor for the position of president. Ultimately, a runoff was held between Sampey and R. G. Lee, the respected and world-renowned pastor of Bellevue Baptist Church in Memphis, Tennessee. The final figures showed that Sampey edged out Lee by little more than a hundred votes. Southern Baptists had expressed their appreciation for Sampey's lifelong ministry and desired that he lead them in the same way he cared for the seminary. Ironically, Sampey was not even present at the time of his election and had to be notified.

In 1942, after nearly six decades of service, Sampey resigned from the presidency of Southern Seminary. During the closing address to his final graduating class, Sampey illustrated the passion of his heart:

> Men, my brothers, there is no work comparable to the preaching of the gospel to lost men. "Go, Tell." Tell what great things the Lord has done for you. The world will listen to such a story. . . . Let the good news fill all lands even in spite of wars. Men are dying without Christ. "Go, Tell!"[8]

On August 8, 1946, just four years into retirement, John Sampey was taken from this world into the next. The new president of the seminary, Dr. Ellis Fuller, conducted the funeral service. Appropriately, Sampey had requested that the funeral center on Christ and that there would be no mention of him. Fuller honored his request and paid tribute to the life and ministry of Sampey through the preaching of the cross of Christ.

21

LEE RUTLAND SCARBOROUGH

July 4, 1870—April 10, 1945
Elected: 1938, 1939

On November 11, 1914, Dr. B. H. Carroll, the founder and president of the Southwestern Baptist Theological Seminary, died. Since 1905, Carroll had led the seminary, first as an institution under the auspices of Baylor University in Waco and then in 1910, when Southwestern Seminary relocated to Fort Worth. Now, four years later, the seventy-one-year-old Baptist pioneer was coming to the end of a long illness. For the previous eighteen months, Carroll had been incapacitated, and his protégé, Dr. L. R. Scarborough, had been acting as president on his behalf. A few days before his death, Carroll summoned Scarborough to his bedside. Scarborough remembered the incident:

> B. H. Carroll, the greatest man I ever knew, . . . a few days before
> he died, expecting me, as he wanted me, to succeed him as president
> of the seminary, . . . pulled himself up by my chair with his hands, and
> looked me in the face. (He) said, "Lee, keep the Seminary lashed to
> the cross. If heresy ever comes in the teaching, take it to the faculty. If
> they will not hear you and take prompt action, take it to the trustees of
> the Seminary. If they will not hear you, take it to the Convention that
> appoints the Board of Trustees, and if they will not hear you, take it to
> the great common people of our churches. You will not fail to get a
> hearing then."[1]

Entrusting the seminary to the hands of the forty-year-old evangelism professor gave Carroll great comfort. For all of his seventy-five years, L. R. Scarborough remained the clarion voice for orthodoxy and evangelism in the Southern Baptist Convention.

Lee Rutland Scarborough was born in Colfax, Louisiana, on July 4, 1870. He was the son of a Baptist minister (George W. Scarborough), and the home was dedicated to Christ and his cause. "The family altar was a regular part of their home life. To [the parents] were born nine children, of whom Lee Rutland was the eighth."[2] The family moved from Louisiana when Lee was four, and when he was still a youth,[3] they moved to a pioneer ranch in west Texas, where Lee attended a log cabin schoolhouse and worked diligently on the farm.

Writing a foreword to Carroll's book, *Inspiration of the Bible*, in 1930, Scarborough reflected on his conversion and his upbringing:

My faith is the faith of a simple, plain Baptist. I accepted from my father and Dr. B. H. Carroll the verbal inspiration of the Bible, the deity of Jesus Christ, His perfect humanity, His atoning death, His bodily resurrection, His second coming. All my studies since have confirmed the simple faith I received from them.[4]

Scarborough was converted in 1887 in a Presbyterian church but was not baptized until he entered college. While a student at Waco, he was baptized at First Baptist Church of Waco, Texas, by Dr. Carroll. It would become the first of many waters through which the men traveled together.[5]

Though he received his bachelor of arts degree from Baylor in 1892, Scarborough was not ordained until 1896, when he was called to become pastor of First Baptist Church of Cameron, Texas. Following his call to his first church and the completion of his degree from Baylor, Scarborough attended Yale University, where he received his A.B. in 1896. Not wanting to become a minister like his father, Scarborough was initially pursuing a law degree. In 1893, he surrendered to the ministry and wrote in a letter to his mother, "I have surrendered to preach. Please show this letter to . . . father."[6]

Scarborough pastored the Cameron church from 1896 to 1899, when he resigned to attend Southern Seminary in Louisville, Kentucky. The death of his brother, however, brought him home and concluded his formal education. The church called Scarborough to serve again until 1901. In 1908, Scarborough was given an honorary doctorate from Baylor, and in 1927 he was invested with an LL.D. from Union University. In 1900, Scarborough was married to Neppie Warren, with whom he had six children.

By 1901, this fiery preacher was called to First Baptist Church of Abilene, Texas. Serving in this historic church, Scarborough saw explosive growth, as his heart for evangelism was infectious to the members. While at First Abilene, Scarborough led a campaign to build two buildings at Simmons College (now Hardin-Simmons University). By 1908, the work of the Lord in Abilene was known throughout Texas, and Scarborough was in constant demand as a preacher.[7]

Meanwhile, back in Waco, Dr. B. H. Carroll was implementing a daring vision for the seminary. Having been separately chartered from Baylor, the seminary was now known as Southwestern Baptist Theological Seminary. Hearing of the tremendous growth at First Baptist Abilene, Carroll remembered that young man he had baptized as a Baylor student. He met with the thirty-eight-year-old pastor and, in his inimitable style, called upon him to become the professor of evangelism for the fledgling seminary. For the next six years Scarborough would work to build the "Chair of Fire" at Southwestern, continuing after the seminary moved to Fort Worth in 1910.

Upon Carroll's death in 1914, the trustees of the seminary prevailed upon Scarborough to become the second president. Since early in 1913, he had been serving in that capacity for Carroll, and he felt prepared for the work. Those early years as president of Southwestern saw Scarborough publish three popular books that reflected his heart for evangelism: *Recruits for World Conquests* (1914), *Volunteers: A Call for Soldiers for Christ* (1918), and *With Christ After the Lost: A Search for Souls* (1919). Under his tutelage, Southwestern was developing a reputation for heartfelt church growth through a passion for the lost.

In 1919, Scarborough was named director of the Seventy-Five Million Campaign for Southern Baptists. Through a concerted effort the Convention was attempting to coordinate all their institutions and outreach in an unprecedented effort of evangelism. Scarborough traveled extensively in the cause and wrote a number of books that served as instructions to state leaders and local Baptists for explaining the new work.[8] Even though the campaign fell short of its intended goal, Scarborough rejoiced in the cooperation seen among the churches in the effort to organize a national purpose and vision.[9]

In addition to serving as president of the Baptist General Convention of Texas (1929–32), Scarborough remained active in denominational life. In 1939, at sixty-nine years old, the senior statesman was elected president of the Southern Baptist Convention. Meeting at the Municipal Auditorium in Oklahoma City, the Convention was led by two Southwestern Seminary faculty, Dr. Scarborough as president, and Dr. I. E. Reynolds, School of Church Music, as leader of the music. In typical fashion Scarborough called the Convention to order on the theme, "He that winneth souls is wise."[10]

At the 1939 Convention, an invitation was extended by the newly formed World Council of Churches for Southern Baptists to join in their social endeavor. A committee of twelve was appointed to prepare a response. The group included such Baptist leaders as Scarborough, John R. Sampey, Ellis A. Fuller, and M. E. Dodd. At the 1940 SBC meeting in Baltimore, Maryland, President Scarborough and the committee presented the response, refusing membership on theological and ecclesiological grounds.[11]

Following his tenure as president of the Convention, Scarborough served as vice president of the Baptist World Alliance (1940–1945), and continued to balance his schedule of teaching, serving as president, writing, and the numerous evangelistic campaigns. Retiring from the presidency of Southwestern in 1942, Scarborough continued to travel, write, and preach. Until his death in Amarillo on April 10, 1945, Scarborough was a tireless minister of the gospel.

The legacy of Dr. L. R. Scarborough continues, not only in the progeny of the almost eight thousand students he taught between 1908 and 1942 but also through his writing and leadership. Such books as *Prepare to Meet God* (1922), *The Tears of Jesus* (1922), *Endued to Win* (1922), *Holy Places and Precious Promises* (1924), *Christ's Militant Kingdom* (1924), *A Search for Souls: A Study in the Finest of the Fine Arts—Winning the Lost to Christ* (1925), *How Jesus Won Men* (1926), *Products of Pentecost* (1934), *My Conception of the Gospel Ministry* (1935), *A Blaze of Evangelism Across the Equator* (1937), and *After the Resurrection—What?* (1942) serve as a standard of evangelistic fervor that Southern Baptists were wise to follow.

His passion for ministers and churches placed academia not in the sphere of the ivory tower but rather on the front lines and dusty trails. His lifelong commitment to "call out the called," the gathering and commissioning of the young men and women called to Christ's service, resonates even today. In recent years Baptist leaders have used Scarborough's legacy to emulate a new call for the surrender. In initiating a new emphasis on the surrender to the gospel ministry, Dr. L. Paige Patterson, president of Southeastern Baptist Theological Seminary, reissued the summons to service. *SBC Life* records:

Patterson's theme of calling out the called is not a unique concept for Southern Baptists. Forerunner L. R. Scarborough . . . coined the phrase during an unprecedented growth in the number of Baptist ministers. Almost a century ago, Scarborough launched an evangelistic initiative urging Southern Baptists to call out the called with the intent of sending God-called men and women to the new territories in the western frontier to plant churches. During Scarborough's campaign, Baptist churches experienced a spiritual awakening that resulted in over 10,000 young people committing their lives to the service of Christ.[12]

22

WILLIAM WISTAR HAMILTON

December 9, 1868—November 19, 1960
Elected: 1940, 1941

W. W. Hamilton was known for his passion to lead unbelievers to faith in Jesus Christ. As professor of evangelism at the Baptist Bible Institute in New Orleans, he illustrated this belief through his own life. In his book *Highway and Hedges*, dedicated to his beloved students, Hamilton compiled stories of how the student body and faculty had impacted the world with the gospel of Jesus Christ.

In one such story Hamilton told how a young soldier who fought in World War I had come home to New Orleans from the bloody fields addicted to alcohol. This bondage consumed the young man's days and distressed everyone with whom he came in contact. His father explained to him that he was disgracing his family and therefore was not welcome at the house. W. W. Hamilton, who was also president of the Baptist Bible Institute, explained what happened next:

> One day he was lying in the gutter, too drunk to care, but conscious enough to hear a motherly woman say to him: "My boy, you need Jesus." He did not know her name, and never saw her again, but he remembered the gray hair, the kindly face, and the sympathetic voice telling him of the Saviour. It was the same message he had heard from his youth. Returning to his home, he attended the revival meeting, walked the road along which he had gone so often with drinking companions, was hardly conscious in his terrible conviction of the long cold night, repented of his sins and trusted Christ as his Saviour, and came to the church the next morning asking the people of God to hear his confession and receive him and help him.[1]

The once-drunken vagabond turned into a soldier of Christ, was called to preach, and entered the Baptist Bible Institute (now New Orleans Baptist Theological Seminary) where he studied evangelism under Dr. Hamilton.

Emulating his mentor, W. W. Hamilton, this student began leading other alcoholics to faith in Christ. He was so successful that one of the local bartenders visited the institute and requested that this young student cease from his evangelism, as it was greatly hindering his business. This, of course, was not possible since Hamilton cheerfully required that all students share their faith through such mission assignments. Yet even if Hamilton had desired to put a halt to these activities, he would have failed. As he said, "So much do these young Christians enjoy such experiences in soul-winning and so eager are they to seek new places and respond to extra calls, that the faculty has had to place a limit upon these practical activities."[2] Evidently, the passion Hamilton had for fulfilling the Great Commission was highly contagious.

William Wistar Hamilton was born on December 9, 1868, near Hopkinsville, Kentucky. His parents, William Perry and Catherine Price (Roach), were devout Christians who reared William in the fear of the Lord. Soon after the birth of young William, the family moved to Bristol, Virginia, where William enrolled in private schools and his parents joined First Baptist Church. When William was ten, the family attended revival meetings held at the church. It was here, after Catherine had counseled her son on salvation, that William made a profession of faith. Years later, after William became professor of evangelism at the Baptist Bible Institute and wrote *Wisdom in Soul Winning,* he dedicated his work to "the good mother who told the ten-year-old boy how to find the Saviour."

Ironically, when it came to furthering his education, Hamilton chose King College, a Presbyterian school in Bristol, Tennessee. In 1890, he received his bachelor of arts degree. Hamilton became increasingly aware of his call to the ministry and consequently enrolled at The Southern Baptist Theological Seminary in Louisville, Kentucky. These three crucial years helped Hamilton develop a passion for evangelism through the teaching of E. C. Dargan and John Broadus.

During his last year at the seminary, Hamilton married Zula Belle Doyle, a young lady who was reared in a Methodist home and remained loyal to her denomination. At the time Hamilton was pastor of two small, rural Baptist churches. When the time came for Zula to join her husband at the church, she also became his first convert. The new bride was baptized by Hamilton at Vinton Baptist Church.

In 1900, after briefly serving two churches in Virginia, Hamilton settled down as pastor of the McFerran Memorial Baptist Church (now Fourth Avenue Baptist Church) in Louisville, Kentucky, where he would shepherd the flock for six years. Once again he was encouraged by seminary faculty who attended the church regularly. In particular, J. R. Sampey, longtime professor of Old Testament, supported Hamilton and convinced the congregation to supply the funds needed for him to attend Bible conferences at Winona Lake, Indiana. The conference motivated Hamilton to participate in a strategic, interdenominational crusade led by churches across the nation.

The success of the Louisville church gave Hamilton instant recognition among Southern Baptists. In 1906, almost immediately following the crusade, Hamilton accepted the position of secretary of evangelism for the Home Mission Board in Atlanta, Georgia. During the next sixteen years in the ministry, Hamilton split his time between the Home Mission Board (1906–1909; 1918–1922) and First Baptist Church of Lynchburg, Virginia (1909–1918).

In 1922, after enjoying the success of both the pastorate and denominational leadership, Hamilton moved south to New Orleans, becoming pastor of St. Charles Avenue Baptist Church. Hamilton remained involved in the Southern Baptist Convention. During the Seventy-Five Million Campaign, the precursor to the Cooperative Program, St. Charles Avenue Church achieved its pledged amount, unlike many other churches across the Convention. The church, inspired by new-found success, proposed building a new auditorium. In 1926, the new building was dedicated, with notables—including E. Y. Mullins, president of Southern Seminary—taking part in the ceremony.

Hamilton's financial acumen, along with his theological expertise, proved to be the perfect combination needed for the struggling Baptist Bible Institute. In 1928, the board of trustees voted to elect Hamilton as president. His assignment seemed impossible, as financial crises overwhelmed the institution. The seminary had one bond note of $85,000 due within a year, $350,000 of total debt, and no institutional endowment whatsoever. The students faithfully followed their president's vision to clear the debt.

Hamilton recalled one night encountering such students:

> One night the president noticed lights on in the classroom. That was against the rules for it was understood that anyone who turned off a light not needed was a member of the institution's Light Saving Crew. The president kept worrying until about midnight when he dressed and went over to put out the lights or to protest. He found it was a group of the students spending the night in prayer for financial help for rescuing the school from its present distress.[3]

God answered their prayer, but not without sacrifice on the part of the faculty. In 1932, half of the ten full-time faculty were dismissed due to financial constraints.

Amazingly, most of the faculty remained with their students, working for little or no pay. The five remaining professors, known as the Chosen Five, also sacrificed over the next decade. At the same time that their salaries were reduced, their workload doubled. This dire situation continued as the Great Depression ravaged the United States. It was not until 1943, a year after Hamilton finished his duties as president, that the institute made its last payment on its property.

In 1940, due to his undying faithfulness in sustaining the struggling institution, Hamilton was honored by his colleagues and elected president of the Southern Baptist Convention. The students of the institute paid tribute to him in the student paper, *Magnet*:

The election of Dr. W. W. Hamilton to the presidency of the
Southern Baptist Convention was a just and beautiful tribute to one of
the most faithful, devoted, efficient and beloved servants of the
denomination. He has served with distinction as pastor, evangelist and
seminary president. As the head of the Baptist Bible Institute he has
molded the lives of hundreds of Christian workers. . . . The Institute
has become one of the greatest agencies for evangelism Southern
Baptists have ever known.[4]

At the height of his accomplishments, Hamilton made a grave error. After presiding over his last Convention, Hamilton married Catherine Hancock, his niece.
Recognizing his mistake, he quickly filed for an annulment, but the damage had
been done. W. W. Hamilton resigned from the institute and accepted the pastorate
of the Gentilly Baptist Church. Later he served as chaplain of Southern Baptist
Hospital in New Orleans, a post he held for fourteen years until his death.

On November 19, 1960, William Hamilton died. Though some have chosen to
focus their thoughts on his late-life indiscretion, perhaps it is appropriate to honor
Hamilton through the words of the board of trustees, who held him both account-
able and in high regard:

We count it a privilege to record on our Record Book this statement of our high appreciation of him and his unmatched services here
in this institution which is dedicated to the training of young men and
women for work in our churches and for carrying the Gospel to the
uttermost parts. We wish for him every blessing that can come from
God whom he preaches and whom he has so winsomely exhorted us to
follow.[5]

23
PAT MORRIS NEFF

November 26, 1871—January 20, 1952
Elected: 1942, 1944

To study the life of Pat Morris Neff—governor of Texas, president of Baylor, and president of the Southern Baptist Convention—is to become immersed in the world of pioneer lore and legend. His biography has almost become mythic with the remarkable events in which he participated, which have now become part of our cultural landscape. For instance, the first Texas state park was built on land donated by his mother in 1916. In 1921, it was named Mother Neff Memorial Park. He vetoed the establishment of Texas Tech University, eliciting the ire of thousands of west Texans. He pardoned the famous blues singer Leadbelly, after the imprisoned guitarist wrote a song to him that became a national hit. He was the first governor to campaign by automobile. His official band, The Old Gray Mare Band, became part of the Texas National Guard and was named the official band of Texas. He started the tradition of live bears serving as the Baylor mascot, when a student bought a bear from a zoo and approached Neff with it. In an era when women had no voice in the judicial system, he appointed an all-woman supreme court to hear a court case. Yet through all of his eighty-one years, Pat Neff remained a faithful Christian, a faithful churchman, and a Baptist.

Pat Morris Neff was born near McGregor, Texas on November 26, 1871.[1] On his father's farm in the fertile land north of Austin, Pat raised cattle and "lived behind the plow," as he often noted in speeches. He received his education in a one-room school during the three winter months each year, ending before the spring plowing. Attending the Baptist church in McLennan County, Neff was converted as a young man and baptized in the nearby river.

Neff attended McGregor High School in the county and entered Baylor University in 1889. He thoroughly enjoyed his Baylor experience and took five years to complete his degree, gaining notoriety as a successful debater. In 1893,

Neff participated in the first intercollegiate debate between Baylor and the University of Texas.[2]

Following his Baylor graduation, Neff traveled to the Arkansas border, where he taught school, and then began work on his LL.B. at the University of Texas. During his years at the University of Texas, he developed lifelong relationships with classmates who would become compatriots in the political arena, Judge William Pitt Hancock, and Senators Earl Mayfield, Tom Connally, and Morris Sheppard.

Receiving his degree in 1897, Neff began practicing law in Waco. In his first year in practice, he continued his education, receiving an M.A. degree from Baylor in 1898. At Baylor Neff continued to develop friendships that would influence the rest of his life. Some of his closest friends were George W. Truett, the future pastor of First Baptist Church of Dallas, and Samuel Palmer Brooks, who would become president of Baylor.

After establishing a successful law practice, Neff was approached by his friends to run for his first political office, as the state house representative from McLennan County. Neff was reluctant at first, as he was just starting to become successful in his law practice, and he was a newlywed. He had married Myrtie Mainer on May 31, 1899, in Lovelady, Texas, and he was unsure if he could wage a successful campaign. From 1901 to 1905, he was a state representative, even serving as the speaker of the house during the twenty-eighth legislature.

Returning home to Waco, Neff was elected county attorney and served from 1906 to 1912. He was obviously well prepared for the task, as his record indicates. As prosecuting attorney, Neff tried 422 defendants, and won convictions in all but sixteen cases. During this time, he also began his twenty-five-year tenure on the board of trustees of his alma mater, Baylor.

Returning to his private law practice in 1912, Neff continued to work on those projects for which he was passionate, including his work as a leader in the state prohibition movement, and was the church clerk at First Baptist Waco.[3] Twice he was offered the position of assistant attorney general, but he declined both offers. Neff felt he had a higher calling to seek.

Noting that the only Democratic candidate for governor of Texas was former United States Senator Joseph Weldon Bailey, Pat Neff entered the 1920 Democratic primary with all the odds against him. He had no funding, no headquarters, and no campaign manager. He was viewed as a "moralist" and a "Christian crusader," with Bailey in complete disagreement with him on the major issues.[4] Neff was for prohibition; Bailey was against it. Neff was for a woman's right to vote (suffrage); Bailey was against it. Bailey had immense funding for his campaign; Neff had no coordinated group of supporters, much less funds.

It was a fierce campaign. Bailey was entrenched in Texas politics and had many connections. Neff only had his church members praying for him, and his car. In that car Neff drove six thousand miles and covered thirty-seven counties never before visited by a gubernatorial candidate. What he lacked in funding or organization, Neff made up for with energy. He was a tireless candidate and debater, and in the runoff, Pat Morris Neff was elected governor of Texas.

Entering the office on January 18, 1921, Neff's first act as governor was a controversial one: he put a moratorium on all gubernatorial pardons of criminals, ending a long-standing tradition in Texas politics.

[Governor Neff] succeeded in increasing funding to rural and vocational schools and establishing Texas Technological College and Texas State Teachers College. He also achieved a reorganization of the Highway Commission and establishment of the park system, which he believed was one of his most important endeavors. In contrast to his predecessors, Neff drastically reduced the number of pardons issued from the governor's office. Twice during his first term he declared martial law to restore order. In January 1922 he sent a Texas National Guard unit and Texas Rangers to the oil boomtown of Mexia to control the bootlegging, gambling, prostitution, and robbery in the area. Later that year he declared martial law to control violence in Denison resulting from a strike by the Federated Railroad Shopmen's Union.[5]

Completing his second term in office in January 1925, Neff had wanted to return to his law practice in Waco.[6] His return home was short-lived, however, as President Calvin Coolidge brought him to Washington to lead the U.S. Board of Mediation from 1927 to 1929. This made his life hectic, as Neff had been elected president of the Baptist General Convention in Texas in 1926, and until 1928 he traveled extensively between Texas and Washington. He also saw his first book published, *The Battles of Peace*.[7]

In 1932, sixty-one-year-old Pat Neff became president of Baylor University. The loss of his dear friend Samuel Palmer Brooks had left Baylor in a quandary, with a $400,000 debt and decreasing enrollment. In the fifteen years of his presidency, Pat Neff set about making radical changes to the Waco campus. Building such facilities as a Bible building, a student center, a gymnasium, and an administrative building, Neff also saw enrollment climb from 2,500 in 1932 to 4,506 in 1947, shortly after the end of World War II.

Toward the end of his tenure as president of Baylor, Neff became the subject of debate among Southern Baptists. In 1942, the Convention meeting at San Antonio had a ground-swell of support for Neff to become president.

It had been more than thirty years since Joshua Levering, another great Christian layman, had served. When the time for nominating a president arrived, E. D. Solomon and J. M. Dawson of Texas both hurried to the speaker's stand. President (William) Hamilton recognized Dr. Solomon, who nominated Pat Morris Neff. Dr. Dawson, with the same purpose, had to be content with seconding the nomination. Without other nominations, Pat Neff was unanimously elected.[8]

Neff was no stranger to Southern Baptist leadership, as he had been elected vice president in 1933. Still he would have to wait some time before he presided over a session of the annual meeting. In 1943, the Southern Baptist Convention meeting, for the first time since 1894, had to be deferred due to the war. In a letter printed in state papers across the nation, Neff wrote:

In these troublous days when the foundations of the world are shaken and nations are torn asunder with war and death, let every Southern Baptist attune his soul to the call of the still small Voice to "be strong in the Lord and in the power of his might." Let us with all courage and undiminished zeal go on with the work which has been committed to us. While we walk in the midst of tribulation and the shadows of destruction lengthen upon the earth, we can yet trust him who created man in his own image; we can depend upon him to lead us out of the darkness; we can "sail ahead, and leave the rest to God."[9]

As the 1945 SBC annual meeting was also deferred due to the war, in 1946, Neff presided over his second Southern Baptist Convention meeting. By the time the session was completed, the seventy-five-year-old Neff was ready to rest. He continued to speak to Southern Baptists, however, until his death on January 19, 1952. He spoke on the radio program *The Baptist Hour,* and in a masterful sermon entitled "Christian Education," Governor Neff revealed some of his core beliefs which served Southern Baptists so ably during his work at Baylor and in the denomination:

Before the first child born in America became twenty-one years of age, Harvard University opened its doors. Above its ancient archway to this day can be read the reason why it was built: "Erected that an educated ministry may not perish from the earth." . . . The difference between Christian education and secular education is not in form but in spirit; not in technique but in traditions; not in curriculum but in character . . . not in minds trained but in destinies determined. If our colleges are to remain Christian, those who teach therein should be Christians. At this point, those in authority should guard the gates with the watchfulness of the cherubim who guarded the Ark of the Covenant. The professor who teaches geology should not only know something about the age of rocks, but he should also know something about the "Rock of Ages." If he teaches botany, he should not only know how to classify a Texas bluebonnet, but he should be able to "consider the lilies of the field." He should be a real human being with a warm, sympathetic heart, and not merely a stilted Ph.D. on some lofty Mount Olympus.[10]

Pat Morris Neff was such a man with a warm, sympathetic heart.

24
LOUIE DEVOTIE NEWTON

April 27, 1892—June 3, 1986
Elected: 1946, 1947

By the time of his death in 1986, few ministers had ever been honored as much as Dr. Louie D. Newton. The list of accolades reads like the memoirs of a wealthy philanthropist or a sixth-generation Baptist preacher:

Shorter College in Rome, Georgia has the Louie D. Newton Medal of Excellence.

Mercer University awards the Louie D. Newton General Excellence Medal at the annual graduation, and the Louie D. Newton Award for Service to community leaders.

In Atlanta, Georgia, there is the Louie D. Newton Center Home for the Aged in the Georgia Baptist Medical Center.

There have been entire doctoral theses written about him at innumerable institutions.[1]

He was the longest-surviving former Southern Baptist president, living forty years after his election in 1946. He remained as the pastor of only one church for his entire pastoral ministry, serving at Druid Hills Baptist Church in Atlanta, Georgia, for thirty-nine years. He served in virtually every capacity known to Southern Baptist life: layman, pastor, associational moderator, State Convention president, Baptist paper editor, denominational leader, trustee, and Southern Baptist Convention president.

The irony is that Louie Devotie Newton never planned on being a pastor and was a layman until he was thirty-seven years old. He was never wealthy. He had no Baptist pedigree. Yet in his ninety-four years, Louie D. Newton became known as Mr. Baptist, and mentored four generations of preachers, writers, and denominational leaders.

Louie Devotie Newton was born in Screven County, Georgia on April 27, 1892.[2] Raised on his parents' farm near the South Carolina border, Louie was saved and then baptized in July 1902 in a stream near Union Baptist Church. After completing his studies in a one-room school in the county and attending McPhaul Institute in Sylvester,[3] Newton traveled approximately one hundred and fifty miles west to attend Mercer University in Macon, Georgia, where he graduated at age twenty-one in 1913.

In the first of many harbingers indicating that Newton was an extraordinary man, Mercer hired him to the history faculty on the day of his graduation. He began teaching history in the fall of 1913, and during the next summer he traveled to Columbia University in New York to begin his graduate studies.[4]

During the next two years, Newton split his time with the summers in New York City and the school year in Macon. During this period (1913–1915) Newton developed his interest in journalism and focused his studies in that field. In the midst of the traveling, Newton found time to fall in love and was married to Julia Winn Carstarphen on April 30, 1915, just a month before receiving his master's degree in journalism.

While Newton was continuing his professorial duties at Mercer, America went to war, and Newton served as "director of the educational activities of the National War Work Council at Camp Wheeler until the armistice."[5] In 1919, the Southern Baptist Convention launched the most ambitious stewardship campaign in its history, the Seventy-Five Million Campaign. In an attempt to retire the looming debt of its institutions, the Convention hired Newton as the publicity director. His expertise in writing and promotion drew the attention of the leaders of the Georgia Baptist Convention. They were looking for a man with special journalistic talents, and Louie Devotie Newton looked like the man they needed.

Since its founding as *The Columbian Star* in 1821, *The Christian Index* (renamed) had been the nation's oldest religious newspaper. Founded by Luther Rice and purchased by Jesse Mercer in 1833, it served as the voice for Georgia Baptists. On January 1, 1920, the Georgia Baptist Convention purchased the paper for $40,000 from B. J. W. Graham, and they were searching for an editor. They elected Louie Devotie Newton.[6] From January 1920 until November 1929, Newton distinguished himself as a fair and popular voice to Georgia Baptists.

For the entire decade Newton was devoted to the *Index* and his church. Serving as the chairman of deacons at Druid Hills Baptist Church, Newton rejoiced at the growth the church experienced under the leadership of Dr. Fernando C. McConnell. He also served as teacher of the men's class, and was a close confidant to the pastor.[7]

When Dr. McConnell died suddenly on January 12, 1929, the pulpit committee approached Newton about becoming the pastor. He declined, noting that he was simply a layman. The committee was intractable and absolutely convinced that the Lord was calling Newton to be their pastor. They approached him a second time, and again he declined. He was the busy editor of a state paper and was not even a licensed minister! Yet the committee would not be denied, and on

March 27, 1929, Louie D. Newton accepted the call to the pastorate of that historic church.[8]

Newton had one stipulation to his call as pastor. He wanted to be ordained at the church where he was saved as a ten-year-old boy. His elderly parents still held their membership at Union Baptist in Screven County, and so on April 20, 1929, one week before his thirty-seventh birthday, Louie D. Newton was ordained in that rural church. More than seventy-five of the leading Georgia Baptist ministers crowded into that church to lead in his questioning and as a show of solidarity to one of their friends and leaders.[9]

For the next two decades, Newton distinguished himself as a pastoral leader in the Georgia Baptist Convention, serving as moderator of the Atlanta Baptist Association and president of the Georgia Baptist Convention. Newton led his church ably through the Great Depression and World War II and still found time to speak to the national concerns of Southern Baptists. In 1943, his concern over alcohol led him to cofound the Georgia Temperance League:

> [In 1943] Secretary of State John B. Wilson chartered the Georgia
> Temperance League on October 19. Methodist Bishop Arthur J.
> Moore, and Georgia Baptist Convention President, Dr. Louie D.
> Newton, both of Atlanta Area led the two denominations in organizing
> this unique joint effort of Christians in Georgia.[10]

There was no Southern Baptist Convention annual meeting in 1945 due to the war, but the messengers gathered in Miami, Florida, in 1946, and Newton allowed his name to be submitted for the presidential election. Against five other candidates Newton was elected and was immediately thrust into the spotlight of controversy and confusion as Southern Baptists struggled to regain their footing after the war effort.

Newton believed passionately in the doctrine of religious liberty, and in 1947, he led in the organization of Americans United for Separation of Church and State. His involvement in this organization and his terse meetings with President Truman following the war led to accusations that Southern Baptists, under the leadership of Dr. Newton, were Communist sympathizers.[11] Though the accusations were completely baseless and false, in 1947, on the eve of his reelection for a second term as president of the SBC, J. Frank Norris, at the Pastors' Conference in St. Louis, Missouri, confronted Newton with the charges.[12] Ironically, Newton's 1947 presidential address to the Convention spoke against Communism, tracing it to the greed and covetousness of Cain in the Book of Genesis.[13] The spurious claims died quickly.

The tenure of Dr. Louie D. Newton was a prosperous one. During his two terms of office, Southern Baptists voted to establish Golden Gate Seminary in California, instituted the rotation method of trusteeship on Convention boards, coordinated a new national calendar organization for SBC promotions, and voted to admit Kansas and Oregon as State Baptist entities.[14] This was a period of unprecedented expansion for the Convention, as they enlarged their vision to include other regions of the country beyond the traditional parameters.

Following his terms in office, Newton continued to pastor and speak on a national level. He would write four books in the next decade, including stirring accounts of missionaries and Baptist life.[15] In 1953, he was named American Churchman of the Year and continued his twenty-five years of service on the SBC Finance Committee.

Newton would also continue to lead his beloved church in Atlanta. Until he reached the age of seventy-six, Newton remained as pastor. On October 1, 1968, Newton retired from the only church he had ever served, and pastors from all over the nation attended the September 26 banquet in his honor before his retirement.[16]

Even well into his eighties, Louie D. Newton continued to serve his Lord. In May 1979, he addressed the summer missionary commissioning service held at Southern Baptist Theological Seminary. Dr. Louie D. Newton died in Atlanta, Georgia, on June 3, 1986.

On May 7, 1947, Newton rose to give the presidential address to the Southern Baptist Convention. It was titled, "Southern Baptists—Yesterday, Today and Tomorrow." In the address, Newton displayed a masterful grasp of the depth and breadth of Southern Baptist history, covering the century of progress they had made to that point. In listing the accomplishments of the task, he noted:

> And from the little band of Baptists who organized the Convention
> in 1845 we behold a great and mighty host a century later . . . with
> churches serving rural and urban life from ocean to ocean and with
> missionary, educational, and benevolent ministries encircling the
> globe. Southern Baptists, yesterday, served with "widening reach and
> heightened power," through designs that centered in the will and to
> the glory of the Father, Son and Holy Spirit.[17]

For a man who spent the first thirty-seven years of his life as a layman and never sought the pastoral ministry, Louie Newton was an amazing student of Baptist life and a testimony to steadfast faithfulness.

25
ROBERT GREENE LEE

November 11, 1886—July 20, 1978
Elected: 1948, 1949, 1950

*T*he seasons were changing in the autumn of 1913 when Bob Lee and Bula Gentry were engaged to be married. Bob sorrowed over the fact that he was financially unable to buy his sweetheart the ring he believed she so deserved. He also was convinced that he needed to build a home in which the newlywed couple could live, and he borrowed $1,800 from one of his professors at Furman University to complete the project. The couple married on November 26, 1913. During their first seven years of marriage, Robert pastored as many as three churches at one time to support his family.

Financial difficulty haunted the young pastor and husband to the point of sleepless nights and anxious days. Indeed, the Lee family had gone into greater debt due to the acute sickness of their firstborn daughter, Bula G. Finally, a break came when Lee was asked by the president and board of trustees of Furman University to chair the Latin department.

This opportunity proved attractive, and Lee resigned his pastorate in Saluda, South Carolina. Lee himself never intended to give up preaching and pastoring but only to double his workload through teaching. Providentially, the trustees at Furman passed a resolution that summer which forbade any professor from pastoring a church. Lee was oblivious of the resolution which passed the board as he was at Tulane University in New Orleans to advance his study in Latin.

Upon returning home, Lee was informed of the auspicious decision. Now Lee had to make a decision which would guide the rest of his life and ministry. Without delay Lee told his wife that he would resign his professorship. Without a pastorate and in debt by approximately four thousand dollars, Lee was nonetheless joyful at being in the center of God's will. His wife likewise believed he had made the right decision. She encouraged her husband, "The Lord never intended that you should dig around among Latin roots. He called you to be a preacher."[1] In 1918, Lee was called to pastor the First Baptist Church of Edgefield, South Carolina. A preacher was reborn.

Robert Greene Lee was born on November 11, 1886, to David and Sarah Lee, sharecroppers in York County, South Carolina. Lee, the fifth child born, was raised in the humble surroundings of the three-room cabin he called home. Lee's parents were devout Christians who made sure the entire family never missed a church service. Furthermore, each Sunday evening served as a worship service at their home, with each able child participating through the reading of the Scripture. At the age of twelve, Lee received Christ as his Savior after hearing a sermon in the morning on heaven and a message in the evening on Christ. He recalled years later:

I went home that night with the most wretched feeling. I could not sleep. I got up in the night, slipped out of the window that opened on the back porch, and went down to the moonlit watermelon patch. It was a beautiful clear night, and I thought of the Heaven beyond the stars and of the hell somewhere in the vast region below.

I had to plow [the next] day. My misery grew until finally I drove out to the end of a long row and dropped the plow down by the side of Barney, my old white mule. I got down in the fence corner, and told God that I felt awfully bad—awfully sinful—and that I wanted to be saved. "If one must accept Jesus to be saved," I prayed, "then I accept Him." There in a fence corner the Lord saved me.[2]

That night Lee went forward at a church service and professed Christ to the entire congregation. On August 5, 1898, Lee was baptized and joined the fellowship of First Baptist Church of Fort Mills, South Carolina.

Almost immediately Lee believed he was called to preach. But until the age of twenty-one, Lee remained on his father's farm unable to pursue a theological education. Lee was self-educated, having immersed himself in the Scripture and consumed any other book he found. His passion to preach led him to study intensely the homiletical style of T. DeWitt Talmadge, nationally known pastor of the Brooklyn Tabernacle, and the narrative style of Sam Jones, a Methodist preacher who honed his sermons by way of personal reflection and passionate expression.

In 1909, after returning home from helping build the Panama Canal, Lee entered Furman University. His college years were filled with new beginnings and spiritual lessons. Along with working odd jobs to pay the bills, Lee served as student pastor at First Baptist Church of Lima, South Carolina. It was also during this time that he met his future wife, Bula Gentry. When Robert finally asked her to marry him, she replied, "I don't know that I could be a preacher's wife. I can't speak in public." He calmly answered her, "Who asked you to speak in public? I can do that. I am asking you to be my wife." She accepted his offer.

In 1913, Lee graduated from Furman with highest honors and married Bula Gentry the same year. After flirting with a professorship at the university, Lee finally settled down as pastor of First Baptist Church of Edgefield, South Carolina.

Learning from the bondage of his own indebtedness, Lee wanted the church to be relieved of its nearly $10,000 liability. One Sunday morning the pastor announced his enthusiastic aspirations: "Next Sunday morning we will pay off our church debt. All gifts must be dough on the barrel head. Nobody must give over five hundred dollars; what he gives more will be returned. But we want everybody to have a part."[3] Though harshly criticized during the next week for his impracticality and youth, the special offering the next Sunday not only paid off the church debts, but the extra $4,000 allowed the church to build their beloved pastor a new home. The church was also unknowingly blessed with hearing one of the most famous sermons ever preached in the United States, "Payday Someday."

After serving the church for three years, Lee tendered his resignation and began his tenure at First Baptist Church of Chester, South Carolina. Though he would stay for only sixteen months, the work of the Lord was substantial and noticeable. There were 415 additions to the church, 300 of these by confession of faith and baptism. Nevertheless, Lee felt called to New Orleans, a thoroughly Catholic bastion. Here Lee became involved in the advancement of the Southern Baptist Convention. He promoted the Seventy-Five Million Campaign, the precursor to the Cooperative Program, and supported the Baptist Bible Institute of New Orleans (later the New Orleans Baptist Theological Seminary).

In 1927, though Lee had served churches for an average of only two years, Bellevue Baptist Church in Memphis, Tennessee, was drawn to the preacher and requested that he shepherd their flock. This began a relationship that lasted thirty-three years. Lee cared for his people with the most diligent of passions. An excerpt from his diary demonstrates his love for God and all with whom he came in contact:

Up at 6. Prayer. Study. Evangelistic service for Junior Department. Had 11 to confess faith in Christ. Preached on "God of Jacob, Our Refuge." Service broadcast. Baptized 2 after morning service. Preached at night—33 additions, baptized 10 at night. Very tired when went to bed. Grieved over news of Lt. Perkins' being killed. First in our church membership to die.[4]

Dr. Lee was also stern at times when he felt God's work was hindered by someone's negligence or carelessness. Perhaps nothing annoyed Lee more than an interruption during the invitation, which he considered to be of utmost importance to the service. He explained:

If I were your dinner guest, and left before the meal was over, without asking to be excused, you would think I was discourteous. And I would be! That's what I think of people who leave just as the invitation is being given for people to accept Christ.

If I walked into the operating room and slapped the arm of the surgeon who was operating on your loved one to save him from physical death, you would think that I was cruel. So do I think that those who attend our services and hinder the effort to enlist Christians in service,

to urge those who are lost to accept the Saviour, by leaving as the
Invitation Hymn begins.[5]

This delicate balance was appreciated not only by his church but also by Southern Baptists nationwide. He was given many responsibilities in the following years, including being elected as president of the Tennessee Baptist Convention (1932–1935) and president of the Southern Baptist Convention (1949–1951). Nicknamed "Mr. Southern Baptist," Lee guided the Convention to new heights.

Though he despised the ecumenical culture emerging among Protestant denominations, enmeshed as it was in liberal theology, he advocated partnership with the growing number of like-minded Evangelicals in the country. As a result, he represented Southern Baptists at the founding of the National Association of Evangelicals and preached at nondenominational evangelical meetings including Moody Bible Institute and Billy Sunday's Winona Lake Bible Conference.

On April 10, 1960, Lee felt it was time to step down as the pastor of the Bellevue Baptist Church. *The Commercial Appeal,* the local paper of Memphis, paid tribute to Lee and his ministry:

> For half a century he has thrown punches at the devil, punches
> containing the same power and vengeance as those of Billy Sunday,
> George Truett, or C. H. Spurgeon. In all of these years, he has never
> quit slugging. He says, "The devil never sleeps." So he has worked
> night and day to bring the gospel to as many people as possible.[6]

Lee was honored for his passion for souls and his desire to preach the incomparable riches of Christ. For the next eighteen years, he traveled the world preaching to thousands and pleading for the lost to come to Christ. Today Lee is remembered for his famous sermon, "Payday Someday," which he first preached in 1919 as a devotional to the Edgefield Church. During his lifetime Lee preached this sermon more than twelve hundred times. Appropriately, here is an excerpt of the sermon used of God in so many people's lives:

> "Payday—Someday!" God said it—and it was done! Yes, and from
> this we learn the power and certainty of God in carrying out His own
> retributive providence, that men might know that His justice slumbereth
> not. Even though the mill of God grinds slowly, it grinds to power. . . .
>
> And the only way I know for any man or woman on earth to escape
> the sinner's payday on earth and the sinner's hell beyond—making sure
> of the Christian's payday—is through Christ Jesus, who took the sin-
> ner's place upon the cross, becoming for all sinners all that God must
> judge, that sinners through faith in Christ Jesus might become all that
> God cannot judge.[7]

The ministry of Robert Green Lee was completed on July 20, 1978, when God called him to his reward. He died quietly in Memphis, Tennessee. The boy born in a three-room cabin to sharecroppers was reunited with his parents in the splendor and riches of glory.

26

JAMES DAVID GREY

December 8, 1906—July 26, 1985
Elected: 1951, 1952

In 1951, legendary football coach Paul "Bear" Bryant brought his team, the Kentucky Wildcats, to the Sugar Bowl to play the Oklahoma Sooners. J. D. Grey, himself a native of Kentucky, was asked to lead the crowd in a pregame prayer, the first of its kind at the Sugar Bowl. Grey seized the moment not for its recreational value but for its cultural significance. The country was at war in Korea in an attempt to contain Communism and retain freedom on at least part of the Korean Peninsula. Grey offered the following prayer:

> Gracious God: We offer thanks to Thee for Thy blessings showered upon our beloved land. We thank Thee for the heritage that is ours as Americans. May we be ever mindful of the glorious tradition which is our blood-bequeathed legacy from the past. Give us, we pray Thee, in this critical hour the true greatness and spiritual strength of our fore-fathers. Grant wisdom to our leaders and courage to all our people. Be with those who bravely fight for our God-given way of life. Put down the forces of evil. Hasten the day when wars shall be no more and "righteousness shall cover the earth as the waters cover the sea." With forgiveness for our national and individual sins, we beg it in the name of Him who is the Prince of Peace. Amen.[1]

This desire to bring people together while praying for the unity and peace of the people would be the lifelong task of the man known around the world as "Saint J. D."

James David Grey was born on December 18, 1906, in Princeton, Kentucky. In 1914, his parents moved to Paducah, Kentucky, where they joined Immanuel Baptist Church. His mother played a profound influence on young J. D. as she continually prayed for the salvation of her son.

When Grey was twelve years of age, he attended a revival service at the family's home church. The evangelist, Dr. John W. P. Givens, preached on the penitent thief, bringing J. D. under deep conviction. When the invitation was given, the young man went forward and professed his faith in Christ. He was baptized shortly afterwards. Six years later Grey accepted the call to preach the gospel and was ordained to the ministry one year later.

During the next seven years, Grey was determined to further his education and knowledge of the Scriptures. In 1925, Grey matriculated at Union University in Jackson, Tennessee. While still an undergraduate, Grey married Lillian Tooke on September 16, 1927, a relationship that produced twin daughters, Mary Beth and Martha Ann. After graduating with his bachelor of arts degree, he and his wife moved to Fort Worth, Texas, where he enrolled at Southwestern Baptist Theological Seminary, eventually earning his master of theology degree in 1932.[2] Along the way, Grey served as pastor of the Vickery Baptist Church in Dallas (1929–1931), Tabernacle Baptist Church in Ennis (1931–1934), and First Baptist Church in Denton (1934–1937).

Grey learned many valuable lessons on shepherding the flock during his formative years but none greater than the lesson of being a source of encouragement to wounded Christians. In fact, he was taught this lesson not by one of his professors but by a Sunday school teacher. He wrote:

A Sunday school teacher wrote in the flyleaf of my Bible a helpful verse I have used to encourage an injured brother:

Men may misjudge thy aim,
Think they have cause to blame,
Say Thou art wrong.
Go on thy quiet way.
God is thy judge, not they,
Fear not, Be strong![3]

As Grey gained recognition from his colleagues, this poem served as a reminder to him to give an erring brother the benefit of the doubt. In fact, Grey became known for his attempt to reconcile Christians in all situations, in all places, in all ways.

In 1937, Grey accepted the offer to pastor First Baptist Church of New Orleans, Louisiana. Baptists were a small minority in a state swamped with Catholics, and Grey purposed in his heart to lead Baptists into the public eye. Over the next thirty-five years, he accomplished this goal and much more. The church grew in attendance from fifteen hundred to over four thousand. The budget of the church increased exponentially from $26,000 to $650,000.

But it was not merely the situation within the church that Grey determined to change. Grey felt it was his civic duty to improve the city to which God had called him. Therefore, he volunteered in New Orleans organizations, including the Boy Scouts, American Red Cross, Association for Retarded Children, Citizens for Support of Public Schools, and Council for a Better Louisiana. City Councilman James E. Fitzmorris Jr., said of Grey, "When others have climbed into their shells, Dr. Grey has spoken his mind. And that's good for a community."[4] Ministers likewise paid tribute to Grey for demonstrating to them the need to be engaged in the community. Walter P. Binns, president of the Baptist-affiliated William Jewell College, asserted:

> There was a time when New Orleans was the graveyard of Baptist preachers because the Baptists were few in number and were so over-shadowed in that Catholic city. The Baptist situation has taken on a new aspect in recent years, and the situation is entirely changed. In seeking the cause for this change we naturally think of the powerful influence of the New Orleans Baptist Seminary and the Southern Baptist Hospital. It is true that these institutions have made a signifi-cant contribution, but the President of Tulane University told me that among all the men of the past or present, living or dead, Dr. J. D. Grey has exerted the greatest influence in bringing about this change in New Orleans.[5]

As New Orleans grew healthier, those around the state took notice of Grey's dedi-cation and service.

In 1949, Grey was elected president of the Louisiana Baptist Convention. Here Grey took up the cause against gambling, because he believed gambling would hurt the people of Louisiana. Grey used his pulpit to denounce this vice per-petuated by the underworld crime community. As one author noted:

> Addressing the Louisiana Baptist Convention, J. D. declared him-self a grateful beneficiary of the First Louisiana Purchase and unalter-ably opposed to the Second. The first brought Louisiana into the United States. The second threatens to sell Louisiana to the gambling interests in and out of the state. The first brought his city into his nation, but the second is an epidemic which could strangle both city and nation. He thankfully salutes the first, but the second will receive his energetic wrath until the last dice lie cold upon unused felt.[6]

Grey eventually lost this battle but gained many allies who honored his leadership and admired his tenacity for defending virtue.

Grey's steadfast faith and maturity were observed nationwide. In 1951, John Jeter Hurt, president of Union University, nominated Grey for the presidency of the Southern Baptist Convention. Jeter, who had been Grey's pastor during his college days, believed Grey was the right man for the job due to his evangelistic zeal, pastoral care, and preaching ability. Though Grey was the underdog against fellow pastor James Storer, he nonetheless won out and became the youngest man elected to the office at that time. Storer, gracious in defeat, joked, "Many people have been beaten by a dark horse. But I was run over by a grey."[7]

In his presidency, Grey officiated over many heated battles on the Convention floor. In all of them, he believed that the most important element of any discussion was the Christian charity people bestowed upon one another. After one imposing discussion, Grey appealed to the messengers to settle their differences:

May the Chair be indulged this: I am so sorry to disappoint you good people of the press over here. But I will give you a story. Let it be said that Southern Baptists are an example of one of the finest of a pure democracy on the face of God's green earth. . . . Let it be said that Southern Baptists in their Convention and through their churches still follow what the First Baptist Church of Jerusalem followed when they said, "We will select a successor to take Judas' place," and no ecclesiastical hierarchy said, "I appoint you," but they voted on the man they wanted. . . . And say to your readers [of newspapers] tomorrow, ladies and gentlemen, that Southern Baptists know what they want to do under God, and we are going to stay together and we are going forward to His glory.[8]

Since both conservatives and liberals respected Grey, Southern Baptists honored his request.

After completing his two terms in office, Grey continued to stay in the spotlight on controversial issues such as race relations and the emerging debate on ecumenism. On race, Grey pleaded with Southern Baptists and Black (National) Baptists, the two largest denominations in the South, to demonstrate Christian love toward each other and bring about harmony "as exemplified by Christ." Grey advocated individual ecumenism, while rejecting denominational ecumenism. To be truly biblical, it had to be personal, and it could not be forced upon people through denominational polity.

In his later years as pastor in New Orleans, Grey developed arthritis and became physically weak. In 1972, after thirty-five years of service, he retired from the pastorate. He remained pastor emeritus of the church until his death in 1985. Known to many as "Saint J. D.," he lived with the belief that a Christian should involve himself in every aspect of life. He affirmed, "A man is free to breathe or not to breathe, but he doesn't lock himself up in an airtight room and stop breathing. It is the same way with religion. Religion is life."[9]

27
JAMES WILSON STORER

December 1, 1884—April 12, 1970
Elected: 1953, 1954

*B*y all accounts the annual meeting of the Southern Baptist Convention in Miami, Florida, on May 18–21, 1955, was a historic, albeit lively, one. In his engaging work *A Messenger's Memoirs*,[1] Dr. Robert E. Naylor provides a fascinating narrative for the gathering at the Dinner Key Auditorium. During the business sessions a report brought by former president Dr. Louie D. Newton from the Committee on Theological Education provoked a melee of discussion concerning the acceptance of state Baptist colleges and institutes as Southern Baptist agencies. The subsequent discussions over the inclusion of tangential institutions, such as the Carver School of Missions in Louisville and the establishment of a Baptist hospital in Los Angeles, California, were also vigorous. As was the case often during the annual meetings, there were heated discussions only because ministers and laymen alike were deeply invested in the various ministries and believed passionately in their viability.

Yet in the midst of all the parliamentary procedures and motions were two remarkable reports. Dr. Baker Cauthen reported that for the first time in history the number of Southern Baptist missionaries overseas topped one thousand, with the exact number being 1,002. Second, a report entitled "Four Major Milestones" gave an extraordinary outline: membership in Southern Baptist churches had topped eight million, Sunday school enrollment six million, and Training Union enrollment two million. The most startling part of the report, however, was the success of the Million More in '54 campaign, which had seen 396,857 baptisms. This was in contrast to the report of 1945, when the SBC had reported 256,699 baptisms. The concerted effort in evangelism had seen a net gain of over 140,000 souls added.[2] Presiding over it all with dignity and grace was a Baptist statesman and gentleman who was born a simple cowboy— Dr. James Storer.

James Wilson Storer was born on December 1, 1886, in the plains of Burlington, Kansas. Together with his family he moved to the frontier of Oregon, where he worked as a cowboy. At the age of twenty-one, he rode his horse to the Calvary Baptist Church in the town of Baker to watch a debate between the Baptists and the Seventh Day Adventists.[3] Though the Adventists never came, young Storer stayed for the service because he enjoyed the music. The next night the cowboy rode the ten miles to the church again and was converted during the invitation.

Within months of his conversion, Storer had surrendered to the call to ministry and was serving as Sunday school superintendent at Calvary. Never having pursued education, Storer felt the Lord calling him, so he entered William Jewel College in Liberty, Missouri, in 1906. Remarkably, within six years, he had completed grade school, high school, and college. Having graduated in the spring of 1912, he married Nora Isobel Wilbanks on December 31.

That same year Storer was called as pastor in Watonga, Oklahoma, with a salary of $900 a year.[4] He earned extra money coaching basketball and baseball. Over the next twenty years, he would serve in pastorates in Ripley, Tennessee; Paris, Tennessee;[5] Greenwood, Mississippi; and Richmond, Virginia. However, the major event in his ministerial life took place on October 1, 1931, when he accepted the call to the First Baptist Church of Tulsa, Oklahoma.[6]

First Baptist Tulsa began as the vision of Baptist evangelist Elihu Lee in 1887. After a protracted meeting, a church was organized the next year, and First Baptist Church of Tulsa grew to become one of the largest and most influential churches in Oklahoma. When the historic church called the forty-five-year-old preacher, it was a wonderful combination of pastor and people that would last until Storer's retirement twenty-five years later in 1956.

The growth and influence of the pastor and the church opened new doors of opportunity for Storer. Beginning in 1938, Storer wrote five books, beginning with the best-seller *Truth Enters Lowly Doors* and culminating in 1953 with *The Preacher: His Belief and Behavior*.[7] Also during his pastorate Storer served as the president of the Oklahoma Baptist Convention (1939–1941), trustee of the Foreign Mission Board, and president of the board of trustees of Oklahoma Baptist University (1941–1956).[8]

In 1953, Storer was elected president of the Southern Baptist Convention at the annual meeting in Houston, Texas. Reelected the following year, Storer presided at the Convention meetings in St. Louis and Miami. The St. Louis Convention in 1954 was noted for animated debate as well, with three rulings by the chair challenged for reconsideration.[9] Yet through it all Storer maintained his calm and humor, allowing the democratic process to work its course.

Retirement usually carries the connotation of a cessation of work. Yet for the seventy-year-old Storer, it was simply another opportunity for ministry. From 1956 to 1967, Storer served as the executive secretary of the Southern Baptist

Foundation in Nashville. Prior to 1927, "the Convention had no adequate method of handling occasional bequests and endowments. . . . In that year the Executive Committee was made the 'fiduciary agency' of the Convention."[10]

The Southern Baptist Foundation was chartered on February 26, 1947, and the first executive secretary was Charles H. Bolton. Following the subsequent leadership of T. L. Holcomb (1953–1956), Storer inherited an endowment of approximately three million dollars. Upon his retirement in 1967, the eighty-one-year-old Storer had tripled the Foundation coffers.[11] Three years after retiring from the Southern Baptist Foundation, James Wilson Storer died in Nashville, Tennessee, on April 12, 1970.

28
CASPER CARL WARREN

May 28, 1896—May 21, 1973
Elected: 1955, 1956

*O*n December 8, 1955, representatives from virtually every Baptist body in America gathered in Chicago, Illinois, to discuss the newly formed Baptist Jubilee Advance, a program created to honor the upcoming 150th anniversary of the first national Baptist Convention in America, the Triennial Convention. C. C. Warren, president of the Southern Baptist Convention and pastor of the largest Southern Baptist church in North Carolina, pioneered this eight-year program that was enthusiastically received by Baptists nationwide. Together they proposed establishing thirty thousand churches in North America by 1964, pledging "to work cooperatively, to witness effectively, and to celebrate worthily." Warren believed that this vision would "give the world a dramatic presentation of what Baptists stand for and what they have done, and to gain a mighty impetus for greater achievements for God's glory in the years ahead."[1]

In 1964, Baptists across the nation celebrated the anniversary of the Triennial Convention. Though the goal was not fully reached, nearly twenty-five thousand churches were constituted. In fact, 1964 was a watershed year within American religious history as Southern Baptists surpassed the Methodists as the largest Protestant denomination in the country. Reflecting on the efforts by thousands of Baptists, Warren articulated the importance of the program:

> Southern Baptists received a needed lesson, that in spiritual unity there are areas in which we can work with other Baptist bodies without the compromise or loss of a single one of their basic tenets. In our own denomination life we were made more aware of the tremendous needs of a lost world and of the fact that each agency while serving in a given area can at the same time join in a common emphasis that advances the cause of our Lord.

Though Warren is most noted for this accomplishment, those who knew him best recognized this pastor as a visionary who led in the establishment of new churches throughout his ministry.

Casper Carl Warren was born on May 28, 1896, in Sampson County, North Carolina, to Richard and Rosella Warren. One of eight children, Warren's father was a deacon at the local Baptist church. When he graduated from high school in 1914, Warren honored the heritage given to him by his parents and enrolled at the Baptist-affiliated Wake Forest College in Wake Forest, North Carolina. His college career was interrupted in 1917 when America became involved in World War I. Warren served his country as a second lieutenant in the Coast Artillery Corp until the armistice was reached a year later.

As Europe celebrated the renewal of peace, Warren returned to Wake Forest College and earned his law degree in 1920. Subsequently, Warren practiced law in Dunn, North Carolina, establishing a lucrative firm. However, the more he volunteered at the local Baptist church, the more Warren's thoughts turned to the ministry. He accepted leadership positions as Sunday school superintendent and president of the Baptist Young Peoples' Union of North Carolina.

Warren finally surrendered to the ministry and was ordained by the Baptist church in Dunn in September 1922. He immediately proceeded to leave the church he served so faithfully to further his education. Warren matriculated at The Southern Baptist Theological Seminary in Louisville, Kentucky, where he received his master of theology degree in 1925, followed by his doctor of theology in 1928.

During his post-graduate studies Warren was privileged to be the assistant to internationally known Greek scholar A. T. Robertson. Also during this time Warren met Mary Lashbrook Strickland. In 1925, the two were united in marriage, a union which brought about three children: Casper Carl Jr., Alva Eugene, and Mary Virginia.

Upon graduation from the seminary, Warren accepted the offer to pastor Lexington Avenue Baptist Church in Danville, Virginia. Ironically, this was the hometown of Warren's wife Mary. In fact, Warren himself proved to be an integral part of the community as the church had more than sixteen hundred additions and built a new auditorium for worship. Here Warren learned a difficult lesson of how important it was for people of all classes and colors to have a pastor and place of worship. Dr. Porter Routh, executive secretary of the Executive Committee of the Southern Baptist Convention and longtime friend of Warren, described a tragedy that Warren encountered:

The charred remains of three little bodies were found in the ashes of a burned tenant house about three miles out from Danville, Kentucky.

A young pastor, who had rushed to the scene after hearing of the tragedy, joined the forty or fifty friends standing around the smoking ruins to bring what comfort he could to the bereaved parents.

"Who is their pastor?" he inquired.

"They ain't got no pastor, Mister. They ain't got no church. They're just poor tenant farmers."

That reply burned hotter than the embers of the fire into the heart of the young pastor. On Sunday morning as he unburdened his heart . . . there came a response on the part of the church to see that church facilities were provided for the people of that community.[2]

This experience, then, compelled Warren to plant new churches around the city in which he was ministering.

After ten years at the Danville church, Warren went on to pastor Immanuel Baptist Church in Little Rock, Arkansas (1938–1943), and First Baptist Church of Charlotte, North Carolina (1943–1958). Both churches grew exponentially, with more than twenty-two hundred additions in Arkansas, while the North Carolina church grew to be the largest in the Baptist State Convention in 1954. Yet what set Warren apart during his ministries was his passion to plant churches. During his thirty years of pastoral experience, Warren led his churches to establish thirty-three new churches.

This zeal gained him the admiration of his colleagues. Along the way he served as president of the North Carolina Baptist Convention (1946–1947), president of the North Carolina Baptist General Board (1950–1953), president of the board of trustees for Southeastern Baptist Theological Seminary (1951–1952), and president of the Southern Baptist Convention Pastors' Conference (1951–1952).

In 1956, messengers to the Southern Baptist Convention elected him president. Here he led the Convention to partner with other Baptist Conventions in beginning thirty thousand new churches through what became known as the Baptist Jubilee Celebration. Consequently, though Warren was known as a dynamic preacher, he resigned his pastorate in Charlotte to devote himself fully to the campaign. In 1964, fifty thousand Baptists from across North America assembled in Atlantic City, New Jersey, to celebrate their efforts. Though the mission was not completely successful, they had many reasons to rejoice. Since 1958, Baptists had gained nearly one and one-half million members. The greatest growth occurred where Baptist were least represented, in the north and west.

In 1959, at the zenith of his ministry, Warren suffered the loss of his wife, Mary. They had been married for thirty-four years. God provided another helpmeet in time as Warren was remarried to Sibyl Brame Townsend in 1962. Indeed, she became his greatest support in his years of retirement. Warren himself viewed this experience as a way to help other men as they grieved the loss of their wives. In particular, Warren was a great encourager to his longtime friend and ministerial partner Perry Crouch, who also felt the pain of losing his wife. Years later Crouch officiated at the funeral of Warren, eulogizing his friend as a "man's man, who knew how to relate to men and to other ministers."[3]

But retirement for Warren did not mean less involvement in the local church. In fact, Warren was the pastor of the newly organized Sharon Baptist Church in Charlotte when he fell ill in the spring of 1973. Five weeks later, C. C. Warren passed away, eight days before his seventy-seventh birthday. A few weeks before he died, Warren spoke to reporters about his legacy. He asserted, "The major joy and task of my life has been to do what's necessary to reach people for Christ."[4] Many Southern Baptists are thankful that this man, born as he said in the "huckleberry patch of Starling Swamp just below Mingo," was called by God to reach a nation with the gospel of Christ.

29
BROOKS HAYS

August 9, 1898—October 12, 1981
Elected: 1957, 1958

*A*s Rev. Joe Ramsey stepped behind the pulpit that evening to preach the immeasurable riches of Christ, the blind Methodist minister did not truly comprehend the impact and influence he was about to have upon Southern Baptists. In the congregation that evening was young Brooks Hays, an eleven-year-old boy born and raised in Southern Baptist life. His grandmother, a devout Methodist, had invited him to an old-fashioned revival meeting sponsored by the local Methodist church. Hays recalled later, "[Ramsey] was one of the most eloquent speakers I've ever heard."[1] That night Brooks Hays accepted the call of Christ to salvation, beginning a spiritual pilgrimage that wedded church and politics.

But that did not make Hays a Methodist. When his parents heard the news of his conversion, they immediately told their pastor in Russellville, Arkansas. At the age of twelve, Hays was baptized according to his profession of faith. Recalling the unpleasant evening, Hays joked, "It was in February and they had not heated the water in the big zinc baptistry, and when I stepped into the water my body turned blue; it almost made me want to be a Methodist."[2] The Baptists had won a man who would become a faithful church member, honest politician, congressional gentleman, and a Southern Baptist Convention president. By the end of his life at the age of eighty-three, Brooks Hays had influenced an entire nation with both his convictions as a Christian and his influence as a statesmen.

On August 9, 1898, Brooks Hays was born in a three-room rented house in London, Arkansas. Born at a time when the Civil War was still fresh in the memories of loyal southerners, Hays recalls his early childhood and contemporary politics: "There is no sadder chapter in the history of southern politics than the cruel and highly effective measures adopted by the white majority around the turn of the century to close the door to the Negro's political participation."[3] His disappointment with elements of Southern culture was further exacerbated by what he saw as irrelevant arguments between denominations over theological disputations such as baptismal regeneration, foot-washing as an essential ordinance, and the eternal security of the saints.

Brooks felt that the "plight of the black people did not appear to trouble the white Christian" very much. Indeed, due to the impact of uncaring and unconcerned Christians, Hays gravitated toward social ethics and away from theological dogma early in his Christian pilgrimage. In fact, when considering whether to study for the ministry or study to be a politician, Hays chose the latter.

In the end Hays served both church and state. A faithful Baptist, deacon, and Sunday school teacher, Hays became a politician who would influence the largest Protestant denomination in the world, the then-eight-million-member Southern Baptist Convention.

Make no mistake, Hays was a southerner who loved his culture and the people. The nurturing of the rural South gave him the family ties and unconditional love he needed as a foundation for his life. Yet he hungered for something that his culture could not give him. Hays went to college in the fall of 1915, determined through education to help his own and all around him. He recalled, "I had suffered with them sufficiently to cling to the determination to work *with* them and *for* them as long as I should live."[4]

Hays earned his bachelor of arts degree from the University of Arkansas-Fayetteville (1919) and his law degree from George Washington University (1922). In the process Hays experienced new ideas and new situations that he carried for a lifetime. Out of his parent's reach, Hays enjoyed "sermon tasting" for the first time in his life. He relished visiting various churches other than Baptist and listening to the preacher. Later in life he explained that it was this "outcropping of an interest in ecumenism that was climaxed forty-eight years later in my acceptance of the appointment as the first director of the Ecumenical Institute of Wake Forest University in 1968."[5] Also during this time Brooks married his lifetime love, Marion Prather.

Hays also beheld a new world politically. Since George Washington University was located in Washington, D.C., it was not difficult for Hays to become enamored with politics over and above his law studies. By 1919, the push for women to vote was reaching its climax. In 1920, Hays watched as the United States Congress refused to ratify the Versailles Treaty, which would incorporate the United States into the League of Nations and out of isolationism. Disappointed with the bitter debate, he believed that the moderates had lost to "die-hard isolationists and the partisans of the League."

This event impacted Hays in such a way that he dedicated the rest of his life to achieving what had failed for years: political *moderation* that brought two sides together to further the unity of the nation and change the old-fashioned ways that hurt the soul of a nation. The ultimate ideal of moderation was best demonstrated fifteen years after Hays was elected to the United States House of

Representatives in 1942. In 1957, the country was in turmoil as blacks demanded equal rights in the school system. Arkansas was center stage. Its governor, Orval Faubus, had blocked the integration of Central High School in Little Rock, causing President Dwight Eisenhower to send troops to enforce the federal mandate of desegregation.[6]

Hays had fought for the abolishment of segregation in all forms of transportation and attempted to repeal the oppressive poll tax requirement to vote. He believed that unity, moderation, and equality must win the day. In 1957, he brought Eisenhower and Faubus together for political discussion. Hays did not consider Faubus to be a close friend, yet he explained, "He's a Baptist, too."[7] In the end, Governor Faubus relented, and integration began at the high school.

Ironically, the principled and biblical position of equality cost Hays his seat in Congress. In 1958, write-in candidate Dale Alford defeated the incumbent by a mere 1,256 votes. The race was highly questionable since nearly 12,000 of Alford's 30,739 votes were made with stickers! A day before the elections, illegal anonymous circulars were dropped from airplanes with the headline, "We know you, Brooks." He was seated between two black Baptist preachers.[8]

Though he was defeated for reelection to Congress in 1958, Hays was elected as president of the Southern Baptist Convention in 1957 and reelected in 1958. Considered the paradigm of racial reconciliation and harmony, Hays was admired by many Southern Baptists for his stance for unity and equality. Indeed, many prominent leaders outside of Southern Baptist life considered him a friend and colaborer in the cause of peace. Martin Luther King Jr. once explained on introducing Brooks Hays, "This is Mr. Hays. He has suffered with us."[9]

Hays's political loss was short-lived. He was called as a member of the board of directors of the Tennessee Valley Authority (1959–1961), followed by an appointment as the special assistant to the president of the United States (1961–1964). When he went to work for the TVA, one Mississippi paper jabbed the Baptist and his image, exclaiming, "We do not know how much Mr. Hays knows about navigation, flood control, or hydroelectric power production, but one thing is for sure, the Baptists now have access to the largest baptismal pool in all the world."[10]

Hays proved more than adequate for the job and even acted as an ambassador around the world for Christ and Baptists. For example, during an official trip with the TVA to the World Power Conference in 1960, Hays contacted some American embassy officials in an attempt to secure greater religious freedom for "our Baptist people in Spain." The former congressman was distraught at the Spanish constitution which asserted that the Catholic faith was the official religion of Spain.

President Kennedy was also impressed by Hays's eloquent attempt at unity and peace. The president once inquired of his special assistant, "What kind of Baptist are you, Brooks?" Hays answered, "An ecumenical Baptist. . . . Just say a catholic Baptist, Mr. President, but spell it with a little *c*."[11] This ecumenicity was seen as

Hays spoke to a varied landscape of religious bodies, including Methodists, Jews, and Catholics.

It was only fitting that Wake Forest University, rich in Baptist heritage, appointed him as director of the Ecumenical Institute in 1968. The politician who had served in government for over two decades had come home to his Southern Baptist roots. Admittedly, Hays knew his form of ecumenical Christianity did not have a favorable hearing among the vast majority of Southern Baptists. His two years at the post were spent attempting to convince Southern Baptists of their need to "break through the old isolation barriers and become a part of the total Christian community."[12]

After an unsuccessful run for U.S. Congress in 1972, Hays and his wife Marion moved to Chevy Chase, Maryland, where they lived until his death on October 12, 1981. He died as he lived his life, in peace. He was buried in Russellville, Arkansas. At the end of his autobiography, published in the year of his death, Hays's final words of inspiration came from his father: "A man's dreams should not die till he dies." Indeed, Hays's dreams of racial equality and religious liberty carry on until this day. Baptists across the globe have the responsibility to carry this vision forth.

30
WILLIAM RAMSEY POLLARD

February 15, 1903—April 19, 1984
Elected: 1959, 1960

$\mathscr{C}$leburne, Texas, is the county seat of Johnson County, approximately fifty miles southwest of Dallas. As a crossroads for the soldiers during the Civil War, it was centered on the wagon trail between Fort Belknap and Fort Graham. Founded as a city in 1867, Cleburne was a pioneering center for commerce and transportation. In 1903, the population hovered around three thousand people, mainly farmers in the outlying areas and traders using the new railroads crossing through town. No one would have fathomed that a child born that year would belie his humble beginnings to travel the world as a minister of the gospel. By his death at age eighty-one, Ramsey Pollard would preach to thousands in Rio de Janerio, Japan, and Hong Kong. He would become the first Southern Baptist president to preach a world tour during his tenure. He would travel hundreds of thousands of miles, and it all began at the crossroads of a small county seat town.

William Ramsey Pollard was born on February 15, 1903, the son of B. O. Pollard, a pioneer police officer in central Texas.[1] At the age of eleven, Ramsey was saved during a revival at First Baptist Church in Amarillo, under the preaching of Dr. Wallace Bassett. Though Ramsey was a strong Christian, he had no desire to become a preacher. In 1920, he moved to Dallas and joined the Cliff Temple Baptist Church. He taught a Sunday school class, attended Oak Cliff High School, and worked in the Baptist Young Peoples' Union. While serving in the church, Ramsey became enchanted with a young woman named Della Pickle. In 1923, following Ramsey's graduation, they were married.

In 1924, the Pollards moved to Tampa, Florida, where Ramsey worked as a bank teller. They settled into a comfortable lifestyle and joined the El Bethel Baptist Church. His gifts as a Sunday school teacher, however, gave him an opportunity that would radically alter his life. A deacon in the church asked the twenty-one-year-old to fill the pulpit one Sunday since the church was without a pastor.

During his preparation for that Sunday, Ramsey sensed the clear call of God and surrendered to the gospel ministry. Amazingly, the church called him as pastor and ordained him on December 16, 1925. For the next four and one-half years, young Pollard learned the pastoral ministry and even served as the moderator of the Tampa Bay Baptist Association.

In 1930, Ramsey was convinced that he needed to pursue his education. Moving to Forth Worth, Pollard entered Southwestern Seminary. While pursuing his degrees, Pollard pastored First Baptist Church of Handley and Evans Avenue Baptist Church in Fort Worth. During this time the Pollards were blessed with the birth of their two children.

In 1939, Ramsey accepted the call of Broadway Baptist Church in Knoxville, Tennessee. For the next twenty years Ramsey became a leader not only on the local level but also on the national scene. Broadway Baptist grew tremendously during this period of time, and Pollard gained a reputation as a popular speaker. His pointed preaching coupled with his humorous and populist style were used by God in many settings.

In 1953, Pollard spoke to the World Youth Conference in Rio de Janerio, Brazil. He addressed assemblies at Glorieta and Ridgecrest conference centers and became a favorite in evangelism conferences. He led crusades in Hawaii, Alaska, and Japan at the invitation of the Home Mission Board (HMB). He also served as a trustee of a number of Southern Baptist entities, including the HMB, Executive Committee, Carson-Newman College, and the Radio and Television Commission. Pollard was literally setting the standard for involvement in Baptist life, serving selflessly with his time and energies.

In 1959, Pollard preached at the annual meeting in Miami, Florida, and was elected to the first of his two terms as president of the Convention. At the invitation of the Foreign Mission Board, Pollard became the first president to conduct a world tour, traveling to many of the major areas of Baptist mission endeavor.[2]

In his 1961 presidential address at the Convention in St. Louis, Pollard roused the messengers with an impassioned sermon. Building on the theme of the militant church, Pollard called Southern Baptists to a new fidelity to the task to which God had called them. In his inimitable style, he exhorted them:

> Now this is no day for timidity; it is a good time for humility, but it is not a good day for timidity. And I want to impress upon you that we are not on an Easter egg hunt and we're not on a Sunday school picnic and we're not on a garden club party. We're on big business for the Lord Jesus Christ and it's no time for compromise. I think some of us have been embarrassed because Baptist people sometimes in places of leadership have compromised what Baptists believe and what the Word of God teaches.[3]

His penetrating analysis did not miss anyone in the Convention hall. Turning his attention to the institutions of training, Pollard continued, "Let us ask God to keep our schools close to the Book. Oh, may God help us see that the Word of God is the way to get people born again—preaching and teaching and living the Word of God!"[4]

It is difficult to overestimate the influence Dr. Pollard had during those days. In virtually every venue of Baptist life, Pollard answered the call to service. In many ways he was one of the most popular preachers in America, and this was reflected in his pastoral ministry. In 1960, he was called to follow Dr. R. G. Lee as the pastor of Bellevue Baptist Church in Memphis, Tennessee. For the next twelve years, until 1972, Pollard led that historic church, and he continued his prophetic voice among Southern Baptists.

Pollard was never shy in expressing his convictions concerning the SBC. Preaching at the 1962 annual meeting, he addressed the perceived liberalism creeping into the seminaries. He said:

If you don't believe the miracles and the Word of God, get out of our Seminaries! I'm not saying that because it is smart. I am not saying that because it's trite. I am saying it because Southern Baptists need to be on guard against false teachers within our own ranks. . . . Your academic freedom stops at a certain point.[5]

His work at Bellevue Baptist was a tremendous investment of his twilight years. In June 1972, approaching the age of seventy, Pollard retired from the pastorate. He remained a member of Bellevue Baptist, and in 1984 when he died, his successor, Adrian Rogers, conducted his funeral.

31
HERSCHEL HAROLD HOBBS

October 24, 1907—November 28, 1995
Elected: 1961, 1962

*H*arold Bennett, in the foreword to Herschel Hobbs's autobiography, *My Faith and Message*, recounts Hobbs's address to the messengers of the 1992 Convention meeting in Indianapolis, Indiana. As is the custom, surviving presidents of the SBC are brought to the platform to bring greetings. At the age of eighty-five, Hobbs was the oldest surviving former president, so he approached the platform first. In his warm and gracious manner, Hobbs summarized his life and beliefs over the seventy-three years of his Christian life:

> I am a Southern Baptist—an old-time Southern Baptist. I have been a Southern Baptist since the day I was immersed in Montevallo Creek . . . into the fellowship of the Enon Baptist Church. I will be a Southern Baptist until the day I die, and I will always be proud to be a Southern Baptist. Having known a little bit of the history of the past, and looking forward to the future . . . I think that Southern Baptists' greatest era is just ahead.[1]

It would be a quintessential Hobbs statement—optimistic, prophetic, humorous, and based on his absolute conviction that God was blessing the work of his denomination. To Dr. Hobbs, the pastor, author, speaker, theologian, and denominational leader, revival was perpetually just around the corner.

Born on October 24, 1907, to Elbert Oscar and Emma Octavia Hobbs, Herschel was the youngest of six children and the only son.[2] Before Herschel was three years old, both his father and his sister Gladys had died, and his mother sold their farm and moved to Ashland, Alabama, to be nearer to her family. A subsequent move to Dry Valley, south of Birmingham, in 1916 brought Herschel to both his education and his faith in Christ.

Attending a two-room school in Shelby County, the Hobbs family also attended the Enon Baptist Church, which was adjacent to the school. During the fall revival of 1919 at Enon, the eleven-year-old Herschel was converted and baptized. The preacher was Ernest Davis, a ministerial student at Howard College, which would later become Samford University. A subsequent move north to Birmingham allowed Herschel and his sisters to attend strong high schools, and in 1926, Herschel graduated from Phillips High School.

After the family joined the Ensley Baptist Church in a suburb of Birmingham, during a youth meeting Herschel met Frances, the woman who was to become his wife. The depth of their Baptist commitment is even seen in their nuptials. Married at 8:30 A.M. on Sunday morning, April 10, 1927, the couple honeymooned at Sunday school, morning worship, the afternoon BYPU and church that evening![3] Also at Ensley Baptist Hobbs surrendered to the gospel ministry, though he would briefly struggle with studying to become a lawyer.[4]

Herschel and Frances served in their first pastorate at the Vinesville Baptist Church in Birmingham in 1929. Moving to the Berney Points Baptist Church that fall, Herschel and Frances entered Howard College in 1930, and both graduated in an accelerated study after just five semesters.[5]

To study the life of Herschel H. Hobbs during the years of 1932–1948 is to see clearly that Hobbs was affected by, taught by, advised by, and mentored by, some of the greatest leaders in Southern Baptist history. Those sixteen years, when Hobbs was 25–41 years old, were not only formative; they were seminal. Though he spent this period of time in anonymity, Hobbs would develop friendships with men who would walk with him through every juncture of the next half century. It was obviously a fond period for Hobbs as well, as his autobiography attests.[6]

Entering Southern Seminary in 1932, Hobbs pastored two part-time Indiana churches and lived in Rice Hall. His studies for the Th.M. and Ph.D. were conducted under the excruciatingly watchful eyes of the giants of Southern Baptist life, Drs. John R. Sampey, A. T. Robertson, and W. O. Carver.[7] His deep and abiding love for these men affected his scholarship and theological acumen in significant ways. He took Hebrew under Dr. Kyle M. Yates. He was immersed in Greek under the tutelage of Dr. Robertson and Dr. W. Hershey Davis. He was a classmate of W. A. Criswell and attended the Criswells' wedding on campus, serving as the getaway driver following the ceremony.[8] Hobbs received the Th.M. in 1935 and the Ph.D. in 1938.

Returning to the Birmingham area following his studies, Hobbs pastored a number of churches, including Crestwood Baptist Church, Calvary Baptist Church in Birmingham, and Clayton Street (now Heritage) Baptist Church in Montgomery.[9] In June 1941, he accepted the pastorate of the Emmanuel Baptist Church in Alexandria, Louisiana, and during World War II, taught adjunctively for Louisiana College. In his New Testament classes, Hobbs remarkably had a significant number of students who would rise to Southern Baptist leadership and would become his lifelong friends, such as Jaroy Weber,[10] W. C. Fields,[11] H. C. Brown,[12] Malcolm Tolbert,[13] Billy McMinn,[14] Ray Rust,[15] and Luther Hall.[16]

In November 1944, Hobbs began a five-year pastorate at the Dauphin Way Baptist Church in Mobile, Alabama, the largest church in the state. With over four thousand members, the church was "second only to Bellevue Baptist in Memphis of all Southern Baptist Churches east of the Mississippi River."[17] The church's rapid growth under Hobbs's preaching was supplemented by revivals with such Baptist luminaries as Dr. R. G. Lee (fall 1947) and Angel Martinez. Hobbs himself preached many revivals, including the first revival in forty-nine years at First Baptist Church in Dallas, after his friend Dr. W. A. Criswell became pastor. The rising influence of the Oklahoma boy was evidenced by the fact that Dr. Lee himself asked Hobbs to nominate him at the 1948 annual meeting. The blessings were mixed, however, in the Hobbs family while at Dauphin Way. The blessed event of the conversion of their first son, Jerry, at the age of nine, was mitigated by the stillbirth of their second son, Harold Elbert.[18]

In 1949, the pulpit committee of First Baptist Church of Oklahoma City unanimously recommended Hobbs to be their next pastor, and thus began a twenty-two year marriage of pastor and people. Amazingly, Hobbs began his tenure at First Oklahoma City with a two-week revival, which he himself preached. Over 140 decisions were recorded in the church, most of which were conversions.

The first decade of Hobbs's pastorate in Oklahoma City was remarkable in every way. The church grew by great numbers and the fury of building programs, educational and discipleship additions, revivals and pastoral duties occupied much of Dr. Hobbs's time. In addition, in 1951, Dr. Hobbs would write the first of over one hundred and fifty books, entitled *Cowards or Conquerors*.[19] Amazingly, Hobbs, as the most prolific of Southern Baptist authors, wrote each manuscript by hand. Covering the vast expanse of New Testament studies, theology, ecclesiology, and Sunday school literature, Hobbs rivaled his hero, Dr. A. T. Robertson, in his prolific ministry.

By 1960, Hobbs's stature in Convention life was such that he had repeatedly turned down offers for nomination for the presidency. In January 1961, he told his wife that for the first time he was open to the suggestion, but he shared this with no one else. He later recounts:

In January of 1961, I received a call from Wayne Dehoney. He said, "Some of us have been talking about who should be the next president of the Convention. We agree that you are the one, and I am calling to ask if you will permit your nomination." I agreed. Then I told him what I had told Frances, but I said that I would do nothing to be elected. He said they did not want me to do anything. All they wanted me to do was to say whom I would like to have nominate me. After thinking it over, I said, "Carl Bates." A few days later I received a letter from Carl asking permission to nominate me. I agreed. That was it![20]

Elected in St. Louis in 1961, Hobbs served at a critical juncture in Baptist life. While the issue of race relations was large on the secular scene, in Southern

Baptist life, the Elliott controversy[21] caused Southern Baptists to address the growing higher criticism that was emanating from the seminaries. At the 1962 Convention meeting in San Francisco, the messengers, along with the Executive Committee, called on Dr. Hobbs to examine the 1925 *Baptist Faith and Message* in light of contemporary theology. The 1963 *Baptist Faith and Message* was presented and approved on May 9, 1963, in the Kansas City Convention hall. Hobbs believed serving as SBC president is the "greatest privilege of service in the Southern Baptist Convention."[22]

Following his two terms as president, Hobbs continued to write. For over twenty-five years, he wrote *Studying Adult Life and Work Lessons* for the Baptist Sunday School Board (1968–1993). He was vice president of the Baptist World Alliance from 1965 to 1970. Though he retired from the pastorate at First Baptist Oklahoma City in 1972, he continued to write, preach, and minister. In the controversy beginning in 1979, Hobbs once again stood to moderate Southern Baptists and affirmed his absolute belief in the Bible. In 1985, he was again called into service on the Peace Committee, and he continued to speak to Southern Baptists through radio broadcasts, conferences, and Conventions.

When Herschel H. Hobbs died on November 28, 1995, his legacy cast a long shadow, but in his heart he always wanted to be remembered as a pastor. Walter Shurden, as Dockery notes, called Hobbs one of the two most influential Southern Baptist theologians of the twentieth century. In comparing Hobbs to the other Baptist theologian, Dr. E. Y. Mullins, Shurden writes:

Mullins served as Southern Baptists' theologian in the first half of this century and Hobbs in the latter half. Both were inspiring preachers, concerned denominational statesmen and strong advocates of Southern Baptist doctrines. Mullins was responsible for Southern Baptists' first confession of faith in 1925 and Hobbs for the confession of 1963. Moreover, Mullins wrote and Hobbs revised the classic statement of Southern Baptist distinctives . . . *The Axioms of Religion*. When, therefore, Southern Baptists want to know "historic" Southern Baptist distinctives, they must return to the writings of these revered leaders. Mullins and Hobbs handled the Word of God reverently, and obediently, seeking to make sure that Baptist distinctives came from the Bible and not from culture.[23]

32
KENNETH OWEN WHITE

August 29, 1902—July 11, 1985
Elected: 1963

*O*n May 12, 1964, the first Sunday after K. Owen White was elected president of the Southern Baptist Convention, a young black man came forward during the invitation desiring to join the fellowship of First Baptist Church of Houston, Texas, where White was pastor. Recognizing the racial tensions within his own city and the country in general, the pastor decided to counsel the young man before allowing the church to vote on the candidate. White learned that the young man had no desire to join for reasons of worship and service; rather, he was sent by the local civil rights organization to test whether African-Americans would be allowed to join white congregations. The church, led by the recommendation of their pastor, rejected the candidate's membership on account of the young man's "selfish motives."

The newspapers immediately circulated stories of protest. Editorials were written, First Baptist Church became enveloped with media attention, and services were continually interrupted by protestors. In a statement to national media outlets, White explained why he recommended the denial of membership:

It is the most difficult thing in the world to know what goes on in a man's heart and what prompts him to do the things he does, but after two conferences with a young Negro who applied for membership at the First Baptist Church, Houston, I sincerely feel that his motivations for requesting membership were not what they should have been. With all due respect to the young man, I believe that he wanted to see if he would be able to join the church where the president of the Southern Baptist Convention is pastor. I do not believe that church membership should be cheapened by accepting for membership those who are not motivated with a sincere desire to worship and serve God through that church. I deeply regret that this situation arose at a time when there is

racial turmoil in other cities and tension in our own city. I feel that
    there could be a wrong time to do a right thing.[1]
In the months to come, the nation was privy to seeing how the church would act
when a sincere black woman requested membership. White, convinced that she
honestly wished to be part of the fellowship, recommended approving her membership. On April 21, 1965, a secret ballot was taken and the church voted,
206–182, not to receive anyone "of the colored race." When the vote was read publicly, segregationists applauded loudly to the dismay of their pastor. Angered by
their joy, he rebuked them stating, "I want you to know that I am wholeheartedly
ashamed of you."[2] White's stand for integration of genuine candidates, though not
accepted by many in his generation, would stand as a model for Southern Baptists
in the next generation.

Kenneth Owen White was born on August 29, 1902, in London, England, to
Malcohn and Ethel White. Malcohn White was a successful physician and lay
preacher within the Methodist Church who moved his family to British Columbia,
Canada, where he served the community as doctor, dentist, justice of the peace,
and postmaster. Kenneth himself took great interest in the activities of the
Methodist Church, so much so that his Sunday school teacher encouraged him to
enter the ministry.

But White had not yet been converted. He accepted Christ as his Savior one
night while working at a sash-and-door factory. That week he had attended a
Baptist revival service which made a profound impact on him. He stated:

During the service two of the ladies in the choir had sung; and the
recurring theme of their song was this: "It was for me that Jesus died
on the cross of Calvary. . . ." There was no light from heaven; there
was no audible voice that spoke. There was no earthquake. There was
no feeling of an electric current playing through my being.

I was alone, just weeping and praying in the darkness; but there
came to me a conviction that I could not shake off, that, if I made this
decision and took this step, it would be necessary to give personal testimony to those godless, profane men with whom I worked in the
shop. This was hard for me; in fact, it looked almost insurmountable.
But I prayed for strength to do it. I have had to pray for strength many
times since that day.

In 1920, though White was reared a Methodist, this experience compelled him to
follow the Lord in believers' baptism, and he accepted the Baptist faith.

In 1921, White enrolled at the Bible Institute of Los Angeles, California (now
named Biola). Here he studied under famed evangelist, scholar, and dean of the
school, R. A. Torrey, whose obsession for winning the lost inspired White to dedicate his life to doing the same. White earned his diploma from the Institute in
1924 and moved to Louisville, Kentucky, where he began attending The Southern
Baptist Theological Seminary. After receiving his bachelor of theology degree in

1926, he married Pearl Woodworth. They would have two children, Stanley Owen and Ruth Marslender. White's wife served as a constant source of encouragement and commitment. In fact, her devotion was particularly evident during one financial drive when she placed her diamond engagement ring in the offering plate when it was passed around.

Upon graduation, White and his wife moved to California where he began his duties at First Baptist Church, Santa Monica, California. But White's desire to further his education consumed him to the point that he moved back to Louisville three years later and began studying toward his master of theology degree. By 1934, White had earned his master's degree, along with a doctor of philosophy in Old Testament from the seminary and a bachelor of arts degree from the University of Louisville. In particular, his work during his Ph.D. prepared White to write three commentaries, *Studies in Hosea*, *The Book of Jeremiah*, and *Nehemiah Speaks Again*.

During the next two decades, White served as pastor of four churches: Central Baptist Church in Gainesville, Georgia (1934–1936), Kirkwood Baptist Church in Atlanta, Georgia (1936–1944), Metropolitan Baptist Church in Washington, D.C. (1944–1950), and First Baptist Church in Little Rock, Arkansas (1950–1953). White's service to downtown churches in Washington, D.C., and Little Rock was noticed by another downtown church which had recently lost their pastor. In 1953, when the Southern Baptist Convention was meeting in Houston, Texas, the pulpit committee of First Baptist Church of Houston took advantage of the opportunity and asked White to preach during their Sunday morning service. Four weeks later White accepted the call to the church, beginning his twelve-year relationship with the congregation.

The church knew that their pastor was a politically and theologically conservative man and stood by him when he fought against liberalism within the community and Convention. In 1962, White denounced *The Message of Genesis*, a recent publication by Midwestern Seminary Old Testament Professor Ralph Elliot. He asserted that the book was a "poison . . . which can only lead to further confusion, unbelief, and deterioration, and ultimate disintegration as a great New Testament denomination."[3] White was not willing to stand idly by as liberals "cast some doubt on the reliability and dependability of the Word of God."

In 1960, White was elected chairman of the executive board of the Baptist General Convention of Texas. The Houston pastor used his position to encourage other Southern Baptists to take a stand against theological liberalism. White's stance resounded with many fellow Texas Baptists, leading to his election as president of the Baptist General Convention of Texas.

In 1963, his notoriety captured the attention of Southern Baptist Convention messengers, and he was elected president of the Convention. Though branded an agitator, White endeavored to lead Baptists to be "even more strongly evangelistic and missionary-hearted."[4] Yet White believed this could not occur unless Southern Baptists were unified on the inspiration of Scripture. He noted:

I have never had any thought but to strengthen our Convention in all of its worldwide responsibilities and opportunities. I took the position which I did in San Francisco in 1962 because it was then and is now my firm conviction that any departure from faith in the reliability and dependability of the Bible as God's Word will in the end rob us of all spiritual power and usefulness.[5]

Over the year of his presidency, White devoted himself to correcting the problem of theological liberalism by working within the Convention structure.

In 1965, White resigned his pastorate in Houston and accepted the position as metropolitan missions coordinator of the California Southern Baptist Convention. Three years later he retired after a full-time ministry which spanned more than forty years. In his later years he remained active within the Convention he so loved, serving on boards of the Home Mission Board, Radio Commission, and Sunday School Board. On July 11, 1985, White died after a long bout with cancer. The man born in London, England, reared in Canada, naturalized as an American citizen, and educated by Southern Baptists was laid to rest in Tucson, Arizona, after a lifetime of dedication to the Lord Jesus Christ and his Word.

33

WILLIAM WAYNE DEHONEY

August 22, 1918—
Elected: 1964, 1965

$\mathscr{A}$s the service began, the electricity in the air was palpable. Communism had ravaged Moscow for over seventy years, and now Billy Graham was preaching a historic crusade. Over the course of three days in 1994, more than forty-three thousand people were converted. In a remarkable moment the Red Army Choir sang, complete with red coats and black coats. Following the service, as the Red Army was boarding its buses, a young woman approached them. Katherine had traveled with her father from America, and she struck up a conversation with them. Eventually, she had the honor of giving many of them Bibles. It was a profoundly meaningful moment in Katherine Evitts's life, yet not a surprising one. Her father had often worked with Billy Graham over the course of three decades. In fact, he had himself traveled the world preaching the gospel. Her father, Dr. Wayne Dehoney, was more than just a pastor, professor, and president of the Southern Baptist Convention. He has been a world ambassador for Christ.[1]

William Wayne Dehoney was born in New Raymer, Colorado, on August 22, 1918. One of three sons born to William Warren and Ruby Northup Dehoney, Wayne moved with his farming family to Cheyenne, Wyoming, and then to Oklahoma City.[2] Dehoney was saved at a Royal Ambassadors meeting at First Baptist Church, Oklahoma City, under the leadership of Dr. M. R. Ham. Shortly after he was baptized into that fellowship, the pastor left, and Dr. T. L. Holcomb became the pastor. The ten-year-old Dehoney became fast friends with the new pastor's son, Luther.

When Wayne was a high school sophomore, his family moved to Nashville and joined First Baptist Church. After graduating from high school, Dehoney entered Vanderbilt University in prelaw studies. His best friend, Luther Holcomb, surrendered to the ministry, and the decision of his friend had a moving effect on Dehoney. Attending the Southwide Student Retreat in Memphis, Dehoney felt convicted of God to surrender to the ministry and made that commitment public in the First Baptist Church. His pastor, Dr. W. F. Powell, encouraged him to continue his studies at Baylor University, but after a year with few preaching opportunities, Dehoney returned to Vanderbilt to complete his undergraduate degree. Back in Tennessee in 1939, Dehoney was called to his first church, the Bethel Baptist Church in Robertson County.

Attending a Baptist Student Union function on the campus of the Peabody University in the fall of 1943, Dehoney became enchanted with a young girl from Madisonville, Kentucky, Lealice Bishop, a freshman at Peabody. A "whirlwind courtship"[3] ensued, and on August 24, 1944, they were married. By this time Dehoney was a student at Southern Seminary and pastoring in Rogersville, Tennessee. Over the next seven years, the Dehoneys would see the birth of three children, Rebecca Ann (1946), Katherine Elaine (1948), and William Wayne Jr. (1951).

Between 1946 and 1950, Dehoney finished his bachelor of divinity studies and pastored the Immanuel Baptist Church in Paducah, Kentucky.[4] In 1950, Dehoney was called to the Central Baptist Church in Birmingham, Alabama, and his life was about to accelerate. God was preparing him for the greatest days of ministry.

When Dehoney arrived at the prestigious Birmingham church, the membership hovered just over two thousand. Within six years that number would double. With relentless energy and passionate preaching, Dehoney was a tireless advocate of evangelism through the Sunday school and social action. By 1956, over twelve hundred people had joined the church, the vast majority by baptism. One of the most unique endeavors instituted by Pastor Dehoney was regular trips to the Holy Land to deepen the Christian walk of his members. In 1955, he started Bibleland Tours (later renamed Dehoney Travel), to enable members to go as economically as possible and to follow the steps of Christ as closely as possible. Also during this time Dehoney became a member of the Baptist World Alliance General Council.

On April 15, 1957, Dehoney assumed the pastorate of First Baptist Church of Jackson, Tennessee. Against all normative ministerial moves, the Dehoneys accepted the call of a church smaller than the one they left because they felt a clear call from the Lord and saw an incredible opportunity for ministry. First Jackson began to grow quickly as well, largely due to Dr. Dehoney's passionate and relevant preaching. In fact, his fearless preaching on subjects from which other preachers would shrink garnered Dehoney a national reputation. Between February and March of 1961, he preached such sermons as "Weighed and Wanting: Immorality in the Home," "Bad Boys and Delinquent Daughters," and "A Faith for the Space Age."[5]

His clarion voice was not lost on Broadman Press, and soon, such books as *Challenges to the Cross*, *Set the Church Afire!*, *Dragon and the Lamb*, *Homemade Happiness*, and *Disciples in Uniform* would come from his pen.[6] By the mid 1960s,

Dr. W. Wayne Dehoney was more than just a pastor in southwestern Tennessee. He was a national spokesman for revival among Southern Baptists.

At the 1964 Convention meeting in Atlantic City, New Jersey, Dehoney was elected to the first of two terms as president of the Southern Baptist Convention. At the age of forty-seven, he was one of the youngest presidents ever elected. As with all his ministerial endeavors, Dehoney worked incessantly in his service to the Convention. In addition to his pastoral work and his writing, Dehoney crossed the country, addressing evangelistic conferences, State Conventions, and ministerial meetings, including the Texas Baptist Evangelism Conference[7] and the Southern Baptist Religious Education Association.[8]

On May 24, 1966, Dehoney gave his final address as president of the Southern Baptist Convention. Facing more than ten thousand messengers in Detroit, Michigan, Dehoney spoke on "The Living God, at Work in His World." Recounting his journeys representing Southern Baptists, Dehoney called Southern Baptists to a renewed fervor for souls:

> God is not dead in the work of Southern Baptists! He is at work, out yonder at the grassroots in the hearts of our people, and in our churches, and in our State Conventions, and in our campus class-rooms, and in our denominational offices. . . . During these two years as your president I have traveled more than 300,000 miles. I have met with thousands of fellow Baptists. . . . We have caught a fresh vision of a lost world. . . . This very Convention is to be the launching pad. Right here in Detroit on Friday night we shall officially begin the Crusade of the Americas that will involve more nations and more churches and more people than any other organized evangelistic undertaking in the history of Christianity![9]

Approaching the age of fifty, Dehoney once again embarked on a new task of evangelistic endeavor. In February 1967, he accepted the call to Walnut Street Baptist Church in Louisville, Kentucky. Beginning an eighteen-year ministry at this strategic church, Dehoney sought to move the membership into "outreach for the unreached" through creative ministries. The results were nothing less than astonishing.

In 1970, the church built a Christian Activities Building, which included a gym, a skating rink, a racquetball court, and six bowling lanes. The building became a home to thousands of inner-city youth. This was a generation before churches would regularly implement such ministries. Dehoney was once again an innovator.

One of the most unique ministries of the church began in 1972. Dehoney led Walnut Street to build an eighteen-story apartment building for the elderly, called the Baptist Towers. In 1984, they followed up with the Treyton Oak Towers, a life-care facility for more than two hundred senior adults. All the while, Walnut Street continued to grow exponentially, and the television ministry of the church became the prototype followed by many churches around the nation.

By the time of Dehoney's retirement from the active pastorate in 1985, Walnut Street Baptist was Kentucky's largest congregation, with more than sixty-three hundred members. In fact, his "retirement" was actually more of a transition. Few people have worked harder in retirement than Wayne Dehoney.

Having led hundreds of trips around the world for churches on mission, Dehoney worked with the Baptist World Alliance and Dr. Nilson Fanini to enable hundreds of churches and thousands of Christians to travel to the mission field.[10] He has published extensively on the spiritual implications and archaeology of the Holy Land. He has continued to travel the world, often preaching crusades and conducting hunting trips. His hunting has brought him into the rare circle of those who have gotten the "big five."[11] He served as senior professor of preaching and evangelism at his alma mater, Southern Seminary. His beloved wife, Lealice, recently served on the board of trustees at Union University, where she graduated after returning to her studies in the fifties. Together they have enjoyed almost sixty years of ministry and now have the added pleasure of four grandchildren and two great-grandchildren.[12] He has also continued writing, adding to the fifteen books he has authored.

For over sixty years, Dr. Wayne Dehoney has continued to call Southern Baptists to innovative evangelism and mission fervor, literally around the world.

34

HENRY FRANKLIN PASCHALL

May 12, 1922—
Elected: 1966, 1967

*T*he year was 1968, and the nation's headlines demonstrated the cultural revolution surging within the heartland of America. War was raging in Vietnam while racial tensions were rumbling on American streets. Southern Baptists, meeting in Houston, Texas, were squarely in the middle of the most controversial topics of the day. As H. Franklin Paschall, the president of the Convention, stepped to the podium, he recognized that his address to the Southern Baptist Convention came at a crucial time to Baptists and the nation. He spoke as a prophet:

So evangelism and ethics go together. It is mandatory that man be personally converted, changed, and that this changed man work for righteousness and social progress in all of his relationships. We must not be so committed to social action as to think that personal conversion is unimportant. And we must not be so committed to personal conversion as to forget the importance of good works in the Christian life.

Many of our critical problems today stem from the age old problem of racial enmity. The tragic events in recent days surely convince us of the frightening proportions of race problems in our country. In Biblical times there was cruel enmity between Jews and gentiles. . . . Hatred of the Jews has continued throughout history. Today there is enmity between whites and blacks.

Ours is an anti-intellectual age. We have made ideas secondary to appetites, passions, prejudices and habits. This persuasion gained momentum with Darwin if it did not begin with him. . . . Freud joined in the apostasy. He contended that man's actions are automatic responses to his unconscious or subconscious needs. . . .
Existentialism also shares in the blame. It puts primary emphasis on

the present. . . . The gospel is the grandest idea ever to dawn on man's mind. It tells man that he came from God, that he was made in the image of God and that though ruined by sin he can be redeemed by the grace of God and receive forgiveness and begin a new life in Christ.[1]

Paschall stood boldly at a time when Southern Baptists needed a man with a prophet's voice and a pastor's heart. Under the leadership of the Nashville pastor, Southern Baptists moved forward with a resolution on racial reconciliation while attempting to halt the detrimental secularism infecting the pews from the likes of Freudianism and existentialism. In the center of any solution lay the gospel of Jesus Christ, without which there was no hope.

Henry Franklin Paschall was born on May, 12, 1922, in Hazel, Kentucky, to Cletus and Eva Paschall. His father was a strong disciplinarian who immersed himself in the Scripture. His mother was a devout Christian of whom he testified, "She may be the best Christian I have known."[2] The family faithfully attended the Oak Grove Missionary Baptist Church, three miles from the Paschall home, where, at the age of fourteen, Franklin attended the customary revival services at the Oak Grove church. After careful consideration about the decision, Paschall proclaimed his faith in Christ and was baptized in an outdoor pool used by several churches in the area.

During his senior year in high school, Paschall sensed that God was calling him into the ministry. After counsel by his father, Franklin matriculated at Union University, in Jackson, Tennessee, a struggling Southern Baptist college dedicated to equipping ministers. In an era of part-time churches, Franklin was quickly sought after by more than one church. In fact, at one time he was serving three different churches, two quarter-time and one half-time.

In 1944, Paschall graduated from Union University. During his senior year he began to court Olga Bailey, who was also a member of the Hazel Baptist Church where he was pastor. Worried about the delicate situation, the couple was married in a private ceremony attended by only a few relatives not including any parents. Olga provided her husband and family with a godly example. Her daughter Sandra recalled:

> She was the ideal pastor's wife. She put God first, her husband second, her daughters third, others fourth, and herself last. She gave everyone as much attention as she was able. One of her most significant activities was the Woman's Missionary Union. . . . Mother provided an atmosphere . . . which freed Daddy from all the frustrations and tedium of daily life. Without doubt, she enabled him to enter sermon preparation, preaching, or other pastoral responsibilities with his mind and spirit unencumbered. With his exceptional talents Daddy would have done well. He far exceeded what he would have been because of her.[3]

Olga allowed her husband to excel spiritually and academically. In fact, in 1949, Paschall received his bachelor of divinity degree at Southern Seminary. All along he remained pastor of the Hazel Baptist Church, though much of his work was delegated to laypeople willing to sacrifice their time and energies in order to keep their beloved preacher.

In 1951, First Baptist Church of Bowling Green, Kentucky, called Paschall as their pastor without even hearing a trial sermon. The second largest church in the Kentucky Baptist Convention, the church had a rich heritage which they believed their new pastor could expand. During his four-year tenure, Paschall led the church to plant several mission churches, grew the church membership to thirty-two hundred, and served as president of the Executive Committee of the Kentucky Baptist Convention.

In 1955, Paschall left Kentucky for the pastorate of First Baptist Church of Nashville, Tennessee. Though he knew God was leading him into the new position, he recognized his ministry was changing from a regional ministry to a national one. Joking about his move a decade later during a sermon at the Nashville church, Paschall illustrated his love for the Bluegrass State. He maintained that Daniel Boone had set up a sign that stated, "Follow Me North." He then explained, "Those who came after him who could read went north into Kentucky. Those who couldn't read ended up in Tennessee."[4] In the years that followed, his relationship with the Nashville church grew to be as strong as his love affair with the churches in western Kentucky.

First Baptist Church, already with a rich heritage, became recognized as having one of the largest Sunday school programs in the nation. In 1970, the church built a new auditorium, with Billy Graham preaching the dedication sermon.

Though Paschall's administrative skills were proficient, his preaching set him apart. In his sermon, "The Gospel for Our Time," he justified his use of expository preaching: "Let God speak to us through every part of Scripture—prophecy, poetry, parable, philosophy, history, signs and symbols, types and shadows—until the light of the glorious gospel of Christ, who is the image of God, shines unto us. Scripture is the fixed fulcrum, and faith is the long lever."[5]

Of the doctrines which endeared him most, the study of the church was the passion of his life. Paschall's work, *Identity Crisis of the Church*, solidified his belief in the local assembly as the primary vehicle from which God works. Furthermore, he believed the Baptist church was modeled from the New Testament church, and therefore "has always existed." This belief in Baptist distinctives repudiated the cultural phenomenon of ecumenism that was sweeping mainline Protestant denominations. In fact, as president of the Southern Baptist Convention, he asserted to reporters, "I do not favor an organization or ecclesiastical union of the churches. A federated church or counterpart to Rome is not the solution to our problems."[6] Instead, the answer was found in following the New Testament pattern of the church which included believer's baptism, faithful preaching and prayer, true worship, and bold witnessing.

In 1966, when the Southern Baptist Convention was meeting in Detroit, Paschall won in a runoff election against ten other candidates. Many believe he was elected as a candidate who was conservative yet could unify a Convention struggling with controversy from the inside and cultural decay from the outside. During his two-year term, Paschall spent much time speaking to congregations across the nation and around the world. In 1967, Southern Baptists asked Paschall to respond to the escalating war in Vietnam. Though most Southern Baptists supported the war to free the Vietnamese from Communism, resolutions backing the efforts of American servicemen failed. By the end of his administration, it was clear that Paschall did not believe his position allowed him to make policy or push his influence; rather, he considered his job as a moderator, keeping the peace, resolving denominational conflict, and advocating harmony among the brethren.

In 1983, Paschall announced his retirement from First Baptist Church of Nashville, but he remained involved in the denomination during the height of the controversy between conservatives and moderates. Paschall was one of the sponsors of a resolution that created the Peace Committee. In 1989, Paschall proposed that Jerry Vines, pastor of First Baptist Church of Jacksonville, Florida, be reelected without opposition if the conservatives agreed not to oppose a moderate candidate the following year.

Franklin Paschall is now advanced in years and travels little because of health conditions. Instead, he remains a faithful member to the church he served as pastor for nearly forty years. Albert W. Wardin Jr., author of the definitive biography of Paschall, *God's Chosen Path*, pays tribute to Paschall:

> God gave him many gifts—radiant personality, keen mind, good memory, love of learning, strong work ethic, and loving family relations—all of which he utilized and even enhanced for the Lord's work. He left his mark on the Southern Baptist Convention as one of its finest pulpiteers, administrators, and denominational statesmen. Truly he had followed God's chosen path.[7]

35

WALLIE AMOS CRISWELL

December 19, 1909—January 10, 2002
Elected: 1968, 1969

𝒯ollowing a "theme interpretation" during the 1994 Southern Baptist Convention meeting in Orlando, Florida, an elderly woman was recognized by the chair during the business session. "I would like to make the motion," the woman began slowly, "that the previous speaker, Dr. W. A. Criswell, be elected . . . Pastor of the Southern Baptist Convention."

The crowd, some twenty thousand strong, rose in an approving murmur, but according to autonomous Baptist polity, the motion was denied. Baptists do not have a bishopric which would allow such a vaulted position, but if ever there was a Southern Baptist who could have been called the Protestant Pope, it was Dr. W. A. Criswell, the venerable pastor of the First Baptist Church of Dallas, Texas.

Such was the influence of Criswell. By the time of his death in early 2002, he was the subject of countless books, articles, dissertations, and studies. Biographies continue to be published, and examinations of his innovative ecclesiology continue to tell the story. Few Southern Baptist Convention presidents have been so scrutinized as W. A. Criswell. A cursory examination reveals eleven tomes and countless articles, variously covering his life, preaching, or ministry.[1] Yet for many, Criswell remains an enigma of immense evangelical influence.

Born in Eldorado, Oklahoma, in 1909, W. A. Criswell was the son of Wallie Amos and Anna Currie Criswell. His father, who worked as a farmer, never called his son anything but "W. A.," but in later years his son would take his paternal name of "Wallie Amos."[2] With the horrific advent of the drought of the first decades of the twentieth century, the once fertile land in Oklahoma became barren, so the family moved to Texline, Texas, in the far corner of Texas, at the crossroads of Oklahoma, Texas, and New Mexico. The elder Criswell opened a barbershop in Texline, and the family began to attend the local Baptist church.

Converted in a revival service in 1919, W. A. Criswell admits that there was never a time when he did not believe he was called to be a preacher and a pastor. Illustrating this, Porter Routh tells the amusing story of twelve-year-old Criswell officiating the funeral service for a beloved dog.[3] In the Baptist church at Texline, Pastor L. S. Hill appointed young Criswell to his first ministerial position, leader of the BYPU.

In 1925, under the watchful eye of his mother, the sixteen-year-old Criswell moved one hundred and twenty miles southeast to Amarillo to attend high school and became a member of the First Baptist Church of Amarillo. Dr. G. L. Yates (1878–1936), the beloved leader of churches in McKinney, Texas; Macon, Georgia; and Decatur, Georgia, was the pastor.[4] Under Yates's mentoring and leadership, Criswell flourished. The young Criswell was licensed to the ministry in 1929 and ordained by First Baptist Amarillo a year later.

Moving another four hundred miles east to Waco to begin his undergraduate work at Baylor University, Criswell also pastored three churches in Marlow, Pulltight, and Mound, Texas. After graduating from Baylor in 1931, he once again moved to Louisville, Kentucky, where he completed two degrees, his master of theology in 1934 and his doctor of philosophy in 1937.[5]

While a graduate student at Southern Seminary, Criswell led two half-time churches, in Oakland and Mount Washington, Kentucky. Routh notes:

> The attractive pianist at the Mount Washington Church was Miss
> Betty Harris. But she was not to be Miss Betty Harris for long. After a
> fast and furious courtship, which was the talk of the seminary campus,
> the pianist became Mrs. W. (A). Criswell.[6]

After receiving his doctorate from Southern Seminary, Criswell moved to Chickasha, Oklahoma, to assume the pastorate of the First Baptist Church. While at First Chickasha, the Criswells were blessed with the birth of their only child, Mabel Ann.

In 1941, Criswell accepted the call of the First Baptist Church of Muskogee, Oklahoma. While in Muskogee, Criswell would later recount, he would come to two decisions that would mark his ministry. First, he became an expository preacher rather than depend on a more topical style; and second, he became convinced of a premillenial eschatology.[7]

The death of Dr. George W. Truett on July 7, 1944, marked a touchstone moment in the life of W. A. Criswell. Happily pastoring in Oklahoma, Criswell was unaware of the machinations happening behind the scenes of the Baptist world. A select number of Baptist leaders suggested the Oklahoma pastor to the pulpit search committee. Yet the task of succeeding Truett was daunting. Criswell was not only an admirer of Dr. Truett; he viewed him as the quintessential Baptist statesman. Few Baptist leaders felt that anyone could follow Dr. Truett without miserable failure. Yet on October 1, 1944, Dr. W. A. Criswell mounted the platform in the hushed church and assumed the pastorate of the First Baptist Church of Dallas, Texas.

The contrast between Truett and Criswell could not have been more defined. Truett was staid and dignified in the pulpit; Criswell was often given to moments of epiphanous emotions and tears. Truett rarely raised his voice above an even speech pattern; Criswell often yelled and shouted. The spectators of Baptist life did not see a bright future for either the church or the thirty-five-year-old pastor. As Patterson writes:

> But as Criswell would say, "The lugubrious prognostications" of his inevitable failure at First Dallas proved erroneous. For the next fifty years Criswell would hold court four times weekly, preaching to a church that burgeoned to twenty-six thousand members with more than six thousand regularly in attendance. More than fifty books would come from his pen, and he would travel the ends of the earth preaching.[8]

During the next two decades, Dr. Criswell led the church on the corner of Ervay and San Jacinto to new heights. In the process he developed quite a reputation as both a pastor and a preacher. His books, which would eventually number fifty-four, became almost required reading for pastors.[9] In 1968, at the annual Convention meeting in Houston, Texas, Criswell was nominated for president, together with Gerald Martin of Tennessee and C. Owen Cooper of Mississippi. Cooper withdrew his name for nomination, and Criswell was elected.[10]

W. A. Criswell presided over the Southern Baptist Convention during one of the most tumultuous times in American history. The Vietnam War heightened the cultural wars that crossed televisions nightly. The issue of segregation in society and church caused church splits and fights across denominational lines. Nowhere did the implications of theology and segregation seem more germane than in the largest Protestant denomination in the world. Into that fray stepped the pastor of a traditional, mostly Anglo church in the center of Dallas, Texas. As Criswell preached the annual Convention message in New Orleans in 1969, he spoke forcefully:

> Charles G. Finney, who had last century's greatest revival, was the most outspoken preacher of his days against slavery. Charles H. Spurgeon sought to alleviate the plight of the helpless poor in industrial England. Dwight L. Moody in America and F. B. Meyer in England were the champions of homeless children. . . . Nor has the record of our Southern Baptist Convention been any different. Our messengers in assembled convocation have spoken out time and again concerning the social and political issues of the day. We have forcefully and emphatically voiced our convictions concerning war and peace, disarmament, human rights and liberties, race, poverty and crime. . . . We are not to cower before the world and the onslaughts of

Satan as though we were craven slaves. We are to press the battle against the enemies of God and of mankind. . . . Christ expects His gospel to march, go, move, conquer, attack.[11]

In the context of that day, this was an unbelievably courageous sermon. Churches in the South were fighting the addition of black converts into membership, and no one in the Convention expected the president to address these things. He could have stayed safely off the topic. Not only did Criswell call the churches of the Southern Baptist Convention to allow anyone regardless of race or background into their churches; he did so in his own pulpit at First Baptist Dallas.

Amazingly, it was not his stance against theological segregation that caused the largest furor at the Southern Baptist Convention. The publication of his book, *Why I Preach the Bible Is Literally True*, which had been published by Broadman Press in January of that year, caused theological faculties throughout the Convention to speak out against his "fundamentalist" leanings of inerrancy.[12]

In the thirty years following his tenure as president of the Southern Baptist Convention, Criswell continued to rise to almost mythic proportions in Convention life. The church membership grew in Dallas, and The Criswell College came to bear his imprint of expository preaching, mission activity, and fervent evangelism. At his death on January 10, 2002, Criswell had literally seen his legacy extend before his very eyes. At the memorial service held at the historic church, Senior Pastor Dr. D. McCall Brunson shared a poignant story:

> My last real conversation with the preacher was two weeks ago. He was on some medication for the pain. His mind was clouded just a little, that great mind that was always so amazingly clear. I walked into the room. . . . It was obvious that he did not know who I was, but with all the strength and all the vitality of life, he looked up at me, and took my hand and he said, "Oh? Are you here for the revival?" I said, "Preacher, I pray so." You see, here was a man in the last days of his life, his mind clouded by medication. Yet his mind had been so saturated down through the years with the things of God that on his heart was the fact that he wanted God to bring revival to his people. That was W. A. Criswell.[13]

He was the author of more than fifty books and the subject of hundreds of others. He remained as the pastor of one church for almost sixty years but was multiplied many times over by pastoral students who covered the globe. Many have considered him the "Protestant Pope."

36
CARL E.
BATES

September 5, 1914–December 21, 1999
Elected: 1970, 1971

"*I* am just a pastor."

For most Southern Baptist preachers, this is the definitive statement of mission and purpose. In the final analysis of ministerial endeavor, serving as a pastor is the highest calling and most honorable service. Yet for one just elected as president of the largest Protestant denomination in America, it is even more striking. In a moment when the lofty accomplishment might become addictive, it bespeaks one who is undeniably centered.

Yet this was the exact statement of Dr. Carl E. Bates in June 1970. Having been chosen over four other worthy candidates, Bates spoke to reporters briefly after the vote. Morris Chapman would later remember:

> I was a young preacher when Dr. Bates was elected president of
> our Convention. In response to a probing question asked during his
> post-election interview, Bro. Bates said, "I am but a pastor." I believe it
> expressed both the humility of his spirit and the joy he felt at serving
> in that high calling. I took him to mean that in spite of all the honor
> associated with being elected president, there was no higher honor
> than to be called "pastor."[1]

This was the heart of the pastor, professor, and denominational statesman.

Carl E. Bates was born on a farm in Amite County, outside of Liberty, Mississippi, on September 5, 1914. Though raised in the Christian home of R. E. Bates, Carl was not converted and baptized until he was in college, at nineteen years old, at the First Baptist Church of Summit, Mississippi. After attending Southwest Mississippi Junior College in Summit, Bates surrendered to the gospel ministry and transferred to Mississippi College in Clinton.

In 1937, Bates entered Southern Baptist Theological Seminary to pursue his graduate degree. While finishing at Southern, Bates served as pastor of Central

Baptist Church in Winchester, Kentucky, where he continued after graduation. On November 15, 1939, he married Myra Mae Gray of Tupelo, Mississippi. He graduated from Southern in 1941 but would return four decades later to pour into the next generations of students as he had received. For the next six years, he served churches in Mississippi and Florida. He would later be awarded honorary doctorates from Mississippi College, Judson College, Wake Forest University, and Baylor University.

From 1947 to 1950, Bates served as pastor of the First Baptist Church of Texarkana, Texas. During this period Bates's renown grew as his heartfelt preaching attracted the attention of Texas Baptists. He continued his work in the denomination on the board of trustees for Wayland College and on the executive committee of the Southern Baptist Convention.

In June 1950, Bates was called to the momentous First Baptist Church of Amarillo, Texas. Started in 1889, First Baptist Amarillo had a tremendous history. Beginning in 1936, a series of three pulpit giants served as pastor.

Dr. J. Howard Williams guided the church from 1936–1940, leading it to develop the largest Baptist Training Union . . . in the Southern Baptist Convention. He later became the president of the Southwestern Baptist Theological Seminary. Dr. Williams was followed by A. D. Foreman (1941–1949) and Carl Bates (1950–1959). During this period the church grew beyond 6,000 in membership.[2]

In his first year as pastor, Bates and the church saw a remarkable move of God. From the summer of 1950 to the summer of 1951, 962 people joined the church, including 379 for baptism. It was an astonishing period of growth, which also included the church's purchasing homes and lots surrounding the church. At the completion of his eight-year term of service at Amarillo, Bates was elected president of the Baptist General Convention of Texas. He served only a portion of his one-year assignment, however, resigning from the church in June 1959 to accept the call to the First Baptist Church of Charlotte, North Carolina.

At First Baptist Charlotte Bates would become a national voice for evangelicals. Almost immediately, Bates was also in demand as a leader in the SBC. He was elected president of the Pastors Conference in 1961. In the summer of 1963, Bates served on the committee that helped frame the *Baptist Faith and Message*. From 1966 to 1968, he served as president of the State Convention in North Carolina. He preached at the SBC Pastors Conference in May 1966 and spoke during the annual Southern Baptist Convention meetings in 1967.

At the Convention meeting in 1970 in Denver, Colorado, Bates was elected on the first ballot and was unopposed in his second term at St. Louis in 1971. It would not, however, be the last time a Bates served on the national Convention stage. From 1976 to 1978, Bates's wife, Myra, served as a vice president of the Southern Baptist Convention, making them the only husband and wife combination ever to serve as Southern Baptist officers.[3]

In his presidential address in Philadelphia on June 6, 1972, Bates proved why he had been so effective as a pastor of growing churches when he gently rebuked those who desired to reinvent the biblical model for evangelism:

I believe we stand upon the threshold of our greatest era. Every organization of our Convention is earnestly engaged in honest effort to serve our people. It is my feeling, however, that the Evangelism Division of our Home Mission Board has brought us back to an approach that is calculated to literally transform the spirit of our churches. For thirty years I have been amused by those who periodically rediscovered Arthur Flake's *Building a Standard Sunday School* and either rewrote and published it or rushed into Convention circles crying, "Eureka!" But [our evangelistic effort] . . . is that house-to-house, person-to-person, day-by-day plan of the New Testament that kept a song in their hearts when their only meetinghouse was a cemetery and their only prospect early martyrdom if they remained faithful.[4]

Following his two terms as president, Bates returned to his pastorate in Charlotte and continued to speak to Baptists throughout the nation. During the summer of 1973, Dr. Bates preached thirteen sermons on *The Baptist Hour* on 418 stations across thirty-five states. In 1977, his advice to young pastors on preaching was published as a series of tapes by Broadman Press.[5] His mentoring of countless young ministers would expand exponentially in days to come.

In 1980, as Bates entered his fifth decade of pastoral ministry, most would assume he would be in the twilight of his years. Yet in 1980, Bates began what was arguably the greatest period of his ministry. He resigned from his twenty-two-year pastorate in Charlotte and became senior professor of pastoral ministries and preaching at his alma mater, Southern Seminary.

At the age of sixty-seven, Bates's voice was still vibrant and strong. For the next five years, he taught the young ministerial students in classroom lectures, chapel messages, and faculty forums.[6] Even following his retirement in 1985, Bates continued to preach well into his seventies. On April 12, 1988, he preached at Southern Seminary's chapel on "Fulfilling the Ministry Which God Has Given You." His final recorded addresses at the seminary were preached at the First Annual Pastors School, including sermons entitled "Withering Gourds in a Dying World," "The Cross in My Church," and the poignant sermon "I Bequeath to My Grandsons."

In 1982, Southern Seminary endowed the Carl E. Bates Chair of Preaching. The chair has been held by such scholars as Kenneth Chafin, Charles B. Bugg, Robert Smith Jr., and Mark A. Howell. In addition, upon his retirement, a dormitory at the Fruitland Baptist Bible Institute was named for Bates.

Following Carl's retirement, he and his wife moved to Asheville, North Carolina, and joined the First Baptist Church. In November 1999, Bates was diagnosed with cancer, and on December 21, he succumbed to the terminal disease. On the eve of the funeral service, his successor at First Baptist Amarillo, Dr.

Winfred Moore eulogized, "He was the best pulpiteer. . . . He was one of the greatest preachers of the Southern Baptist Convention. People in Amarillo still talk about his preaching."[7] Forty years removed from that church, and his legacy continued.

37
OWEN
COOPER

April 19, 1908—November 9, 1986
Elected: 1973, 1974

It all began with a fertilizer plant. Owen Cooper, president of Mississippi Chemical Corporation in Yazoo City, dreamed of helping the Indian people arise out of their poverty and meet the needs of the growing population on the Asian subcontinent. Indeed, India at the time received more subsidies from the United States than any other nation in the world, and Cooper knew this charity could not continue indefinitely. He convinced the company's board of directors to put up the $300,000 needed to begin a study into the feasibility of this project.

India became the benefactor of the largest fertilizer plant in the world. In fact, it generated so much assistance to the farmers that the Indian government built another plant that eclipsed the first. Through the vision and ingenuity of Cooper, India succeeded in becoming largely self-sufficient. Yet, far more important than the physical needs of the Indians, Cooper had also opened an avenue to mission work with the people. The Foreign Mission Board of the Southern Baptist Convention was only permitted to send missionaries into the nation if they could help meet the physical needs of Indians. Now the plant served not only as a corporate headquarters but also as a missionary center. Don McGregor, longtime friend of Cooper, elucidated on the new opportunities:

> The Foreign Mission Board began to pick up the salaries of the
> Indian evangelists. And, at Cooper's insistence, they began to send
> itinerant missionaries into the country for three-month visits to super-
> vise the work. There are hundreds of Baptist churches in India today
> because of the foresight and insistence of Owen Cooper. It all began
> with a fertilizer plant.[1]

To his closest friends, Cooper was a missionary after the like of the apostle Paul. Though he supported himself through his own innovation, his true concern was with the advancement of the kingdom of God.

Owen Cooper was born on April 19, 1908, in Warren County, Mississippi, to William and Malena Cooper. Growing up on a dairy farm gave Owen the knowledge he needed to pursue a career in agriculture. In 1929, Cooper graduated from Mississippi State University with a bachelor's degree in agriculture. Cooper, desiring to balance his education, furthered his education and received a master's degree in economics and political science from the University of Mississippi and a law degree from the Jackson School of Law (now Mississippi College School of Law). All degrees would serve Cooper in the years to come, both in the political arena and in the religious field.

Those college years illustrated plainly Cooper's leadership and love for his denomination, serving as president of the Baptist Student Union for one year. Moreover, the BSU held special meaning to Cooper, for it was through a Union Convention in Jackson, Mississippi, that Cooper met his future wife, Elizabeth Thompson. Cooper knew from the start that she was the woman for him. After their first encounter, Cooper remarked to his secretary, "I've just met the lady I am going to marry." On September 2, 1938, after only a few months of courtship, they began a relationship that would span nearly half a century.

In 1939, shortly after graduation, Cooper was appointed executive director of the Mississippi Farm Bureau Federation. Cooper soon envisioned a farmer-owned cooperative that would become the Mississippi Chemical Corporation. Cooper became its first and only president until his retirement in 1973. During his tenure, the company became the largest business ever chartered in Mississippi.

Cooper wanted to succeed in his secular affairs for one purpose: to support and participate in any cause he believed advanced the kingdom of God. Therefore, he served on numerous boards, agencies, and organizations, believing it was time for the laypeople of the Convention to stand up and lead Southern Baptists into new growth. The following list, found in an article published by the *Baptist Record*, the official paper of Mississippi (Southern) Baptists, lists some accomplishments of Cooper during his lifetime:

Local

- Deacon at First Baptist Church, Jackson, Mississippi
- Director of Sunday school and Church Training at First Baptist, Yazoo City, Mississippi
- Moderator of his association in Yazoo City, Mississippi
- Baptist Student Union director at Millsaps and Belhaven colleges

State

- President of the Mississippi Baptist Convention
- Chairman of the Christian Education Commission of Mississippi Convention
- Trustee of the Mississippi Baptist Hospital

- President of the state Sunday school organization

National
- Member of the executive committee of the SBC for twenty-one years
- Trustee at New Orleans Baptist Theological Seminary
- Member of the board of the Southern Baptist Foundation

International
- Vice president for the Baptist World Alliance
- Secretary of the men's department of the Baptist World Alliance
- President of the Pan American Union of Baptist Men[2]

When asked if there was any office in Southern Baptist circles that he had not filled, he replied, "I've never been an officer in the Woman's Missionary Union."

Cooper found inspiration in laying the groundwork for others to lead in the cause of Christ. Though he spent most of his adult years within the state of Mississippi, his greatest passion seemed to be for the people of India and their impoverished physical and spiritual condition. Cooper not only built a fertilizer plant that made the Indian people self-sufficient, but he also convinced the Foreign Mission Board to support the national pastors with its resources. Though the opposition was great, his persistence won out. He explained his motive for the enormous task: "I could not honestly feel comfortable seeing the work started by William Carey possibly die for want of $300 a month support."[3]

In 1972, the growing admiration for Cooper led to his ascension to Southern Baptist Convention president. Appropriately, it was fellow church member and renowned comedian Jerry Clower who nominated him for the post. He jokingly testified:

He didn't come up here to Philadelphia in no watermelon truck.
He had held every office there is for a layman to hold in his local
church. He doesn't go around talking about church. He's involved. He
was in B.Y.P.U. He was in Training Union. He is in Church Training;
and if they had voted for Quest, he would be in that.[4]

Cooper did not waste any time in pleading to Baptist laypeople of the desperate need for their involvement in mission work. During his Convention sermon, Cooper explained to the messengers:

We must recognize that the task of winning the world for Christ
cannot be done by "paid" persons alone. Their efforts and their leadership must be supplemented by an increasing number of committed lay
people who are willing, able, and eager to share their faith.[5]

In 1973, Cooper retired from Mississippi Chemical Corporation. By the end of his life, he had spoken in churches in every state as well as on every continent. He had visited mission churches in forty countries around the globe and led mission trips at home in places including Montana, California, and Ohio. In 1985, the Mississippi Baptist Convention awarded Cooper the title "Layman of the Century." The next year, on November 8, he succumbed to cancer. The citation given to Cooper for his service represents well his influence:

> Scarcely a country exists that he has not touched, for the better, spiritually and physically. . . . His vision, his compassion, and his faith are extraordinary. He picks up dreams and makes them realities. He sees no impossibility, because he knows God.[6]

38
JAROY
WEBER

December 27, 1921–February 6, 1985
Elected: 1974, 1975

$\mathscr{I}$n the late winter of 1985, state papers throughout the Southern Baptist Convention ran a brief obituary. Beneath the scant five paragraphs lay the testimony of a man who had not only given over four decades to the preaching of the gospel ministry but had also dedicated himself to the evangelism and mission vision of the Southern Baptist Convention. Dr. Jaroy Weber was more than just a Baptist preacher and denominational leader; he was a statesman and a gracious Christian gentleman.

Born in 1921 in Shirley, Louisiana, Weber was raised in a Christian home. His father, Edward Weber, was an active layman in St. Landry Baptist Church and sent his son to the Acadia Baptist Academy. He was converted in his early teen years, and by the time he was in high school, he had surrendered to the ministry. Rather than immediately entering college, Weber felt led to leave his home state and travel to Texas, to become a pastor.

The period of the fall of 1938 to the winter of 1939 was eventful for Jaroy Weber. At the age of seventeen, he became one of the youngest full-time pastors in Texas, as he accepted the pastorate of the Little Cypress Baptist Church in November 1938. On February 17, 1939, he married his sweetheart, Nettie Wiggins of Beaumont, Texas. That same year he was ordained by his home church, St. Landry Baptist Church, and in July 1939, he accepted the call to the North Orange Baptist Church. *The Baptist Standard* recorded:

[North Orange Baptist Church] was organized [in 1939], and
under the leadership of Brother Weber, began to grow very rapidly.
During this time [1939–1942] the pastor has led the church in building an auditorium, education building and pastorate, all of which has been paid for and the church is free of debt. The present membership is 500, with 450 enrolled in Sunday School and 150 in B.T.U. At the

age of 21, Brother Weber is one of Texas' leading young pastors. He is doing a very fine work in Orange.[1]

This partnership between pastor and people would see a remarkable work of God. Though he was barely out of his teens, Weber's passionate preaching and visionary leadership pressed this embryonic church to unrivaled heights. He remained at North Orange for ten years, and the ministry flourished. In 1940, the membership hovered around 150 but by 1942 had risen to 500 due to numerous revival meetings led by Weber. By the time he left North Orange in 1948, the membership had risen to an astonishing 2,622, with more than 800 enrolled in Sunday school and 325 in BTU.[2]

Resigning from North Orange in 1949, the Webers moved back to his home state of Louisiana when he accepted the pastoral call from First Baptist Church of West Monroe. Not only did Weber become pastor of one of the more prominent churches in Louisiana, but he also committed to complete his education. In 1950, he received his bachelor of arts from Louisiana Baptist College, and he received his bachelor of divinity from Southwestern Baptist Theological Seminary in 1954. It was a difficult time for Weber, as his travels between West Monroe and Fort Worth almost overloaded his schedule. To add to the weight of his calendar, the Webers continued to see their family expand. Their two sons, Jaroy Weber Jr. and Billy, had been born during the Orange pastorate, and in 1950, their daughter Nettie Beth was born.

The West Monroe church was blessed of God during Weber's ten-year service. The church grew from fewer than 4,000 members in 1949 to 4,458 in 1958. Also during this time the Sunday school attendance grew to 2,237. In 1957, Louisiana Baptist College conferred a doctor of divinity degree on him.[3] As Weber continued to lead his church, he was also getting opportunities to expand his influence across the state and denomination. A popular preacher in conferences and Conventions, Weber poured himself into calling Baptists to continuous evangelism through the local church. This tenet of his ministry led to his first denominational position.

On August 22, 1960, Dr. Jaroy Weber resigned from the West Monroe church to become secretary of evangelism for the Louisiana Baptist Convention.[4] Though he would only serve in that capacity for a year, Weber was already seen as a clarion voice for revival among Southern Baptists. At the age of forty, Weber was poised to see the greatest blessings of his ministry.

In 1960, Dr. T. A. Patterson had resigned as pastor from the historic First Baptist Church of Beaumont, Texas. The inimitable Patterson, who would serve as the executive secretary of the Baptist General Convention of Texas, had led that church since 1946, and his fifteen-year tenure had been marked with substantial growth. Now First Beaumont was in a quandary. Who could follow such a giant in the pulpit and the pastorate? The search took some months and was marked with some measure of controversy. In *And God Gave the Increase*, William Estep noted:

A. W. Shannon, chairman of the pulpit committee, brought the recommendation [of Weber], stating, "that the committee feels, without reservation, the hand of the Lord leading them in inviting Dr. Weber to come before the church." Dr. Weber preached at both services on May 21 [1961]. The following Wednesday the church met in a called conference for the purpose of considering the recommendation of the pulpit committee. There was, apparently, considerable opposition to Weber. One member stated that he felt the church was not ready to call a pastor and asked for a delay in issuing an invitation. . . . Another suggested that the vote be taken by secret ballot. Both moves were defeated by a vote of the congregation.[5]

Seated in the balcony during the fracas was the nineteen-year-old son of the former pastor. Paige Patterson had remained in Beaumont to finish his final year of high school and was living at the YMCA. He had heard the disparaging comparisons between the candidate and his father. Dr. Weber, with his flair for communication, had made some grammatical mistakes in his sermon that had displeased some of the more staid members of the church. Recognized by the chair, the young minister mounted the platform to speak, and people assumed he would speak against Weber. Instead Patterson noted that Weber was clearly a man of God, and Patterson believed this was the man God had called to the church. When the vote was finally taken, 369 voted for the report and 157 voted against it.[6]

Weber remained at First Beaumont until 1966, and the five years were marked by revival and growth. The entire sanctuary was remodeled in 1964, and numerous revival meetings saw tremendous results. From March 31 to May 19, 1963, Weber "traveled to Japan where he participated in the New Life Movement."[7] When Weber announced in 1966 that he had accepted the call to another church, First Beaumont unanimously voted to ask him to reconsider. The country preacher and the city church had truly been a blessed union.

From 1966 until 1978, Weber served two churches with distinction. From 1966 to 1972, he was the pastor of the Dauphin Way Baptist Church in Mobile, Alabama, and from 1972 until September 1978, he was pastor of the First Baptist Church of Lubbock. These prestigious churches also saw their pastor become a leader in the Southern Baptist Convention. In 1974, he was one of seven candidates nominated for the presidency. As Naylor writes: "Those nominated were W. O. Vaught, Landrum Leavell, Clifton W. Brannon, Kenneth L. Chafin, Dotson M. Nelson, Jr., Daniel Sotelo, and Jaroy Weber of Texas. After a run-off between Weber and Chafin, Weber was elected."[8]

As the country was preparing to celebrate its bicentennial, the Southern Baptist Convention was also planning to mark the occasion. Through his two terms Weber used the historic event to call Southern Baptists to revival and a renewed fire for souls. In his 1975 presidential address entitled "Let the Bells Ring," he forcefully spoke of both the religious liberty that formed America and the responsibility of the church to address the social concerns in which they were mired.

> We must speak to the social problems of the world but our speaking must be in the context of Biblical Rev[elation] and not from the lips of liberal sociologists, philosophers or theologians. We take our stand upon the principles laid down in scripture and not from the proclamations of unbelievers who propose a cause supported only by their demand for notoriety. The Bible has already spoken directly or by implication to every social problem [that] could ever confront ancient or modern man. "Thus saith the Lord," is adequate guidance for every generation.[9]

Preceding his sermon, Weber's daughter sang a solo, and immediately following his address, the official replica of the Liberty Bell was rung while the messengers stood with prolonged applause.

The following Convention in Norfolk was memorable. It was held just two weeks before the bicentennial. The theme of the Convention was religious liberty, and on June 15, 1976, at 3:00 P.M. President Gerald R. Ford rose to the platform.

> President Weber escorted [President Ford] to the platform while the Convention messengers stood to greet him with applause. . . . At the end of [President Ford's] address, our president again escorted President Ford from the Convention while the messengers stood and applauded as an expression of their appreciation.[10]

On September 27, 1978, after forty years of pastoral ministry and denominational leadership, Jaroy Weber retired from the pastorate. But he did not stop preaching. The fifty-seven-year-old founded and served as president of Church Ministries Association in Dallas and advised churches in areas of pastoral searches. On June 10–16, 1982, he led the Home Missions Conference in Glorieta, New Mexico.

On February 6, 1985, Dr. Weber died in a Dallas hospital of a stroke. Albert McClellan summarized the ministry of this Louisiana country preacher when he said, "Jaroy Weber, affable and understanding, was one of the greatest pastors of his generation."[11]

39
JAMES LENOX SULLIVAN

March 12, 1910–
Elected: 1976

$\mathcal{D}$uring his senior year at Baptist-affiliated Mississippi College, James Sullivan was the captain of the football team. Though a small private college, the team was known for its tenacity and determination to win. The experience of the game taught Sullivan many lessons in life, including integrity and perseverance. In the most memorable instance, Sullivan recalls a game with Mississippi State University which taught him those lessons. His team was winning by the slimmest of margins, one point, when Mississippi State advanced the ball to the opponent's one-yard line. He recalled:

> We held them four consecutive plays to get possession of the ball and punt out. The unbelievable thing was that the safety man caught the ball and ran back to our one-yard line. This means we had to hold them four more consecutive times. I was in the linebacker position on defense. This means that we had to hold them eight consecutive times on defense within the one-yard line! We did so and the final whistle blew before we got opportunity to punt the ball out of the end zone. Nevertheless, we won the game. Of course, there was great rejoicing because ours was a small college playing one of much larger size with bigger men. So much for athletics.[1]

Sullivan acknowledged that his coach, Stanley Robinson, "had a profound influence on my life because of the quality of man that he was."[2] In the years that followed, Sullivan himself was called upon to lead Southern Baptists, a responsibility he assumed with the highest integrity and character.

James Lenox Sullivan was born on March 12, 1910, in Lawrence County, Mississippi. Grateful that he grew up in "the buckle of the Bible belt," Sullivan also recognized that the family name was rich in heritage. His father's legacy is illustrated through the name given to that section of the state, "Sullivan's Hollow."

His mother's side received a land grant from the government as compensation for their military services fighting against the British Crown during the American Revolution.

His parents also reared James to be a devout Christian. His church experiences as a child typify Southern Baptist life. He enrolled in the now-forgotten Sunbeams, which taught children to appreciate mission work, and the Baptist Young People's Union (BYPU). In fact, the pastor of the Tylertown Baptist Church played a significant role in the conversion of young James. Sullivan had heard his pastor preach a poignant sermon he felt was directed at his own needs. That day Sullivan rode his horse to Lover's Mountain where he secluded himself from everyone else. He explained:

> I tied my horse to a nearby tree and spent literal hours in meditation and prayer trying to come to that point of personal decision on my own. The day was drawing to a close. Still I felt that I had not received the answer for which I was questing. If I were to go back to BYPU and church that evening, however, I had to be on my way. So I mounted the horse and was riding home alone. I had gotten in sight of the church when I actually experienced a change of mind, heart, attitude, and feeling. Burden was turned to joy. Doubts were removed by a vibrant faith which has continued with me throughout my years.[3]

That night eleven-year-old James came forward during the invitation and was baptized shortly thereafter.

When Sullivan was seventeen years old, he accepted the call to the ministry. Though he knew God had impressed upon him the call almost simultaneously with his conversion, he waited until the end of his high school years to publicize his decision. In 1928, Sullivan enrolled at Mississippi College, where he received his degree four years later. He emerged as a leader within the college and community. He served as pastor of the Baptist church in Clinton, where the college was located, while also playing linebacker for the football team. Finishing his undergraduate work, Sullivan decided to further his education, matriculating at The Southern Baptist Theological Seminary, where he earned his master of theology degree in 1935.

In 1935, after finishing his education, Sullivan married his childhood sweetheart, Velma Scott. Sullivan testified that the two met in his hometown when she was just one-and-a-half years old. He stated:

> I went home to tell my Mother that there was the prettiest little girl I had even seen up at Mr. Scott's house. I didn't know then who she was, but I liked the way she looked. It turned out that this beautiful young girl who impressed me so at first sight still does. She is my wife and the mother of my three children. In fact, she has been an indispensable helpmeet to me through my years in the gospel ministry. She is the only girl I ever dated, and the only girl with whom I have

ever been in love. I counted that meeting one of the most fortunate days of my life when I met her at a time she was too young to have an opinion about me. She and I never had but five formal dates. The fifth one was the wedding date.[4]

For the next eighteen years, Sullivan served as pastor of churches in Kentucky, Tennessee, and Texas. In 1947, he accepted the pastorate of the Belmont Heights Baptist Church in Nashville, Tennessee. This would begin a lifelong relationship between Sullivan and Tennessee Baptists which was only briefly interrupted when Sullivan served First Baptist Church of Abilene, Texas.

In 1953, Sullivan led the Abilene church in incredible growth and into a million-dollar building campaign. Following encouragement from the likes of W. A. Criswell, Sullivan agreed to succeed T. L. Holcomb as the president of the Baptist Sunday School Board (BSSB; now LifeWay Christian Resources). Sullivan always recognized that his job was to encourage Christians through supplying local churches with the materials needed for the task. In his book *Rope of Sand with Strength of Steel*, he wrote:

> The most important organizational unit of the denomination is the local church. Although the units of organization called associations, statewide bodies usually called State Conventions, and the nationwide Southern Baptist Convention have their places, we cannot overemphasize the importance of a local congregation. The local church is more vital than all other areas combined. It is at the local level that "the water hits the wheel." If work is not done there, it is not done anywhere. If it is done well there, its successes become the denomination's strength.[5]

The accomplishments under his leadership demonstrate Sullivan's desire to assist the local church. In 1954, the Sunday School Board led in the Million More in '54 campaign, attempting to reach a total of one million additional people with the gospel of Christ. Though the goal was not met, the endeavor retains in history the recognition as the largest Sunday school movement of recorded religious history.

However, political and theological controversies were also on the horizon. Politically, racial integration caused much turmoil among the Southern churches. The Sunday School Board became immersed in the *Becoming* episode. *Becoming*, a publication of the board, produced an issue with a cover picturing a black man with two white female college students. Sullivan ordered the issue pulled not because of the depiction but because of visual problems and the age difference, he felt, was too exaggerated among the people on the cover. Though he recommended that younger students of both races be used for the newly revised picture, the national media accused Sullivan of advocating segregation.

Theologically, nothing was more tumultuous than the publication of *The Message of Genesis*, written by Midwestern Baptist Theological Seminary Professor Ralph Elliot. Sullivan believed it was unwise to revise the work, which denied the historicity of the first eleven chapters of Genesis, since "we would have been tampering with curriculum material for a theological school."[6] In the end, the reputation of the BSSB was diminished in many churches, though, in the mind of Sullivan, not permanently scarred. The same resiliency he demonstrated as the captain of the Mississippi College football team aided him in the tough days of Convention controversy.

In 1975, Sullivan retired from the Sunday School Board. In the same year he was honored for his conspicuous leadership, being named one of the vice presidents of the Baptist World Alliance while also serving as chairman of the Division of Evangelism and Education. The next year Southern Baptist Convention messengers paid tribute to Sullivan by electing him president of the Convention, though he could serve for only one term due to ill health.

Dr. Sullivan has preached on every continent and in every region of the United States. Though now more than ninety years old, Sullivan remains active at First Baptist Church of Nashville. On June 12, 2001, he was awarded the M. E. Dodd Award for lifetime achievement for his support of worldwide missions through the Cooperative Program. Always devoutly loyal to Southern Baptists, he is considered one of the premier statesmen of the Southern Baptist Convention. When asked about the incredible changes which have occurred in the culture, Sullivan reminded Christians, "One thing that has not and will not change is the message of the church. As long as we keep the message consistent and the spirit Christ-like, God can use us."[7]

40
JIMMY RAYMOND ALLEN

October 26, 1927–
Elected: 1977, 1978

As Dr. Jimmy R. Allen rose to deliver his first presidential address on June 13, 1978, in Kansas City, his voice rose to a fevered pitch when he described the excruciating existence of mankind, deep in the throes of sin and desperation:

There is a yearning in the land. Out of our confusion created by unkept promises and unfulfilled hopes, there is a hunger of spirit. We are weary of the burden of sin and guilt. We are yearning for meaning in lives which are empty and jaded. The fear of death is often exceeded by the fear of life. The time is right for harvest. The battered and used woman at the well . . . returns from her experience with Jesus to shout to other battered and used people, "See the One who knows all about me and still gives me the refreshing water of life." And they are pouring out of the Samaritan villages of our world . . . hungry to know him.[1]

His words bespoke compassion for the hurting and disenfranchised, and his call to action illustrated his heart for reaching to the most neglected people on the planet. For over seven decades Jimmy Allen has lived his sermonic rhetoric. Few men have ever led churches into the deepest bowels of humanity to share the love of Christ as Jimmy Allen has. Few men have ever empathized so fully with the downtrodden and ignored. And few ministers have experienced such tragedy as this man of God or survived with such joy.

Jimmy Raymond Allen was born on October 26, 1927, in Hope, Arkansas.[2] As the only child of Rev. and Mrs. Earl Allen, he lived most of his formative years in Dallas, Texas, where his father pastored a number of prominent churches. Being raised in a pastor's home often repels the children of the minister, but Jimmy Allen flourished in the environment. Surrendering to the gospel ministry in his youth, Allen entered Howard Payne University in Brownwood, Texas, in 1944, and graduated with his bachelor of arts degree in 1948.

In his senior year at Howard Payne, he met a freshman, Wanda Ruth Massey, who would become the love of his life. Married in 1949, the Allens began a series of pastorates that would eventually lead to a long life of denominational service.

During his college years, Jimmy often led student revival teams from Howard Payne, often preaching in small rural churches around Brownwood. Attaining a reputation as an engaging speaker, Allen was pursued by a number of churches, eventually pastoring Fairview Baptist Church of Evant, Texas, and the Duffau Baptist Church in Hico, Texas. He resigned from Duffau to become the associate pastor of the First Baptist Church of Dublin, Texas.

Following his graduation in 1948, it did not take long for Allen to become a much sought after preacher and leader. The Baptist General Convention of Texas (BGCT) appointed him secretary of the Royal Ambassadors, a position he served from 1948 to 1950. Immediately following his service with the State Convention, Allen accepted his first full-time pastorates, the First Baptist Church of Van Alstyne (1951–1952), and the First Baptist Church of Willis Point (1952–1956). During this time Allen completed his master's degree at Southwestern Seminary in 1958, and the young couple had three sons, Michael Wayne, Stephen Ray (Skip), and Kenneth Scott. Allen would later receive his doctor of theology degree from Southwestern Seminary as well.[3]

Yet his effectiveness in leading churches and pastors would not allow him to serve in this singular capacity for long. In 1960, at the age of thirty-three, Allen was asked again to serve his State Convention. Between 1960 and 1968, Jimmy Allen served as executive secretary of the Christian Life Commission of the BGCT. It certainly was a formidable position for such a young man, but Allen attacked the work with vigor. In his capacity as executive secretary, Allen called Southern Baptists to a deeper sense of worldwide ministry. In 1966, he was asked to serve as a special observer at the United Nations. That same year he wrote one book, *The Menace of Gambling*,[4] and contributed to another, *Peace, Peace*.[5] During his eight years of service, Allen traveled throughout the United States and Europe, speaking in symposiums and conferences on religious and international affairs. He also served on the planning committee for the White House Counsel on Civil Rights.[6]

On January 1, 1968, Allen assumed the pastorate of the nine-thousand-member First Baptist Church of San Antonio, Texas. Since its founding in 1861, historic First Baptist San Antonio had been led by such ministerial luminaries as Charles Roy Angell (1933–1936) and Perry F. Webb (1937–1961).[7]

The move was not without a considerable strain on the family, initially. Wanda Allen shared her stress in an interview following her husband's election to the Southern Baptist presidency. "She spoke candidly . . . including an emotional breakdown she suffered after the Allens moved to San Antonio in 1968."[8] Having recovered after nineteen months, Mrs. Allen spoke of the pressures of returning to the pastorate and the difficulty of readjusting to the rigors of the ministerial fish-bowl. "I never could have come through this without the support of our church friends and my husband. . . . When I was out of touch with God, these people through their concern and prayers, were keeping God in touch with me."[9]

Yet it was this authenticity with the people they served that endeared the Allens to the people of First San Antonio. Dr. Allen called the church to a wider and more involved ministry, and the people responded in an unprecedented fashion. The church established, "a medical clinic, a literacy program, work with internationals, counseling and a program which [fed] . . . as many as 150 people a day."[10] In addition to the social work the church was doing, they also baptized between three hundred and six hundred people a year. By 1978, the work of the church and Dr. Allen had gained national prominence, and he was nominated and elected to the presidency of the Southern Baptist Convention.

On the last day of 1979, Allen resigned as the pastor of the San Antonio church and became the president of the Radio and Television Commission of the Southern Baptist Convention. As a pioneer of religious broadcasting, Allen founded the American Christian Television System (ACTS), which gave local churches access to television broadcasting. In 1988, Allen won an Emmy for the best special program produced on daytime television with "China: Walls and Bridges." He served as host of *Life Today* for eight years.[11]

During this period the Allen family experienced its greatest trials and tragedy. When Allen was interviewed following his election to the presidency of the SBC, he was asked his opinion on a number of controversial subjects, including homosexuality. Singer Anita Bryant had raised the question within Christian circles at the time, and the controversy had become prominent. From his lifelong commitment to working with those considered the "untouchables," Allen noted that he "was on record as upholding 'God's design' of heterosexuality . . . but homosexuals should be viewed with 'concern and compassion' and said homosexuals are ministered to in [First Baptist San Antonio]'s street ministry programs."[12]

Though his words were spoken in 1978, five years before knowledge of the AIDS virus and its impact on both the homosexual and heterosexual communities, Allen spoke with prescience. His own family would be shaken by this horrible disease.

In 1985, his daughter-in-law, Lydia, discovered that she had contracted the HIV virus after receiving a blood transfusion during the birth of her first son, Matthew. Not only was Lydia diagnosed HIV-positive, but also Matthew and her newborn son, Bryan. When her husband, Scott, shared the family crisis with the church at which he was serving on staff, he was fired the next day. The church did not want their children even to attend the Sunday school, for fear of the disease. Scott, Lydia, and the two sons moved in with the Allens in Fort Worth. Three months later Bryan died. Within a few years Lydia and Matthew died. Scott became embittered toward Christianity following their treatment by the church. A short while later the Allen's middle son, Skip, announced that he was homosexual and within a few years was also diagnosed as HIV-positive.

In 1995, Dr. Allen took the courageous step of writing a book entitled *The Burden of a Secret*,[13] which chronicled their struggles and tragedy. Dr. Allen's quintessential openness and genuineness once again sparked Christians to action. Between 1995 and 1999, more than twenty-five hundred churches have started AIDS ministries. Before she died, Lydia and her family helped found Bryan's House, a program designed to meet the needs of HIV-infected children. The Allens have also helped start Lydia's House, another center in southwestern Ohio.[14]

During the 1990s, Dr. Allen became the visiting professional scholar at Vanderbilt University First Amendment Center, and chaplain of the Big Canoe Chapel (1992–2002). While at Vanderbilt, Allen coauthored *Bridging the Gap Between Religion and News Media*, which won the Wilbur Award. In his retirement he serves on the board of trustees for the Freedom Forum First Amendment Center, though at the age of seventy-five, Dr. Allen shows no signs of slowing down. He has preached on reaching the "untouchables" in thousands of churches and assemblies. With his typical clarity and authenticity, Dr. Allen continues to challenge churches to follow the steps of Jesus in reaching those who have been traditionally shunned. As Carolyn Weatherford Crumpler noted: "Dr. Allen has remained sturdy and true through many difficulties . . . and thereby encourages others facing similar tragedies."[15]

41
ADRIAN PIERCE ROGERS

September 9, 1931—
Elected: 1979, 1986, 1987

*S*eminary training could never have prepared Adrian Rogers for the pain he and his wife were about to experience after graduating from New Orleans Baptist Theological Seminary. Called to a church in Ft. Pierce, Florida, the Rogers family included three children: Steve, Gayle, and Philip. In fact, Philip was only two months old when they settled into the new parsonage. That first Mother's Day began as Rogers preached on the blessings of a Christian home. Rogers remembered what happened after that:

Joyce was out in the kitchen preparing our lunch after the service. And I was in the living room reading. Suddenly I heard her distraught voice. "Adrian! Come here quickly! Something is wrong with Philip."
I leaped to my feet. She had our baby boy in her arms. He was not breathing. His face had a blue cast to it.
"What's wrong?" she cried.
"I don't know. You call the hospital and tell them I'm coming."
I put our little boy inside my coat to keep him warm. With eyes blinded by tears, I screeched out of our driveway and sped to the hospital emergency room. "Please help me," I cried to a waiting nurse as I burst through the heavy double entrance doors to the hospital. Kind hands took Philip and rushed him to a nearby room. I knelt outside the emergency room door and prayed for God's mercy, not caring who saw me or what they might think.
After a while, an attending doctor came out of the room and walked over to me. He laid his hand upon my shoulder and shook his head. "He's gone. There was nothing we could do. We tried."
It was one of those sudden "crib deaths."

Joyce was standing in the doorway of our house when I returned alone. The look on my face told the story. Mother's Day had turned into a day of incredible grief and confusion for us. The tragedy was so sudden and so stark. We did the only thing we knew to do. We knelt and called out to the Lord for help.[1]

Nearly forty-five years later, Adrian and Joyce Rogers have ministered to countless parents who have lost young ones. Reminding Christians that suffering is an integral part of the Christian walk, he explains, "And if He has healed you, remember that your scars may be your greatest ministry!"[2]

Adrian Pierce Rogers was born on September 9, 1931, in West Palm Beach, Florida. The third child born to Arden and Rose Rogers, Adrian grew up in the heart of the Great Depression. Though his mother was a Christian, she was private in her faith and did not express her beliefs to her son. Adrian earned the reputation of a troublemaker and school-yard brawler. One evening when Adrian was fourteen years old, someone invited the Rogers family to a revival crusade at the Northwood Baptist Church. That night Arden Rogers stepped out during the invitation and accepted Christ as his Savior. Adrian was convicted himself, and when his father took that step of faith, he too came forward to receive Christ into his life. They were both baptized shortly thereafter.

Still Rogers did not find complete peace. He continued in his old ways of street fighting. Furthermore, though Rogers had made a public profession of faith, he began doubting the validity of his salvation. He admitted that he knew little of this grace he received and was not counseled sufficiently the night of his conversion. After two years of doubting his salvation, Rogers settled it once and for all. He stated:

> I remember stopping one night on the corner of 39th St. and Calvin Avenue in West Palm Beach after I had walked my girlfriend home from church. I stopped and prayed, looked straight up into the sky and I said, "God I don't know whether I am lost and the Holy Spirit has me under conviction, or whether I am saved and the devil is trying to make me doubt it, but I am going to get it settled tonight and once and for all, now and forever, I trust You as my personal Lord and Savior. If I have done it already I still am saved but if I haven't I am saved tonight. I don't look for a sign, I don't ask for feeling; you promised to save me by your grace and I stand in that and that settles it it's done. Thank You." From that time on I have had the assurance and I really believed I was saved when I went forward there. But I got that cleared up and then I began to pray about God's will for my life. [In] my middle year in high school I felt God calling me to preach.[3]

Rogers, sure of his relationship with God, accepted the call to the ministry and began to preach immediately. While in high school Rogers preached his first sermon in the same church where he was saved, baptized, and later on, ordained and married. His first sermon, "I Dare You," used the life of Daniel to charge the congregation to be bold in their witness. The sermon lasted only fifteen minutes, though Rogers felt he had exhausted the entire Bible.

Rogers desired training for the ministry and enrolled in the Southern Baptist-supported Stetson University located in his home state of Florida. The university gave Rogers both a football and ministerial scholarship. But Rogers forsook the football scholarship after his first year and accepted his first pastorate at the First Baptist Church of Fellsmere, Florida, a rural church in a town of six hundred people.

Also during his college years Rogers married his childhood sweetheart, Joyce Lewis Gentry. As he jokingly says, "I met Joyce in the fourth grade but didn't get serious until the sixth grade." Joyce was faithfully by his side during Rogers's most important decisions as an adolescent. She was present when he accepted Christ and was baptized. She was at the Ridgecrest Conference Center in North Carolina when Adrian came forward to accept the call to preach. She was a cheerleader when Adrian played football at Palm Beach High School. In 1951, the two were married.

In 1954, after graduating with his bachelor of arts in religion, Rogers, his wife, and their firstborn, Steve, moved to New Orleans Baptist Theological Seminary, where he received his bachelor of divinity. By the time of his graduation, the Rogers family had two more additions, Gayle and Philip. Sadly, young Philip died before his first birthday, a result of crib death. The Rogers were devastated by the sudden tragedy and leaned completely on the mercies of God. In time they had one more son, David, who is now a missionary in Spain.

In 1964, after faithfully serving the Parkview Baptist Church in Fort Pierce, Florida, for six years, Rogers accepted the invitation to pastor Merritt Island Baptist Church, home of the nation's space center. Over the next eight years, Rogers led the church in enormous growth, increasing the Sunday school from three hundred to nearly two thousand. Rogers was thoroughly content in this ministry, but a persistent pulpit committee from the historic Bellevue Baptist Church, Memphis, Tennessee, led in the past by Baptist stalwarts R. G. Lee and Ramsey Pollard, convinced Rogers to accept their offer to become the new pastor.

In 1972, Rogers began his ministry at Bellevue Baptist Church, a relationship that has now spanned three decades. At the time of his arrival, Bellevue was in a state of decline. The Sunday school had decreased from twenty-seven hundred to less than thirteen hundred. The auditorium, which would seat three thousand, was only half full on Sunday mornings.

The church grew so quickly that Rogers found himself preaching three times each Sunday morning due to the limited capacity of the auditorium. The church relocated to its present four-hundred-acre location and built a new auditorium that was nearly three times as large as the old auditorium. Today Sunday school attendance has reached a historic high of more than ten thousand, with total membership surpassing twenty-eight thousand. Furthermore, Bellevue illustrates love for the lost around the world, giving more than four million dollars annually to missionary causes. Rogers himself has visited a number of countries, including Korea, Romania, and Nicaragua. Many of the members also go on short- and long-term mission trips.

In 1979, messengers gathered in Houston, Texas, and elected Rogers president of the Southern Baptist Convention. Though electing a conservative as president was far from unprecedented, Rogers was the first conservative who planned to implement necessary changes in the Southern Baptist Convention agencies through the nomination process. He promised to submit for consideration only the names of those who believed the Bible was the infallible and inerrant Word of God and in turn would also only nominate for other committees those who would stand for the total inspiration of Scripture. These nominations then filtered down to the seminaries and agencies, returning the Convention to its conservative roots.

With his election in Houston, Rogers in many ways was the forefather of the Conservative Resurgence. Rogers served honorably for the next year but declined to run for reelection due to time constraints within his church and family. But in 1986, Rogers was once again elected as president of the Convention, serving in this capacity for the next two years. Perhaps Rogers's greatest contribution to Southern Baptists was in serving as chairman of the Baptist Faith and Message Committee formed in 1999 by the Convention president Paige Patterson. The committee worked diligently, as Rogers clarified the purpose of the committee:

We reviewed the confessional history of our denomination and considered the challenges faced by the Baptists of this generation. We were guided by the rich heritage embodied in the 1925 and 1963 editions of the Baptist Faith and Message. We have sought to retain all the strengths of that noble heritage, to clarify the truths there expressed, and to address the needs of our own times.[4]

In 2000, the messengers of the Southern Baptist Convention meeting in Orlando, Florida, overwhelmingly approved of the confession, reaffirming Southern Baptist heritage.

Indeed, this vote also solidified the legacy of Rogers in standing for the "total truthfulness and trustworthiness of the Bible." Today Rogers remains one of the premier pastors in the country. His media ministry, *Love Worth Finding*, has been broadcast worldwide for more than fifteen years. Adrian Rogers combines the unique qualities of standing for the integrity of the Word of God while living with integrity through the Word of God.

42
BAILEY EUGENE SMITH

January 30, 1939—
Elected: 1980, 1981

In 1980, the First Southern Baptist Church of Del City, Oklahoma, accomplished something unprecedented in Christian history. That year the church baptized two thousand people, an achievement not experienced before or since by any church. Under the leadership of Bailey Smith, the church was focused on the task of glorifying Jesus Christ by reaching as many people as possible with the gospel of the Savior.

After being elected president of the Southern Baptist Convention that summer, Smith brought this same passion to Southern Baptists. In 1982, during his last presidential address to the Convention messengers, Smith preached a sermon entitled "Southern Baptists' Most Serious Question." Here, he expressed his desire to glorify Christ through the finished work of the cross:

The greatest man that ever lived was Jesus;

The greatest love ever shown came from the heart of Jesus;

The greatest wisdom ever spoken came from the mouth of Jesus;

The greatest forgiveness ever bestowed flowed from the power of Jesus;

The greatest humility ever exemplified was born in the will of Jesus;

The greatest and most profound thinking ever acquired came from the mind of Jesus;

The greatest and most cherished teaching ever taught was exhibited in the knowledge of Jesus;

The greatest service and cost of discipleship ever rendered was ministered in the name of Jesus;

The greatest strength ever portrayed rose from the power of God in Jesus;

The greatest words ever proclaimed sprung out of the abundance
of the heart of Jesus;
The greatest obedience ever exercised to the Heavenly Father was
in the will of Jesus;
The greatest commitment ever dedicated to God was in the spirit
of Jesus;
The greatest acceptance ever felt was opened in the heart of Jesus;
The greatest healing ever administered was shown in the compas-
sion of Jesus;
The greatest model ever imagined to pattern our lives after was
shown in the image of Jesus;
The greatest man that ever lived was JESUS.[1]

Without a doubt Smith is the ideal personification of a Christian who has an unwavering, single-minded commitment to fulfilling the Great Commission.

Bailey Eugene Smith was born on January 30, 1939, in Dallas, Texas, the first
son of Frances and Ezell Smith. Smith was privileged to be reared in a family rich
in Christian tradition as both of his grandfathers, James Bailey Smith and A. F.
Lucky, were pastors. In fact, his father was the pastor at Elam Baptist Church in
Dallas when Bailey received Christ at ten years of age. Convicted that he had never
made a personal confession of faith, Smith was led to the Lord by his father when
they were sitting at the dinner table. The next Sunday his father baptized him.
Sadly Smith lost both of his parents while they were relatively young. Later in life
he testified about the tragedies:

Sometime ago, I stood at the graves of my young parents. My
Mother was in the hospital for routine surgery, but died there at forty-
one years of age. My preacher father, examining the foundation of his
new auditorium, had a piece of reinforcement wire to strike him in the
eye and he fell dead at fifty-five years of age. They are buried side by
side.[2]

In 1957, Smith knew God was calling him to preach the gospel. He surrendered to
the call the next year and began preaching immediately. His first sermon was delivered at the Alexander Road Baptist Church in Rylie, Texas, a small town south of
Dallas. There he preached "Tangent Christians" to a crowd of one hundred and
fifty, encouraging Christians to mature in their faith and grow in the knowledge of
Christ.

Interestingly, Smith preached that same message in 1962 in El Dorado,
Arkansas. At that service Tom Elliff—soon to be his brother-in-law and to follow
him in Del City and as SBC president—was called to preach.

In 1958, Smith enrolled at Ouachita Baptist College in Arkadelphia, Arkansas.
As a freshman Smith began to pastor two half-time churches, the Rehoboth Baptist
Church in Barton, Arkansas, and Brickeys Baptist Church in Brickeys, Arkansas.
Since both churches were located deep in the country, Smith had to drive

approximately 180 miles each way while earning a mere twenty-five dollars a week. Yet he was grateful for each Sunday he was allowed to serve as the people showed him genuine love and respect. His early success enabled one church to build a new auditorium. The church then had bragging rights as the first church in the area to have an indoor bathroom.

In 1962, during his senior year, Smith met Sandy Elliff. On June 8, 1963, the couple was united in marriage in Little Rock, Arkansas. Ironically, Sandy was the third consecutive generation to meet her husband while attending Ouachita College. Her grandmother met her husband as did her mother, Jewell. Nearly two years after the wedding, Bailey and Sandy welcomed into the world the first of three sons, Bailey Scott. Steven Wayne was born in 1968, and James Joshua in 1974. Today all three sons serve the Lord in the gospel ministry.

In 1964, the Smith family moved to Fort Worth, Texas, and Bailey enrolled at Southwestern Baptist Theological Seminary. The next three years equipped Smith to become one of the premier preachers in the Convention. In particular, Smith purposed to take every preaching course offered by the seminary in order to hone his skill as an expository preacher. He also furthered his pastoral experience, serving at the First Baptist Church in Crowley, Texas, until 1966.

After serving as pastor of the First Baptist Church of Hobbs, New Mexico, for five years, Smith, only thirty-four years old, was given the opportunity to pastor the second largest church in the Southern Baptist Convention, the First Southern Baptist Church of Del City, Oklahoma. Over the next twelve years, Smith baptized nearly eleven hundred candidates annually, and he baptized more than two thousand in 1980. He led the SBC in baptisms those twelve years. The church experienced such phenomenal growth that a new auditorium that seated seven thousand was built; this was the largest in the nation at that time. Smith also became a noted author, writing a national best-seller, *Real Evangelism.*

As his church topped fourteen thousand in membership in 1980, Smith was called upon by fellow conservatives to run for president of the Southern Baptist Convention. The Conservative Resurgence had begun in 1979 when Adrian Rogers, pastor of Bellevue Baptist Church, was elected to the presidency. But the following year, Rogers decided not to run for reelection. Even though Smith's church was known for its evangelistic ministry, he was a virtual unknown outside the Southwest. When Smith was elected as president, it stunned many messengers who opposed his candidacy, but it illustrated the strong support conservatives received from the messengers.

Smith knew that he could "rally the troops" through the presidential messages he would preach. In fact, many believe his powerful sermon during the Pastors Conference the day before the election helped him seal the vote. In 1981, Smith preached "The Worth of the Work," a sermon based on the fourth chapter of the Book of Acts. He encouraged Southern Baptists to look ahead to a bright future while holding fast to the Word of God. He explained:

If the Bible is the Word of God at all, it is the perfect Word of
God, because God will not give a word of flaws and mistakes. . . .
I know we must never get bogged down in anything that keeps us from
missions and evangelism, but I also know that no soldier wants to go
into Battle with a defective weapon. We can have confidence in the
Word of God. We do have a Bible worth believing—66 Books, 1,189
chapters and 31,175 verses, all true inspired Word of God without any
mixture of error. Praise God for His wonderful, infallible Word.

Our denomination has a great and joyful future fulfilling the Great
Commission of our Lord Jesus Christ. Your church has a future worth
living because the gates of Hell shall not prevail against it. You have a
great future because if you have put your faith in Jesus Christ, you can
rest assured that what He said is true, "In my Father's house are many
mansions, if it were not so I would have told you. I go to prepare a
place for you that where I am there you may be also."[3]

These words of evangelism and encouragement rang true in Smith's own life in
ministry. While he was president of the Convention, he personally saw six thousand
professions of faith.

In 1985, at the height of his ministry in Del City, God compelled Smith to
enter full-time evangelism. Smith left his twenty-thousand-member church and
began an evangelistic organization "committed to the uncompromising proclamation of the gospel of Jesus Christ." Through a variety of venues including church
revivals, crusades, Bible conferences, and overseas ministries, Smith has witnessed
God work in the hearts of thousands of men and women. He has gone on thirty-
four mission trips to preach the gospel, including one in which he preached to one
hundred thousand people in South America.

Smith is most noted for his message, "Wheat and Tares," which expounds on
the difference between saved people in the church (wheat) and those who are lost
and yet in the church (tares). This is still his most requested sermon, and Smith
has seen forty thousand people receive Christ after this message was preached.
Through his example, Bailey Smith has led Southern Baptists into the twenty-first
century with a new fervor to win people to saving faith in Jesus Christ.
Appropriately, Smith was recently honored by Southeastern Baptist Theological
Seminary, which established the Bailey Smith Chair of Evangelism to pass his
legacy on to the next generation.

43
JAMES T. DRAPER JR.

October 10, 1935—
Elected: 1982, 1983

*O*n a hot summer day in 1947, young Jimmy was once again enjoying a week at the Piney Woods encampment in southeast Texas. Annually, the youth group of Central Baptist Church of Jacksonville, Texas, where Jimmy's father was the pastor, would make their pilgrimage for five days of physical recreation and spiritual renewal. During one evening service Jimmy sensed that God was calling him into the ministry. Jimmy worried that he had to know exactly what type of ministry he was called to do and so stayed silent about God's working in his life. Two years later, during a summer youth revival, Jimmy surrendered to the call of God.

Eight days after his public proclamation, fourteen-year-old Jimmy was preaching his first sermon at the First Baptist Church of Mixon, Texas, a small congregation only ten miles from his home church, Central Baptist Church in Jacksonville. The evening service was moved to an earlier time because so many from Central Baptist wanted to hear him preach. Jimmy recalled that terrifying evening:

> I had carefully prepared a message that was parts of sermons I had read and from my dad. I preached, "What shall I do with Jesus, who is called the Christ," from Matthew 27:22. I had it down to thirty minutes . . . and preached it in twelve minutes! My father slipped out to hear me and then left and got back to Central Baptist Church in time to preach the evening service there. And, I got through so quickly, that I got back in time to hear him preach![1]

Little did young Jimmy know then that thirty-five years later, as president of the Southern Baptist Convention, he would be preaching in front of thousands of Baptists who eagerly awaited his message.

James T. Draper Jr. was born on October 10, 1935, in Hartford, Arkansas. Blessed with a rich Christian heritage, Jimmy's life and ministry were influenced by Jimmy's grandfather and father more than any others. He explained:

> Without a doubt my father and grandfather were the most pro-
> found influences in my life. Both were Southern Baptist pastors. Both
> were solidly conservative preachers who believed in the complete
> inerrancy and reliability of the Scripture. . . . I learned more just
> watching my dad [in the pastorate] than probably all my years of col-
> lege [and] seminary put together.[2]

Not surprisingly, Jimmy was not even six years old when his mother and father led him to Christ. Jimmy confronted his parents one night after revival, telling them of his need to be saved. However, his parents never pushed Jimmy into making a pub-lic profession of faith. Due to his admitted shyness as a child, he waited until he was nearly nine years old before making his decision in front of his church. Shortly thereafter, he was baptized by his own father.

By the time Jimmy was seventeen years old, he had preached for three years at any place God gave him opportunity, including rest homes and rescue missions. In fact, before Jimmy went to college, he conducted twenty-two revivals. As Draper's ministry continued to grow, he matriculated at Baylor University in Waco, Texas. Providentially, during a revival service in August 1955, Draper met his future wife, Carol Ann. Though they saw each other only twice a month on the weekends, Jimmy and Carol Ann were engaged during Christmas 1955. They were married nearly seven months later, on July 14, 1956.

Draper accepted his first pastorate when he was only twenty years old. During his nearly two years of ministry at the Steep Hollow Baptist Church near Bryan, Texas, the young pastor did not baptize a single person. Draper, looking back on that time, now believes that God was teaching him to be an effective pastor. He explained:

> God was teaching me how to be a pastor . . . We had a profession
> of faith or two, several of them toward the end of that time, but our
> church didn't have a baptistry, so they were not baptized before
> I left. . . . God was teaching me a lot of patience and how to minister
> to people, how to care for people. I had my first funeral there at that
> church, and learning how to visit, nurture, and love and minister to
> people in the church was a lesson that I needed.[3]

In 1957, Draper graduated from Baylor with his bachelor of arts degree and moved to Bryan, Texas. Later that fall he and Carol Ann experienced the birth of their first child, James Randall. They also moved from Bryan to Fort Worth, where Draper began attending Southwestern Baptist Theological Seminary. In 1961, fol-lowing in the footsteps of his grandfather and father, Draper graduated from the seminary with his master of divinity degree. By this time he and Carol Ann were the proud parents of two more children, Bailey Ray and Terri Jean.

During the next decade Draper served as pastor of University Park Baptist 'hurch in San Antonio, Texas (1962–1965); Red Bridge Baptist Church in Kansas v, Missouri (1965–1970); and First Southern Baptist Church in Del City,

Oklahoma (1970–1973). Unlike his first pastorate, Draper was able to see many people converted to faith in Christ. In fact, Red Bridge Baptist led the Missouri Baptist Convention in baptisms for three years consecutively. The same was true in Oklahoma as First Southern Baptist averaged more than six hundred baptisms annually. The patience Draper had learned early was now bringing forth fruit as his ministry matured.

In 1975, after serving two years as associate pastor of First Baptist Church of Dallas, Texas, under the leadership of legendary Southern Baptist expositor W. A. Criswell, Draper was called as the pastor of First Baptist Church of Euless, Texas. During his tenure there, Draper, who had always been a great supporter of Southern Baptist mission giving through the Cooperative Program, gained a great passion to be involved in missions personally and through his local church. In the last twelve years of his ministry in Euless, the church sent hundreds of their members on mission trips overseas as well as in the United States.

Draper himself became intensely involved with mission work in Kenya. During one mission trip to Mombasa, which was predominantly Muslim by tradition, Draper experienced a harvest like he had never seen in his ministry at home. He was able to participate as thousands of Muslims found peace with God through Christ, and then, along with local pastors, helped baptize the new converts in the Indian Ocean. In one particular case he spoke to a Muslim man who reminded him of the cost of accepting Christ as his Savior:

> We witnessed to [the man] and he told me, "You don't know what
> you're asking. If I do what you ask me to do, I will lose my job, I will
> lose my family, I may lose my life." I just talked with him a little bit
> more and he left. He came back and said, "I am ready. I want to pray
> to receive Christ." It was wonderful.[4]

This mission trip in 1986 changed Draper profoundly. Since then, he has traveled throughout much of the world, including Taiwan, Hong Kong, Brazil, Argentina, and much of Europe, preaching the gospel of Christ. Ironically, in his college days, Draper and his wife dreamed of becoming missionaries, but she did not meet the educational requirements of the International Mission Board at the time. Now much of that dream has been fulfilled.

In 1982, Draper was nominated to be president of the Southern Baptist Convention. To be sure, he was placed in the midst of the theological controversy over the authority and reliability of the Bible. Not the most well-known of the conservatives, he was forced into a runoff with Duke McCall, perhaps the most well-known Southern Baptist in the world at the time. Describing the unexpected outcome, Richard Land, now president of the Ethics and Religious Liberty Commission, stated after the vote:

> But when Jimmy Draper beat Duke McCall—I mean if there was a
> man who was Mr. Establishment Southern Baptist in the years from
> 1943 to 1982, it was Duke McCall, president of what became New

Orleans Baptist Seminary at age thirty, executive director of the Executive Committee from 1946–1952, and then president of Southern Baptist Theological Seminary from 1951–1981, and the current serving president of the Baptist World Alliance, and running against him was Jimmy Draper, pastor of the First Baptist Church of Euless, Texas. . . . It was when Jimmy Draper beat Duke McCall that they began to take the Conservative Resurgence seriously. It was when Jimmy beat Duke that the conservatives began to think, *We might actually be able to win.*[5]

Draper won handily and, as president, made missions and evangelism his emphasis. Indeed, in *Authority: The Critical Issue for Southern Baptists,* he stipulated that any rejection of the Bible's infallibility or reliability would lead to diminishing evangelism. In the end Draper trusted God's Word while honoring the biblical heritage given to him by his father and grandfather.

In 1991, while serving in one of the most successful churches in the Convention, Draper believed God was calling him to be president of LifeWay Christian Resources. Now more than a decade later, Draper continues to serve faithfully in that position. LifeWay has tightened the standards of publishing while increasing the quality of its products. Yet, when asked about his greatest accomplishments while serving Southern Baptists in this capacity, he answers passionately:

> We founded an international department. . . . We've trained national consultants in thirty-one different countries in the last four years. We send more than one hundred people overseas on mission trips each year. When we go on mission trips, we go strictly to do one-on-one witnessing and, out of that, church planting. Just the trips we have taken in the last four years, we have seen over 36,000 professions of faith and 121 churches started.[6]

Though Dr. Draper was never called into career missions, it is obvious to those who know him well that wherever he has served, he has focused on missions. This, then, will be his legacy, pointing lost people to Christ while pointing Christians to the field ripe unto harvest.

44
CHARLES F. STANLEY

September 25, 1932–
Elected: 1984, 1985

*W*hat do you do when more than half of your deacons and Sunday school teachers simultaneously resign from their positions? In January 1972, First Baptist Church, Atlanta, Georgia, gathered for a special business meeting where half the church leaders resigned. Tensions ran high as the newly elected pastor, Charles Stanley, was asking the congregation to give him the authority to appoint all church officers. Some of the leaders deeply resented this move since it would take away the power structure they had exercised for generations.

One man in particular felt so passionate about the vote that he threatened Stanley, warning him not to overstep his boundaries. That night, the man was so infuriated at losing power that he backhanded Stanley, stunning the congregation. But Stanley never lost his temper. He knew God was in charge of the situation.

The congregation quickly came to the defense of their new pastor and protected him vehemently. Within ten days the old power structure vanished as thirty-eight deacons, half of the Sunday school leaders, and all of the Women's Missionary Union leaders left the church.

Through this event God began to bless and grow the church. Before the ugly incident, one group of deacons controlled the church. Before the incident, the church was on a steady decline in membership. Since the incident, First Baptist Church of Atlanta has seen phenomenal growth as the congregation trusted their pastor's vision and were able to exercise their own spiritual gifts. Ultimately, the church was released from the bondage of a small power base that was stifling the work of the gospel. Today, services led by Charles Stanley can be heard in every nation around the world, every day of the year.

Charles F. Stanley was born on September 25, 1932, in Danville, Virginia, to Charles and Rebecca Stanley. When Stanley was just nine months old, his father passed away suddenly, leaving his mother to rear Charles by herself. She trusted

God in the difficult times, praying with young Charles every night without fail. The family struggled financially and moved frequently, living in seventeen different locations within Danville the first sixteen years of Charles's life.

Rebecca also took her son to the local Pentecostal Holiness church each Sunday. One morning, when a female evangelist was in town, Charles came forward at the invitation to receive Christ as his Savior and Lord. F. A. Dale, pastor of the Danville church, introduced Charles to the crowd and asked the twelve-year-old to tell the people what God had done in his life. Charles explained, "I don't know everything he's done for me, but I know he's saved me."[1] Then Charles began crying since he had found peace with God.

Immediately Charles knew that God was calling him to the gospel ministry. To think that one day he would preach the gospel of Christ consumed his mind. But Stanley was too shy to admit to anyone the conviction God had put on his heart. During this time Raymond Barber, a good friend who was a Baptist, played a pivotal role in Charles's life. While they were sitting in a baseball field one day, Charles, then fourteen years old, confessed to his friend that he was called to preach. Barber responded that he too was led by God to preach. The two have continued to be friends ever since, though Barber is now retired from the ministry.

As Charles began to mature as a Christian, F. A. Dale, the only pastor he had known, left the Danville church. Charles did not get along well with the new preacher and asked his mother if he could begin attending Moffett Memorial Baptist Church in Danville. How she responded made an indelible impression: "Well, Charles, if you can live just as holy in the Baptist church as you can in the Pentecostal Holiness church, that's fine." Stanley joined the Southern Baptist church, beginning a relationship that has now spanned nearly six decades.

The pastor of Moffett Church took a deep interest in Charles and his calling. In fact, the pastor was able to secure a four-year scholarship for Charles at the Baptist-affiliated University of Richmond. In 1950, the young preacher entered the university, deciding to major in history. In the next four years, God affirmed His call on Stanley. Through the classroom, friends, and his own journey, Stanley knew that God was working in his life. In fact, one night during his senior year, Stanley recalls experiencing the presence of God so greatly that he knew God was speaking to him "loudly, clearly, unmistakably."

In 1954, Stanley received his bachelor of arts degree and moved to Southwestern Baptist Theological Seminary in Fort Worth, Texas, where he enrolled in the bachelor of divinity program. Though there were several Southern Baptist seminaries closer to him, Stanley specifically chose Southwestern because it seemed to be the most theologically conservative Southern Baptist seminary. In 1955, Charles married his longtime sweetheart, Anna. Two years later Stanley graduated from seminary and moved the family to North Carolina, where he served as pastor of the Fruitland Baptist Church for the next two years. He was also given the opportunity to teach homiletics and evangelism at the Fruitland

Bible Institute, an undergraduate Baptist institute devoted to training preachers for the ministry.

For the next ten years, Stanley was the pastor of three Southern Baptist churches: the First Baptist Church in Fairborn, Ohio (1959–1962); followed by First Baptist Church in Miami, Florida (1962–1968); and finally the First Baptist Church of Bartow, Florida (1968–1969). In fact, Stanley had not been in Bartow for a year when a member of the First Baptist Church of Atlanta called and asked him to consider relocating once again to become their associate pastor.

Stanley repeatedly rejected the offer from the church, but God continued to convict Stanley that it was his will for him to go to Atlanta. On September 30, 1969, the Stanleys and their two children, Andy and Becky, moved. Looking back upon that difficult time, Stanley maintains, "I came because I had to and not because I wanted to." Providentially, this began a relationship that has now lasted more than thirty years.

Not only was Stanley hesitant about moving to the Atlanta church, but much of the congregation was equally hesitant to accept him. The traditional church had gained a liberal reputation as their pastor, Dr. McClain, was known for his theological liberalism. Yet, perhaps because the church was steadily declining in membership, the congregation, with the approval of their pastor, agreed to call Stanley in order to help rejuvenate the downtown congregation. Within a year of his coming, McClain resigned from the pastorate as he was frustrated with the apathy in the church. Stanley was immediately asked to be the interim and, less than a year later, was voted in as pastor with 65 percent approval.

Though many people left the church the first year, First Baptist has grown exponentially during Dr. Stanley's thirty-three-year tenure. The church is also a generous supporter of missions, both within the Convention, and of parachurch organizations such as Campus Crusade for Christ. In 1978, the Christian Broadcasting Network contacted Stanley and offered him free air time on the cable network. Four years later, IN TOUCH Ministries was born, a media ministry that now reaches across the globe to millions of listeners and viewers.

When the controversy within the Southern Baptist Convention was at its height in the 1980s, Stanley's notoriety among Southern Baptists nationwide offered conservatives a candidate, admired by thousands for his integrity, who could continue the theological resurgence. Stanley agreed to run for president, only to withdraw his name literally hours before the crucial vote. Conservatives rallied in a hotel room, praying through the night for the will of God. When morning came, Stanley joined the group and declared, "Men, I have been running from God. I don't want to be nominated today, but God told me before I left my room this morning that I have no choice if I'm going to obey Him. I don't want to be nominated, but I'm at least willing. Since He has told me, I must do it. Let Him humiliate me if He wants to. I will be nominated."[2] Though an outsider and underdog against his opponents, Stanley received 52 percent of the vote. Of the pivotal election Jerry Sutton explained why Stanley defeated two well-known Southern Baptists who were devoted to the denomination:

> What [moderates] . . . failed to understand was that Stanley was not considered marginal by Southern Baptists. He was only considered marginal by denominational executives and those who controlled the machinery of the Southern Baptist Convention. For the average mom-and-pop Southern Baptists, Charles Stanley was one of their heroes and was also one of the great leaders among Southern Baptists.[3]

Stanley, who had fought liberalism in his church, now gained the national spotlight as the herald of conservatism.

The next year, in 1985, history was made. The largest religious meeting in history took place in Dallas, Texas, as Southern Baptists registered more than forty-five thousand messengers, with many more coming as spectators. Moderates declared "holy war" against the Fundamentalists, and Stanley was their premier target. Winfred Moore, pastor of First Baptist Church of Amarillo, Texas, advertised himself as a compromise candidate in whom both parties could trust. Due in large part to the endorsement by evangelist Billy Graham, Stanley won the election with 55 percent of the vote, solidifying the Conservative Resurgence as a steadfast movement.

After his presidency was completed, Stanley once again concentrated wholly on his local church and media ministry. Many have honored him for his diligent work over more than five decades. In 1989, he was named Clergyman of the Year by Religious Heritage of America. He has now authored more than forty-five books, selling nearly four million copies. Personally, his greatest accomplishment comes perhaps through his son, Andy, who is pastor of the Northpoint Community Church in Atlanta. The congregation, a fairly new fellowship, now runs an average of more than seven thousand each Sunday.

IN TOUCH ministries, which has received numerous awards from the National Religious Broadcasters, has become the focal point of Stanley's passion. Today it is produced in thirty languages around the world, with a goal of reaching 92 percent of the word's population as the program is translated into one hundred different languages. IN TOUCH is also creating an interactive discipleship institute which can be used internationally. Ultimately, Dr. Charles Stanley has the desire to "lead people into a growing relationship with Jesus Christ and to strengthen the local church." It is his goal to get the gospel to "as many people as possible, as clearly as possible, as irresistibly as possible, and as quickly as possible—all to God's glory."[4]

45
CHARLES JERRY VINES

September 22, 1937–
Elected: 1988, 1989

This rain is surely going to keep every person away, the young man thought. *No one is going to hear me preach, and that is probably a good thing.* The sixteen-year-old preacher boy was just moments away from preaching his first sermon. On this dark, rainy Wednesday night at the Pleasant Grove Baptist Church in Carroll County, Georgia, in 1953, the young man had brought his friend, Charles Vaughn, to lead music for him. As ten people who fought the storm made their way into the small sanctuary, the young man asked Vaughn to add more hymns, to stretch out the time because he knew his first attempt at preaching was going to be short. He was right. He preached for fifteen minutes. In his mind, it was the longest fifteen minutes of his life, yet he knew preaching and pastoring were his calling.

Thirty-five years later, that once-timid teenage preacher boy named Jerry Vines would become the forty-fifth president of the Southern Baptist Convention. And no one could question his skill as a preacher and exegete of God's Word.

Charles Jerry Vines was born on September 22, 1937 in Carroll County, Georgia. Saved in 1946 at the Tabernacle Baptist Church under the preaching of Pastor John Tippett Jr., Vines was also greatly influenced by his grandfather, W. O. Johnson, a country evangelist. His grandfather spent hours teaching young Jerry about the premillenial return of Jesus Christ. By 1953, Vines was preaching throughout his county and was ordained by Tabernacle in August 1956.

In the fall of 1957, the twenty-year-old Vines was called to his first pastorate, First Centralhatchee Baptist Church in Heard County, Georgia. The church, located on Church Street in Franklin, Georgia, was surrounded by dirt roads. All sixty members voted to call the neophyte preacher as pastor and to pay him $37.50 a week.

Vines had only one book besides the Bible in his library, George W. Truett's *Quest for Souls.* Still Vines was already displaying the expositional passion that would drive his ministry. In the eighteen months he was pastor of First Centralhatchee, the church grew to over one hundred, and Vines preached through the Book of Romans.

In 1959, Vines accepted the call to the Bethesda Baptist Church in the same county. The church also experienced growth almost immediately, but Jerry Vines has fond memories of the church and the pastorate for additional reasons. On Homecoming Sunday in May 1960, Vines stood to preach to a packed church on "Jacob's Ladder." Looking out into the congregation, Vines became spellbound by a young woman. "She was the most beautiful girl I had ever seen," Vines would later recount. "She looked like a movie star with that beautiful blond hair. Right at that moment I fell off the ladder."[1]

As soon as the service was over, Jerry ran to the back of the church to greet members and visitors and sought the name of the young woman. Seven months later, on December 17, 1960, Jerry Vines and Janet Denney were married in College Park, Georgia. Within seven years of their nuptials, the Vines were blessed with four children, Joy, Jodi and Jim (twins), and Jon.

Almost immediately after the wedding, the Vines felt called to New Orleans Baptist Theological Seminary. Having received his undergraduate degree at Mercer University, Vines was often perplexed by his religion professors' disdain for "that prayer meeting school" in Louisiana. For Vines their distaste for the seminary was enough for him to want to see what God was doing there.

It certainly was not an easy road for Vines. Even though he was a classmate with future Southern Baptist leaders such as Paige Patterson, Jim Henry, Jimmy Jackson, and Fisher Humphreys, he rarely had time to socialize. Poor as the proverbial church mouse, Vines worked on the ground crew for the seminary, cutting grass and cleaning apartments. Still, the sparse pay of local country churches was not enough to support a family, and in the fall of 1962, the Vines family decided to return home to Georgia.

Every person to whom Vines spoke at the seminary warned Jerry not to leave. "You will never return," they warned. "You will never complete your education." But Jerry Vines was determined to sharpen his skills in the pulpit. Having become the pastor of the Second Baptist Church of Cedartown, Georgia, Vines began to commute to New Orleans Seminary every week. This was not an easy task. His church was almost five hundred miles away, so the schedule was tenuous and excruciating. Every Friday Vines would board a train in New Orleans and ride all night to get home. Arriving in Cedartown early on Saturday morning, he would run home, shower and shave, and then spend his Saturdays on visitation. He averaged thirty visits a day each Saturday and would then preach and lead the church all day Sunday.

Early Monday morning Janet would pack Jerry a lunch, and he would board the train in Cedartown and ride all day to New Orleans, studying for the next day's classes. Apparently, however, the grueling schedule inspired Jerry Vines. During the ten months he continued this schedule until he received his bachelor of divinity degree,[2] Vines maintained a high A average, and the church baptized 110 people in the same period!

Even before his graduation from New Orleans Baptist Theological Seminary, Vines's reputation as an expository preacher was spreading. From 1971 to 1976, Vines was pastor of one of the most influential churches in Alabama, the Dauphin Way Baptist Church in Mobile. The church grew quickly during his tenure, with crowds traveling great distances to hear Vines preach through books of the Bible. His ability carefully to expound a text and explain its implications raised Vines's prominence in the Southern Baptist Convention; and during his time at Dauphin Way, Vines first preached at the Pastors Conference at the annual meetings.

Following his tenure in Alabama, Vines was called as senior pastor of the West Rome Baptist Church in Rome, Georgia. For the next eight years, Vines led the church in continuous growth through soul-winning and the Sunday school. In 1976, Vines was elected president of the Pastors Conference at the Southern Baptist Convention; and during his tenure at West Rome, Vines began his literary legacy. Having written twelve books, many of which have become best-sellers, Vines is one of the most prolific authors in the Convention. His two volumes on preaching, *A Guide to Effective Sermon Delivery* and *A Practical Guide to Sermon Preparation,* have become standard textbooks on homiletics in many colleges and seminaries.[3]

In July 1982, First Baptist Church of Jacksonville, Florida, finally received the word that Jerry Vines was open to accepting the co-pastorate. The senior pastor, Dr. Homer Lindsey Jr., had pursued Vines for over a year, but Jerry and Janet did not feel the Lord had released them until that summer. It was the beginning of an over twenty-year pastorate for Vines, with two of the most powerful preachers in the Southern Baptist Convention sharing the leadership in downtown Jacksonville. It was also the beginning of a period of unprecedented growth for the church. In the years that followed, First Baptist Jacksonville grew into one of the largest churches in Southern Baptist history, often baptizing more than one thousand people a year.

In 1988, the Southern Baptist Convention was embroiled in the deepest controversy since the beginning of the conservative resurgence in 1979. The two candidates for the presidency were inerrantists, and with the Convention meeting in San Antonio, Texas, it was in the backyard of Dr. Richard Jackson, senior pastor of the North Phoenix Baptist Church in Phoenix, Arizona. Few people gave Vines a chance to win the election, even among the conservative leadership. The media focused on the meeting, with hundreds of representatives converging in the Baptist Press room.

When Vines was elected president on the first ballot, the national scrutiny was overwhelming. Through the initial days of hostile questioning and controversy,

Vines was unflappable. The secret of his calm assurance came from a moment in the middle of the strife. Vines recounts:

> One morning, Janet and I were having our quiet time. It was during a period when the secular media was pressing on all sides. Then, I said to Janet, "These people who are attacking—I don't know them, and they don't know me. If I were to die today, they would not shed a tear or attend my funeral. Thus, the only ones I have to worry about pleasing are Jesus, my family and my church. I am going to ignore the critics. I am going to do what I believe is right."[4]

During his tenure as president of the Southern Baptist Convention, two themes emerged from Vines's leadership: a call to fidelity to the Bible and a renewal of soul-winning efforts. In sermons preached across the country, Vines constantly reiterated the need for regular, passionate, and door-to-door visitation as found in Acts 20:20. Perhaps his most famous moment, however, was his sermon, "A Baptist and His Bible," preached at the Southern Baptist Convention in 1987. Even in the analysis of secular historians, the sermon was a masterful display of biblical rhetoric. As Vines reached the epiphany of his defense of biblical authority over against the tools of biblical skepticism, he offered a final illustration:

> Years ago, in the days of the old camp meetings, a preacher set out after the evening service to find his way along the edge of a dangerous cliff to the cottage where he was to spend the night. He had no lantern. . . . An old farmer, sensing the preacher's predicament, lighted a bundle of pine branches, handed them to the preacher, saying, "Take this, it will light your way home." . . . Do you see this Book? It is a lamp unto your feet. . . . There will be times when the winds of unbelief may seem to almost put out its glow. Storms of skepticism may threaten to engulf it. There may even be times when you are tempted to lay it aside and make your way unaided. . . . But, my Baptist brothers and sisters, hold on to your Bible. It will see you home![5]

Kell and Camp call the sermon, "the finest national statement on biblical inerrancy we found. . . . A gifted orator of the New South School of Southern Baptist preachers, Vines was the perfect combination of country preacher and gifted scholar of the Bible."[6]

Poignantly, Dr. Vines had come a long way since his days of sleeping and studying on the train to New Orleans, eating a sack lunch. His more than twenty-year tenure in Jacksonville and his influence among a new generation of Southern Baptist ministers continues.

46
MORRIS HINES CHAPMAN

November 21, 1940—
Elected: 1990, 1991

*T*he young groom stood nervously at the altar, awaiting the beginning of the marriage ceremony. August 31, 1963, had blossomed into a wonderful day for a wedding, and Bellevue Baptist Church in Memphis, Tennessee looked resplendent. The esteemed pastor, Dr. Ramsey Pollard, looked much younger than his sixty years. Having served as a pastor since his ordination in 1925, Dr. Pollard had administered countless weddings. The year he arrived at Bellevue, he was serving as the president of the Southern Baptist Convention.

The day of that particular wedding, Pollard had completed his two terms as president and was enjoying the anonymity of the pastorate, as much as the pastor to thousands could. Pollard smiled as the young man, recently graduated with a bachelor of music from Mississippi College, watched the doors in the back of the sanctuary. Finally the doors opened, and a radiant young woman named Jodi entered. Little did Dr. Ramsey Pollard know that twenty-seven years later that young man would follow in his footsteps as president of the Southern Baptist Convention.

Morris Hines Chapman was born on November 21, 1940, in Kosciusko, Mississippi. Saved and baptized at the age of seven at the First Baptist Church of Laurel, Mississippi, Chapman had known since the age of twelve that God was calling him into vocational Christian ministry. Still, as he completed high school and entered Mississippi College, he was unsure about the exact nature of that call. To add to the dilemma of his decision, Chapman experienced the personal trauma of a broken home. Chapman would later recount the painful period in 1958:

> On occasions when I rode to and from school with my Dad, he would sometimes say, "Son, I may have to move out of the house, but if I do, I know you are a big boy, and you will take care of your Mother and brother." Beginning in the seventh grade, these became words all too familiar to me. . . . During my senior year in high school, my parents' incompatibility became intense enough that Dad rented a room

in an elderly lady's house and moved many of his personal belongings from our house. He never came home.

I want to be quick to add that to my knowledge neither parent was ever unfaithful. The incompatibility was about them, no one else. On occasions they sought professional counsel, but for some reason they were unable to find resolution to their problems. After twenty-one years of marriage, the tension had taken its toll. My parents were granted a divorce on the grounds of their incompatibility, and my brother and I moved with our mother from Kosciusko to Jackson, Mississippi, the summer after I graduated from high school.[1]

Struggling with the call of God on his life, and dealing with the heartbreak of familial strife made that time difficult for Chapman. Yet his faith in Christ carried him through the rough waters. Though he had no money for college, God provided the means through miraculous interventions and perfectly timed employment.

Serving as a summer youth minister at the Highland Baptist Church in Laurel, Mississippi, Chapman was asked by the pastor to preach the annual Youth Sunday message at the end of summer of his senior year at Mississippi College. In the two months before that fateful Sunday, Chapman struggled with both the message he should preach and God's perfect will for his life.

Finally he laid out a fleece before the Lord. He did not want to bargain with God, but he was scheduled to graduate the next spring with a bachelor of music degree, and he was unsure what the next step in his life would be. Desperate to know God's will for his life, Chapman asked God for two people to make a decision during the invitation. If they did, then Chapman would take that as God's leadership for him to preach. After fervently preaching that Sunday, Chapman saw three come forward; two teenagers accepted Christ, and one surrendered to foreign missions. Chapman knew God had given him the answer.

Many times since that day, as Chapman has noted in sermons, God has affirmed that call, but it became clear that night. In 1964, Chapman was licensed by the First Baptist Church of Borger, Texas, under the leadership of C. E. Wilbanks, and in 1967, he was ordained by the Bellevue Baptist Church in Memphis.

This call by God has had a profound effect on the Southern Baptist Convention. After getting married, the Chapmans moved to Fort Worth, Texas, where Morris began his graduate work. In 1967, Chapman began his first pastorate at First Baptist Church of Rogers, Texas. The young couple, who had already been blessed with their son Christopher in June 1964, had a daughter, Stephanie, in 1968. Shortly after arriving at the Rogers church, Chapman realized that people were getting saved, and it was now his responsibility to baptize them. His wife, Jodi, came to the rescue:

In seminary class the professor taught us how to baptize, but I was never chosen to practice in the baptistry. Now the time had come. One

Saturday I said to my wife Jodi, "Honey, would you put on your swim-
suit and go down to the church with me? The baptistry has been filled
with water, and I need to practice baptizing." I baptized Jodi in a
marathon baptismal practice. It must have been a rich biblical experience for her because I baptized her "seventy times seven." . . . The
custodian was cleaning the auditorium, and each time I put Jodi under
the water and raised her up, I looked out to the custodian and said,
"How was that?" Several hours later we returned home. Jodi was
waterlogged, but I felt ready for the big day, my first baptizing! I have
had the privilege of baptizing many people over the years. I wish they
all could have known the sacrifice Jodi made in order that I might not
drown them.[2]

Chapman's ministry at the Rogers church was fruitful, including baptizing
forty people in one year—5 percent of the town's population. In 1969, Chapman
began a five-year pastorate at First Baptist Church of Woodway, near Waco, Texas,
where he remained until 1974.

In 1974, at the age of thirty-three, Chapman became pastor of one of the most
prominent churches in the Southwest, First Baptist Church of Albuquerque. While
serving at that distinguished church, Chapman was elected president of the New
Mexico Baptist Convention, at the young age of thirty-five. Also during this period
he completed his doctor of ministry degree at Southwestern Baptist Theological
Seminary.

In 1979, Chapman was called to First Baptist Church of Wichita Falls, Texas,
which had been led by such Baptist luminaries as James Landes, Landrum Leavell,
and William Pinson. Chapman established himself as a leader within the
Convention. By 1986, he was elected as president of the Pastors Conference of the
Southern Baptist Convention and also saw his first book published, *Youth Affirm:
The Doctrine of Christ*.[3]

For all of the blessings which God had brought to his ministry at the First
Baptist Church of Wichita Falls, Chapman seemed an unlikely candidate for the
presidency of the Southern Baptist Convention. As the Convention meeting at
New Orleans loomed in 1990, John Bisagno announced that he was going to nominate Chapman as a candidate for president. The Convention was in the midst of
one of the most furious media onslaughts in history, and the moderate faction of
the Convention was proposing Daniel Vestal as their candidate, one equally well-
known as a soul-winner, pastor, and preacher. The night before the election, many
conservative leaders gathered around Chapman in a prayer time. That night
Chapman thought, *If I am not elected, the Conservative Resurgence may collapse
at my feet*.[4]

The next afternoon, after a rousing nomination by Bisagno, Chapman was still
unsure of the outcome. As he entered the Louisiana Superdome, he happened by
the evangelist Manley Beasley:

> [Beasley] was sitting in a wheelchair on a concourse looking down
> upon the field; he was growing increasingly weak and died a year
> later. . . . That fateful afternoon, Manley said, "Brother Morris, you
> have walked by faith. You are about to walk by sight. You are going to
> be elected."[5]

Brother Manley's words proved prophetic. Chapman was elected by the largest margin of victory for a first-term conservative nominee since 1979.

A month after his election as president, Chapman experienced one of the most remarkable missionary trips in recent history. Participating in the Kenyan Coast Crusade in Mombasa, Kenya, the Chapmans spent two weeks with the missionaries, indigenous pastors, and other Southern Baptists, preaching in a series of meetings. Along with their traveling partners, Jimmy and Carol Ann Draper, the Chapmans were amazed by the thousands of people who responded during the four-week crusade. On the final Sunday afternoon of the Kenyan Coast Crusade, all the ministers entered the Indian Ocean and baptized thousands of new believers.

This revival had a profound effect on Chapman. Upon his return to the United States, Chapman had a renewed fervor to see Southern Baptists lead the nation to a spiritual awakening. America had not seen a spiritual revival in his lifetime, and he began to redouble his efforts to call Southern Baptists to renewed faith and repentance. Believing God was calling him to lead the Convention to dedication and reconciliation, Chapman had the 1991 Convention meeting in Atlanta dedicate the entire Wednesday night session to "A Call to Prayer for Spiritual Awakening in America."

During his two years as president of the Southern Baptist Convention, Chapman attained the reputation as a fair and gracious moderator of the public sessions. He allowed messengers to speak regardless of viewpoints and emphasized the need to be respectful in the public meetings. He was so equitable as he presided over the sessions at the Convention that the trustees of the Executive Committee felt led to ask him to serve as the president and chief executive officer of the Executive Committee in 1992. He has served in that capacity since that day.

While pastoring his first church in Rogers, Texas (1967–1969), Chapman used to meet three men in his study every Sunday morning. Wray Durnal, Alton Green, and B. F. (Bruinie) Harbour were three strong deacons in that small country church. They had prayed for each of the men who had pastored them, many of whom were novices in the ministry. As they knelt with the young Chapman, they earnestly prayed that God would use their pastor to lead people to a saving knowledge of Jesus Christ and a deeper walk with him. Forty years later the evidence of God's honoring that prayer is apparent. As Chapman himself notes:

> If God had not intervened in the life of a seventeen-year-old boy
> whose heart's desire was to obey his call, I may never have gotten
> started on what has been an incredulous journey filled with God's

abundant blessings. I cannot imagine the turns my life might have taken had God not saved me at the age of seven, claimed me for the gospel ministry when I was twelve, and provided a way for me to go to college when I was seventeen. To this day I am amazed at the marvelous grace of our loving Lord.[6]

47
HOMER EDWIN YOUNG

August 11, 1936–
Elected: 1992, 1993

At the 1993 annual meeting of Southern Baptists, the president appointed a theological task force as part of a study, examining the direction of the Southern Baptist Convention. The Theological Study Group, cochaired by Timothy George and Roy Honeycutt, sought to "move beyond the recent denominational controversy into a new consensus rooted in theological substance and doctrinal fidelity."[1] The task was further expressed as a desire to "foster a renewed evangelical confessionalism that is rooted in the historic orthodoxy of the early church, the Reformation, the Great Awakenings, and the distinctive principles of Southern Baptists."[2] The committee consisted of the chairmen and such Baptist leaders as William Bell, J. Walter Carpenter, Stephen Corts, Mark Coppenger, Carl F. H. Henry, Herschel H. Hobbs, Richard Land, R. Albert Mohler, and William Tolar.

In October 2002, three thousand pastors and church leaders gathered in Houston, Texas, for the North American Mission Board's Church on the Cutting Edge: A 21st Century Legacy conference. With more than one hundred speakers, the conference was to help churches present the gospel to an increasingly secularized culture and effectively speak to a new generation.[3]

What do these two seemingly unrelated events have in common? While one attempted to draw clear theological directives and implications from biblical study, doctrinal fidelity, and historical accuracy, the other attempted to build churches with practical advice and biblical principles. Yet both events had one common factor: each was led by Dr. Ed Young, the senior pastor of the Second Baptist Church of Houston, Texas. While a church growth conference and a call to theological confession might seem contradictory on the surface, they are melded seamlessly in the life and work of this innovative pastor, the forty-seventh president of the Southern Baptist Convention.

Born in Laurel, Mississippi, on August 11, 1936, Homer Edwin Young was profoundly influenced by his mother. Reading the Bible to her children and leading them in family devotions, she deeply impacted the life of her son. Each day, using *Open Windows*, the family would pray for missionaries and specific family requests.[4]

In 1947, the eleven-year-old boy was attending Vacation Bible School at First Baptist Church in Laurel, when Pastor Gates's wife shared the gospel message with him. Edwin was saved during that Vacation Bible School and baptized in a service that followed. In those first years of Edwin's Christian life, he was also influenced by his Sunday school teacher and junior high school coach, Floppy Bishop.

Young preached his first sermon at the Baptist church in Petal, Mississippi, just outside of Hattiesburg. Edwin's father ran a country store, and one of his customers was pastor of the small, quarter-time church. Young approached the task of preaching to those sixty people with the same fervor that he later demonstrated when preaching to thousands. He had read *Iron Shoes*,[5] a book by Charles Roy Angell, the venerable pastor of First Baptist Church of San Antonio (1933–1936) and Central Baptist Church in Miami (1936–1962). The sermon in that book entitled "The Second Mile" became the outline for his first sermon on the Christian life of service.

Entering the University of Alabama in 1955, Young was pursuing an engineering degree when the Lord called him to preach. Young surrendered to the gospel ministry and transferred to Mississippi College. The summer following his freshman year, he served as youth director, and later associate pastor, at the Northside Baptist Church (later renamed Woodland Hills Baptist Church) in Jackson, Mississippi. He was licensed to preach by Woodland Hills in 1957 when he was twenty-one and graduated from Mississippi College in 1958.

On June 28, 1959, Ed married Jo Beth Landrum, and the newlyweds moved to North Carolina where he began his studies at the Southeastern Baptist Theological Seminary in Wake Forest. He was called to his first full-time pastorate at First Baptist Church of Erwin, south of Raleigh. He would later recall:

> I preached a youth revival in this church. They were without a pastor, and unbelievably they called me! I remember the laymen in that church who loved God. They taught me how to visit door-to-door. They taught me personal evangelism. They were so encouraging in everything that I did. My first son, Ed, was born while we were there. Those two and a half years in that first church were so important to me because they were excited and I was excited, and in that textile village God really did a work in my life.[6]

Receiving his bachelor of divinity degree from Southeastern in 1962, Young moved his family almost three hundred miles west to assume the pastorate of First Baptist Church, Canton, North Carolina. From 1963 until 1969, Young led the church.

During this time the Youngs were blessed with the birth of their second son, Benjamin Blake, in June 1963. Their third son, Clifford Wesley, was born in August 1972.

From 1969 to 1971, Young pastored First Baptist Church of Taylors, South Carolina, near Greenville. In 1971, he was called to the historic First Baptist Church of Columbia, South Carolina. The church, one of the oldest in the state, was founded in 1809, and the sanctuary was built in 1859 under the leadership of their pastor, Dr. James P. Boyce, the fifth president of the Southern Baptist Convention.[7] As the pastor of one of the largest and most prestigious churches in South Carolina, Young quickly rose to leadership. Serving on the General Board of the South Carolina Baptist Convention, Young was also conferred with the first of six honorary doctorates, in 1973, from Furman University.[8]

In the early spring of 1978, Young was approached by a pulpit committee from Houston, Texas. The meeting would serve as a harbinger for one of the most blessed unions of pastor and people in Southern Baptist history. Ed Young was about to become pastor of the Second Baptist Church in Houston, Texas.

In March 1927, 121 people covenanted to start a new church. In 1928, the fledgling congregation purchased the property of the St. Paul's Methodist Church in downtown Houston. Second Baptist Church of Houston, Texas, was born. Under the leadership of such pastors as Dr. E. P. West (1927–1932), Dr. F. B. Thorn (1932–1945), Dr. Kyle M. Yates (1946–1956), and Dr. James S. Riley (1956–1976), the church had grown tremendously, and had relocated in 1968 to the crossroads of Woodway and Voss.[9]

Following Dr. Riley's departure in 1976, the search committee began to search diligently for a new pastor. The next two years were transitional ones for Second Baptist, but by 1978, the committee had finally voted unanimously on the candidate: Dr. H. Edwin Young. In June 1978, Young accepted the call and became their pastor.

Almost immediately Young's vision for a relevant proclamation of Christ began to take effect. In 1979, the church began a weekly local television broadcast, and in 1982, radio broadcasts were added. At the advent of the 1980s, the church auditorium was overflowing with two morning services, and in 1986, they moved into their new worship center. Young's preaching, often including humor and illustrations to supplement the exposition, was drawing large crowds, and the publication of his first book, *The Lord Is . . . ,* broadened his influence. The church was growing so quickly that by 1989, the church purchased a second location in west Houston. These innovations affected the vision of many pastors around the nation.

By 1982, many pastors in the Convention were turning to Dr. Young for leadership in church growth and evangelism. The television ministry, renamed *The Winning Walk* in 1989, became a nationwide ministry, and his writing continued to help mentor Christians in their daily walk.[10] In June 1982, Young served as president of the Pastors Conference, preceding the annual Convention, and he was serving in numerous leadership roles, including the executive board of the Baptist General Convention of Texas, and the resolutions committee, among others.

In 1992, Young was elected to his first of two terms as president of the Southern Baptist Convention. His ability to lead a church nearing thirty thousand members was helpful to his leadership as president. Observing the weighted bureaucracy of the Convention organization, he appointed a study group to bring recommendations to make the organization of the entities of the SBC more efficient and effective. Young also called Southern Baptists to "restate their doctrinal foundations" to an increasingly vacuous culture, and the Theological Study Group was formed. During his two years as president, the Convention also focused on evangelism and missions, specifically reaching metropolitan areas.

One would imagine that the years following his tenure as president would give cause to some gradual decrease in activity in Ed Young's life. Instead, the years have only seen him working as diligently as ever. Second Baptist Houston has helped start 122 churches in Mexico. In 1999, the church became "one church in two locations," and the west campus at which Dr. Young also speaks is now running over five thousand in attendance. Combine this relentless schedule with the presence of seven grandchildren, and one can imagine the pace at which he travels.

If there is a final testament to Dr. Ed Young's legacy, it can be found in his sons. All three of the Young boys are in full-time Christian service. Their oldest son, Ed, is pastor of one of Texas's largest churches, the Fellowship Church in Grapevine. Ben Young is the singles pastor to the largest singles department in America, leading twelve thousand singles at Second Houston, and the host of the nationally syndicated radio show, *The Single Connection*. Finally, the Young's youngest son, Cliff, is the lead singer of Caedmon's Call, a best-selling Christian band. For Ed Young, it is more than a family ministry; it is a family legacy of faith.

48
JAMES BASCOM HENRY

October 1, 1937—
Elected: 1994, 1995

*A*s another spring season emerged in Melvin, Alabama, the newly elected young pastor, a recent graduate of Georgetown College, never imagined the awkward situation in which he was about to place himself. Indeed, no amount of seminary education could have prepared Henry for what he was about to encounter. Mt. Pisgah Baptist Church was a small congregation without a baptistry. Candidates for baptism waited for warm weather before they made their public professions of faith through immersion in the living waters.

Henry had recently led Lucille, who lived "within a stone's throw of the church," to faith in Jesus Christ as her Savior and Lord. Now that spring had arrived, the church eagerly marched to the local river to celebrate the decision with her. Years later Henry recalled what happened next:

> The town had a big flood in the place they used to baptize, and it
> had been filled in with some loose sand. While I was standing there,
> I started getting sucked under with that loose sand. I nearly lost
> Lucille and me at the baptism. It scared me as my first baptism.
> I thought I was going to lose my candidate and I was going to disap-
> pear from the horizon and never be in the ministry again. But I some-
> how got her back up. By that time I was about up to my neck in water
> and nearly went under with her. I struggled to the shore. I will never
> forget that experience.[1]

Out of those humble waters emerged one of the premier pastors in the Southern Baptist Convention who led Southern Baptists to appreciate their heritage while looking toward the future. He explained in one press release, "The more Southern Baptists know what the denomination is about, its history, and its value in God's sight, the more committed people will be to the SBC."[2]

James Bascom Henry was born on October 1, 1937, to James William and Kathryn Fisher Henry. Though his father did not become a Christian until late in life, his mother was the most profound influence young Henry had. She consistently took him to Sunday school and church, giving him a Christian heritage on which to build. Indeed her prayers were answered when, during an old-fashioned tent revival, he came under conviction and accepted Christ as his Savior. In August 1946, when he was eight years old, Henry made that decision public at the Hopewell Baptist Church in Springfield, Tennessee. The next February James was baptized at First Baptist Church of Nashville, Tennessee.

Shortly thereafter James sensed a calling on his life to the ministry. After two years of discipleship by both family and church, James believed God was setting him aside for the ministry. James went through high school and college never truly dwelling on the call while being consistently reminded of it by the Lord. Finally, while he was teaching school, he approached his pastor, explaining how God was working in his life. His pastor clearly expressed his belief, stating, "The devil never put it on anybody's heart to preach the gospel."

The next Sunday Henry made the decision known to his church, but he had not yet notified his fiancée Jeanette of the decision. At the time Henry was living in Florida and teaching school while Jeanette was continuing to study at Georgetown College in Georgetown, Kentucky. In 1957, the two had met on the campus of Georgetown College and begun to date. By 1959, plans for marriage were in place as James was nearing graduation from the college. Providentially, the same day James went forward to solidify his call, Jeanette went forward, recognizing that God was dealing with her concerning the same situation. The two were married on December 27, 1959, in Cave City, Kentucky.

Obeying God's call on his life, Henry enrolled at New Orleans Baptist Theological Seminary in 1960 to prepare for the ministry. In the same year he accepted the call to his first pastorate at Mt. Pisgah Baptist Church in Melvin, Alabama.

Trouble ensued within the church soon after Henry's arrival. The young pastor believed that God's love reached out to anyone, regardless of color or class. In the 1960s, the South was immersed in racial tension. At Mt. Pisgah one man pushed for Henry's termination because he preached the love of God for all men. The church stood behind their pastor. Amazingly, no one in the congregation would even second the man's motion. Henry decided to leave the decision in the members' hands. He stated, "When I first went into the ministry, I said that I did not want people voting on me, and I don't want to cause that kind of hurt in the church." Ultimately, the man left the church and never came back.

In 1963, Henry graduated from New Orleans Seminary. After a brief pastorate at the Hollywood Baptist Church in Sledge, Mississippi, he was called to pastor Two Rivers Baptist Church in Nashville, Tennessee, just a few miles from the church where he was ordained. Henry quickly settled into the position and saw

God reap a harvest. As one of the top baptizing churches in the state, with services broadcast on two television stations, Two Rivers became a lighthouse of the Tennessee Baptist Convention.

Henry was utterly content with the ministry God had given him in Nashville. His extended family lived nearby, and his children were all reared in the city. However, in 1977, Henry received the call to the First Baptist Church of Orlando, Florida. At first he was reluctant to accept the offer due to the wonderful ministry at Two Rivers. But that summer Henry spoke to a Fellowship of Christian Athletes youth camp at Black Mountain, which included students from the Orlando church. They were so thrilled with his preaching and pastoral qualities that they went home and placed his name in nomination to the pastor search committee.

In 1977, Henry began serving at the First Baptist Church in Orlando, a relationship that now spans more than twenty-five years. For his caring leadership to the flock, he has been awarded numerous honors including Minister of the Year by the Greater Orlando Baptist Association (1995) and Floridian of the Year (1997). The church regularly leads the entire Convention in Cooperative Program offerings, giving nearly one million dollars annually to the program. In 1985, Henry led in the building of the new auditorium which seats fifty-five hundred. Today the church is known as one of the landmarks of Orlando and one of the flagships of the Southern Baptist Convention. Yet Henry remains true to his humble roots and compassionate personality.

In 1994, Henry was elected president of the Southern Baptist Convention. Running against Fred Wolfe, another conservative who was pastor of Cottage Hill Baptist Church in Mobile, Alabama, Henry won by a large margin due to his endearing personality, loyalty to the Convention, and his promise to create peace within a battle-worn Convention. In 1995, Henry was part of accomplishing the goal of restructuring the Convention for the future. He was also grateful for a resolution on racial reconciliation, in which Convention messengers apologized for "racism of which we have been guilty, consciously or unconsciously." More than any other privilege, Henry counted it his highest honor to introduce world-renowned evangelist Billy Graham, who spoke to the messengers during the 150th anniversary of the Southern Baptist Convention.

Today Henry's passion for the lost has grown as his ministry has matured. It is now his desire to train young ministers and encourage them as they set themselves aside for one of the most important jobs in the world. He explains:

> If the Lord wills in his providence, I would like to spend some time
> mentoring or teaching, going to colleges or seminaries, spending some
> time with some guys, or maybe have them come to the church where
> I can pour some of my experiences through the years to encourage
> guys to pastor. I read in an article yesterday that in one of our schools
> only 7 percent of the guys in schools wanted to be pastors. Some of
> their presidents have shared the same concern. A lot of them are in

the ministry, but a decreasing number is feeling led to pastor. I am a pastor, and so if God gives me life and health, I'd like to spend some years encouraging young pastors, to learn some things I learned, and to pass on those things to that generation. I'd love to do that. I have a heart to do that.[3]

On Dr. Henry's twentieth anniversary at First Baptist Church, the members set aside $70,000 as an endowment to make his dream a reality. Five years later the church honored their pastor once again by setting aside an additional $30,000 to the task of training young preachers and encouraging others in ministry. The legacy of Jim Henry will most likely be one of soul-winning and compassionate shepherding. He is truly one of the few pastors willing to help train a generation of bold preachers in a generation of bland uncertainty.

49
THOMAS DAVID ELLIFF

February 21, 1944—
Elected: 1996, 1997

*S*unday, November 25, 1962, was an important day in the life of the young preacher. Twenty-two years old, the young man faced an ordination council at East Main Baptist Church in Eldorado, Arkansas. As he scanned the congregation, he saw many familiar faces. In actuality, few faces were unfamiliar to the Ouachita Baptist University student, for he was serving as the part-time youth and music worker in the church and had led in this capacity for some time.

This ordination of a young man surrendered to preach, an event which has taken place hundreds of thousands of times in Southern Baptist churches, *was* unique. His family was neither surprised by his call nor by his surrender. Tom Elliff's father was a preacher, his grandfather was a preacher, his brothers were preachers, his brother-in-law was a preacher, and his uncle was a preacher. Yet few in this family would have ever guessed that the next four decades would find Tom serving as a pastor, a foreign missionary, and as the forty-ninth president of the Southern Baptist Convention.

Thomas David Elliff was born on February 21, 1944, in Paris, Texas. His parents, J. T. and Jewell Elliff, had moved often in the ministry, and eventually J. T. would serve as pastor of the Bethany Baptist Church in Kansas City, Missouri, and retire as the director of missions for the Capital Baptist Association in Oklahoma City, Oklahoma.[1] Thomas's grandfather, A. P. Elliff, was a longtime Arkansas pastor who also retired after serving as a director of missions in Louisiana, though retirement was a relative term since he preached until he was ninety-two years old!

Raised in a devoutly Christian home, Tom was saved when he was seven years old[2] and, by 1962, was volunteering in churches, working in areas of youth and music. That year Elliff entered Ouachita Baptist College, located on the banks of the Ouachita River in Arkadelphia, Arkansas. It was an exciting time at Ouachita, as their history explains:

During the administration of Dr. Ralph Arloe Phelps, Jr.
(1953–1969), the curriculum was revised and expanded, a graduate
program was added, the endowment was doubled, and the student
body reached a record high of 1,671 . . . in the fall of 1966. . . . In the
spring of 1965, the status and name were changed to Ouachita Baptist
University.[3]

That fall of 1962, Elliff had asked Bailey Smith to preach the youth crusade at his church. Bailey, who was five years older than Elliff, was dating Elliff's sister Sandy and would marry her the following June. During that crusade, the eighteen-year-old Elliff began to consider God's perfect will for his life. God's will for Thomas David Elliff was full-time service in the gospel ministry.

His ordination became a family affair, as well as big news in the community. His grandfather was well-known as a doctrinal preacher and was often invited to preach on the importance of theology and doctrine at brush arbor meetings. He had even drawn up 150 questions necessary for the ordination of a preacher, and young Elliff did not receive any mercy during his ordination. His was a two-hour inquisition, which included many of the men in his family as well as his future brother-in-law.[4]

Immediately upon being ordained, Elliff was called as pastor of the Southside Baptist Mission in Warren, Arkansas. Warren was a small sawmill community, and First Baptist Church in Warren sponsored the new mission across town. The leaders in the mission literally cut a house in half, moved it across town, reassembled it, and used the bedroom and the living room as the sanctuary. The members affectionately joked that they were the only church in the country with a bathtub in the ladies restroom.

In 1966, Elliff graduated from Ouachita and was serving as a graduate teaching fellow in the history department. He was also the new pastor of the Martindale Baptist Church in Little Rock. Commuting seventy miles between church and school, Elliff was a busy man. In October 1965, Elliff had fallen in love with a sophomore, Jeannine Kaufman Thomas. One month later he proposed marriage, and they were married on August 20, 1966.

At the end of the 1966–1967 school year, the Elliffs were called to Vickery Baptist Church in Dallas, Texas, and Tom entered the master of divinity program at Southwestern Baptist Theological Seminary in Fort Worth.

By the time Tom graduated from Southwestern in 1971, he was serving as pastor of the First Baptist Church of Mansfield, Texas, and was now the father of two daughters, Beth (1968) and Amy (1970). The church grew rapidly under Elliff's leadership, and his emphasis on missions and theology left a lasting impression on the church. Dr. Rick Garner, executive pastor at First Mansfield, states, "The Lord used Dr. Elliff profoundly at First Mansfield. He led the church to build an expanded auditorium. His ministry resulted in exponential growth of children and families, including a bus ministry transporting over 200 people weekly."[5]

In 1972, Elliff was called as pastor of Eastwood Baptist Church in Tulsa, Oklahoma. It was a remarkable church, and the next nine years were a wonderful time for the Elliffs. In addition to seeing the birth of two more children, Sarah in 1975 and Jon in 1976, the Elliffs also saw God bless their ministry tremendously. By 1980, the church had grown from approximately six hundred to over twenty-six hundred in worship attendance, and the heavy emphasis on prayer and missions had a tremendous impact on the lives of the people and their pastor.

By 1981, Elliff could have settled into the routine of a successful pastorate. Certainly the blessings of God were evident at Eastwood, and the church was reaching around the state and the world in its evangelistic and mission endeavors. Yet that year the Lord began to impress upon the Elliffs that He was leading them to do something rare in denominational leadership. He was leading them to leave the confines and comforts of a megachurch and denominational leadership and to minister in anonymity in Bulawayo, Zimbabwe.

On January 1, 1982, Tom, Jeannine, Beth, Amy, Sarah, and Jon arrived in Bulawayo. It was 8,986 miles from Tulsa as the crow flies, but it was an entire world and culture away. The Elliffs were sent by the International Mission Board to reach the Ndebele people among the Zulu in the southern part of the country. The region was near the crossroads of Botswana and South Africa, and the work was, in the words of Elliff, "wonderful."[6]

Reaching those precious souls was a fruitful ministry for the Elliffs, and sensing they were directly in the center of God's will gave them a great sense of liberation. Nine months after arriving, tragedy struck. As Tom was working, his wife and children were driving to a mission kids retreat when they had a terrible car wreck. The car spun out of control and flipped several times. Beth, the oldest child, was severely burned. Police reports would later indicate that they had been victims of sabotage. For nine months the Elliffs watched their daughter slowly recover until they were able to return home.

Though they had left the mission field, the Elliffs' mission fervor did not diminish. Called as pastor of the Applewood Baptist Church in Wheat Ridge, Colorado, Elliff immediately set out to lead the church in a worldwide vision.[7] The church's current senior pastor Calvin Wittman writes:

> All pastors leave their mark on the churches they serve—some to a greater degree, some to a lesser degree. The mark many leave is no more than a footprint in the sand that will soon be faded by the tides of time. Others leave a mark more akin to a footprint in stone, unmistakable and indelible. Such was the mark Tom Elliff left at Applewood Baptist Church.

> Tom's commitment to the inerrancy of Scripture and his passion for expository preaching raised the bar for all who would follow. During his tenure at Applewood, Tom led the church to build an education building, to continue the church's passion for volunteer mission

endeavors, and to maintain their commitment to missions giving. Applewood remains the number one church in Colorado in Cooperative Program missions giving and in the top one hundred churches in the SBC in gifts to the Lottie Moon Christmas Offering. The legacy Tom Elliff left at Applewood can be felt to this day.[8]

In 1985, Elliff became the pastor of the First Southern Baptist Church of Del City, Oklahoma. Bailey Smith had pastored the church from 1973 to 1985, and had left to enter full-time evangelism. First Southern Del City had long been known as an evangelistic church, and Elliff set out to lead the church in continuing evangelism and discipleship, with a special emphasis on prayer, missions, and family ministry.

As the Del City church continued to prosper, Elliff was able to bring his unique ministry of missions and doctrinal preaching to denominational leadership. In 1988, he served as the chairman of the committee on order of business, and in 1990, he served as president of the SBC Pastors Conference. His passion for spiritual awakening, lighted by such mentors as Manley Beasley, E. F. Hallock, and R. G. Witty, became the onus for an awakening in the SBC when he became president in 1996.

During his tenure the Convention appointed a committee to add a "Family Amendment" to the *Baptist Faith and Message,* approved the covenant between the SBC and its seminaries, and established nationwide Call to the Cross gatherings on each seminary campus and at the Home Mission Board. Elliff's influential writing ministry includes books on the family, prayer, and discipleship.[9]

As evidence of Elliff's heart for spiritual awakening, his presidential address on June 9, 1998, at the Salt Lake City Convention called Southern Baptists to lives of holiness, which births a passion for the harvest of souls.[10] In the midst of an era of programs and formulaic church growth, Elliff said, "The lack of holiness will render us absolutely powerless regardless of our personal charisma, human energy, understanding of the culture, or methodological expertise."[11]

As he approaches the age of sixty, Elliff continues the ministerial legacy of his family. Even though the family faced devastation while on the mission field, the families of the four children, including eighteen grandchildren for Tom and Jeannine, are actively serving in the ministry. Tony and Beth Cox serve at First Southern Del City, where Tony is a deacon. Jon Elliff is a pastor in Lanesville, Indiana. Sara is married to Greg Mann, who is associate pastor at Hillcrest Baptist Church in Cedar Hill, Texas. Most remarkably, David and Amy Jarboe serve as IMB missionaries in Cambodia. Four generations—many ministers and missionaries—and one gospel of Christ.

50
LEIGHTON PAIGE PATTERSON

October 19, 1942–
Elected: 1998, 1999

*A*s the gavel hammered down on the lectern, the 2000 Southern Baptist Convention gathered in Orlando, Florida, came to a close. Finishing his second and final term as president, Dr. Paige Patterson, an avid sportsman, looked forward to an exhilarating and refreshing time hunting big game in Zimbabwe. Inundated with his duties as president of the Convention while also leading one of the fastest growing seminaries in the world as president of Southeastern Baptist Theological Seminary, Patterson finds his respite in the open bush of Africa.

During one hot summer day, the situation became much more dangerous than Patterson could have imagined. Patterson, accompanied by two professional hunters and two trackers, encountered a 430-pound lioness looking for a meal. She believed she had found it in the president of the Convention. Immediately, the two trackers, who were unarmed, sprinted for their lives away from the location. The three remaining hunters took aim and fired. Unfortunately, they either missed or hit the lioness in an area which did not phase her appetite. Finally, as the lioness came within fifteen feet of Patterson and his guides, he took perfect aim and killed the lioness. Ironically, this seems to be just an average day in the life of one of the most colorful figures in Christian history.

Leighton Paige Patterson was born on October 19, 1942, in Fort Worth, Texas, to Thomas Armour (T. A.) and Roberta Patterson. When Paige was four, the family moved to Beaumont, Texas, as Tom Patterson assumed the responsibilities as pastor of the First Baptist Church.

During the next seventeen years, much of Patterson's future was shaped through circumstances and providence. Patterson remembers falling under the conviction of the Holy Spirit at the tender age of six, yet he did not respond to the call of salvation until three years later. Just before Easter Sunday, the Beaumont church was having revival services led by Fred Brown, an evangelist from Chattanooga, Tennessee. On Good Friday, Paige came forward during the invitation and asked Jesus Christ to be his Savior and Lord.

Providentially, another person came forward during the invitation that same night who unquestionably would have the greatest human impact on Patterson's life in the future. Dorothy Jean Kelley was an eight-year-old girl whom Patterson had met two years earlier. Patterson told his father the day the two were introduced that she was the one he was going to marry.

Dorothy was eyewitness to every major decision Patterson has made in his life. She was saved during the same service and baptized two days later on the same Easter Sunday. The following Wednesday, nine-year-old Patterson committed himself to the ministry. Eleven years later, on June 22, 1963, the couple, who had never dated anyone else, were married at the same church where both were converted.

After Patterson's surrender to the ministry, he was able to watch and learn from many famous preachers who visited his father's church. Evangelists such as Angel Martinez taught Patterson the urgency of personal evangelism. However, Patterson's parents had the most profound influence in the areas of evangelism and missions. "Honey" Patterson, as she was affectionately known, bestowed upon her son an urgent compassion needed for the lost. He recalls:

> Mother was very, very deeply committed to the missionary task and
> kept that before us always. [As] she would sit in front of the television,
> which in those days was black and white, she would see a news report
> and weep and cry because all those people were lost. It made an
> indelible impression on me.[1]

What his mother taught him in the heart, his father taught him through action. In 1959, when Patterson was only seventeen, his father took him on a preaching tour of the world. Visiting thirteen countries, Patterson believes this trip made an impact on his life that no other journey ever made.

In 1961, after invaluable evangelical and doctrinal exposure, Patterson matriculated at Hardin-Simmons University in Abilene, Texas. The professors quickly introduced him to liberalism, neoorthodoxy, and pluralism within theological thought. Known for his theological conservatism, Patterson felt confident to challenge the scholars in their beliefs, which polarized some students and faculty.

While he dedicated himself to earnest study, Patterson also immersed himself in practical experience. In 1962, he began his first pastorate at the Sardis Baptist Church in Rotan, Texas. At this rural church Patterson gained valuable experience. He stated, "It was a difficult ministry evangelistically because there was not a large population in the area, but it was an opportunity to preach regularly and to minister to my people who were among the sweetest on earth."[2]

In 1965, Patterson graduated with his bachelor of arts degree. Though he had every intention of enrolling at Southwestern Baptist Theological Seminary, the same institution in which his father received his doctor of theology degree, he sensed that God was calling him to a different school. The Pattersons visited New Orleans Baptist Seminary and immediately were impressed to pursue their graduate studies there. In particular, Patterson admired H. Leo Eddleman, president of the institution. He maintained, "The one thing I knew about Dr. Eddleman was that he was the only president of any of the seminaries at that time who had made an attempt to deal with the liberalism problem. He had not succeeded fully, but he had worked at it."

Patterson also knew that the city of New Orleans would give him ample opportunity to minister to people from all walks of life. In 1965, he enrolled at the seminary. Along with his studies Patterson assisted in opening a coffeehouse in the French Quarter of the city. Here he was able to evangelize those least fortunate, including prostitutes, biker gangs, drug addicts, and runaways. Patterson also served as a counselor to many ministerial students on campus who were shaken in their faith due to questionable doctrine taught in the classroom. Patterson, known for his stance for theological fundamentals, also became known for his evangelical compassion.

While at New Orleans Seminary, Patterson was quickly noticed for his leadership qualities. In the fall of 1967 at the Café du Monde, Patterson was introduced to Paul Pressler, a layman and circuit judge in Houston, Texas, who was visiting President Eddleman. Pressler, in his book *A Hill on Which to Die,* described the meeting:

> The conversation was between four individuals who had a mutual interest in reaching people for the Lord Jesus Christ. We shared our hearts with each other. It was also a time for ones who had experienced liberalism in the Southern Baptist Convention to share their mutual concerns about the effect this was having on the proclamation of the gospel.[3]

This then began a relationship that helped return the Southern Baptist Convention to its roots.

In 1970, two years after receiving his master of theology degree from New Orleans Seminary, Patterson assumed the pastorate of First Baptist Church of Fayetteville, Arkansas. Here Patterson demonstrated his heart for the lost, baptizing 239 people in the next five years.

The church was a challenge to Patterson as seventy Ph.D.s regularly attended the service. Patterson emphasized missions, and the Fayetteville church planted six churches in Canada and one in New York City. Much of this work was done through the youth and college ministry. In fact, fifty-two students from this group committed themselves to the ministry during Patterson's tenure.

In 1975, Dr. W. A. Criswell pursued Patterson, who now held a doctor of theology degree from New Orleans Seminary. Criswell asked Patterson to take control of the Criswell Bible Institute, a fledgling, unaccredited institution with only eight full-time students. Over the next seventeen years Patterson established a first-rate accredited institution which granted undergraduate and graduate degrees. The curriculum illustrated Patterson's commitment to the inerrancy of the Bible, personal evangelism, and global missions. The school moved into the newly remodeled facilities of the old Gaston Avenue Baptist Church.

During his time at Criswell College, Patterson became immersed in the controversy of the Southern Baptist Convention. He and Paul Pressler were the architects to turn the Convention back to its biblical roots of inerrancy and infallibility. Toward the conclusion of his seventeen-year tenure, the trustees of the institution criticized Patterson for his involvement, which caused him to be absent from the school for prolonged periods of time. The trustees believed that Patterson was hindering the school because he was spending an inordinate amount of time with denominational difficulties and not raising funds for the school. For this reason, Patterson was fired from Criswell College in 1991. After an incredible backlash from both students and prominent pastors across the nation, Patterson was reinstated.

In 1992, at the height of his difficulties, Patterson was chosen to succeed Lewis Drummond as president of Southeastern Baptist Theological Seminary in Wake Forest, North Carolina. This former bastion of liberalism was under investigation from the accrediting agencies, and the student body had dwindled down to fewer than five hundred.

Patterson was able to turn around the institution by once again emphasizing missions and evangelism. Now ten years later the seminary is one of the fastest growing seminaries in the world. Ryan Hutchinson, vice president of administration at the school, explains the transformation:

> The meeting of the Board of Trustees this Monday and Tuesday will mark the 10th Anniversary of Dr. Patterson's service as President of Southeastern Baptist Theological Seminary. God has greatly blessed SEBTS during this time, and has used Dr. Patterson to guide this institution to a point of being the greatest seminary on earth. Over the past ten years our student body has grown from 500 to 2,300 students, we have completed over $18 million in construction/ renovation, we have taken the lead in placing students full-time in some of the most difficult mission field locations in the world, we have seen hundreds of churches planted both stateside and abroad with tens of thousands coming to know Christ and are preparing to embark on the largest project of Dr. Patterson's tenure, a new 59,000 sq. ft. Campus Center projected at a cost of $6.3 million. Of course, the greatest accomplishment is the sending out of thousands of students who understand the complete authority and sufficiency of God's Word and have a passion to proclaim the Gospel of Christ to this dying world.[4]

In 1998, Patterson was honored by Southern Baptists, who elected him president of the Convention. During the next two years, Patterson accomplished two major feats. In 2000, Convention messengers overwhelmingly voted to revise the *Baptist Faith and Message* in order to clarify its doctrines and answer new challenges of the present generation. Patterson said, "[*The Baptist Faith and Message, 2000*] is a testimony to the twenty-first century for what Baptists say about the Bible." Second, Patterson mobilized Southern Baptists to refocus their efforts in the big cities of America, a much neglected field in a Convention in which 80 percent of churches reside in rural communities. He explained, "Great metropolises of our own nation have burgeoned into some of the world's most demanding mission assignments." Southern Baptists have overwhelmingly responded to both of these emphases, dedicating themselves to fulfilling the command of the Great Commission in the new millennium.

Dr. Paige Patterson is considered by many as one of the most influential and recognizable Baptists in the world. He has ministered in over eighty countries around the world and witnessed to nine different heads of state, including Yasser Arafat. He has written more than a dozen books and contributed to numerous publications. Yet, when asked what he considers his greatest contribution in life, he unequivocally states, "My students [who] are now all over the world." He is truly a pastor to pastors, a scholarly theologian, and a passionate evangelist.

51
JAMES GREGORY MERRITT

December 22, 1952–
Elected: 2000, 2001

*I*t was a service like no other. A month shy of his twenty-fifth birthday, he was serving in his first pastorate at Macedonia Baptist Church in Tick Ridge, Kentucky, just outside of Vanzant. Having been called as pastor by the forty-five active members a year before, the preacher wanted this baptismal service to be memorable.

On the Sunday following Thanksgiving in 1977, he had asked a sister church if they could use their baptistry, since Macedonia did not have one. The church had agreed, but they had forgotten to fill it up. Now, the preacher faced over a hundred people, all eager to see their newly converted family members and friends be baptized, and the preacher had no place to baptize them.

Suddenly, a member asked, "Why can't we baptize in the river?" The snow on the ground, the freezing temperatures, and the ice covering the river would have seemed to give a silent answer; but the preacher agreed. Standing in icy waters, with his lips turning blue and shivering uncontrollably, James Gregory Merritt baptized twelve people in a service that must have seemed interminable to him at the time.

It was an inauspicious moment in the ministry of the man who would become the fifty-first president of the Southern Baptist Convention, but few things in the life of Dr. James Merritt fit easily in a paradigm. He was the first SBC president to be born after World War II and one of the first to speak entirely to a Boomer generation.

After his election in 2000 at the meeting at Orlando, Merritt threw himself into calling Southern Baptists to evangelism and missions. In the subsequent two years, he became the first SBC president in history to visit all fifteen regions of the world during his tenure.

Born on December 22, 1952, in Gainesville, Georgia, James Gregory Merritt was saved while watching the 1961 remake of *The King of Kings* in the Royal

Theatre in his hometown. His mother had taken him to see the movie starring Jeffrey Hunter, and during the crucifixion scene, he began to ask, "Why were they crucifying Jesus? He had never done anything to deserve that." Even in his nine-year-old mind, Merritt had heard the story many times in his home, but he could not fathom why anyone would do that to Christ. Sitting in the darkness of that theatre, the Holy Spirit spoke to James, "Your sins crucified Jesus." At that moment of conviction, he was saved.

Baptized in August 1962 at Oakwood Baptist Church in Georgia, James Merritt was a reluctant preacher. He had always wanted to be a lawyer and even received his B.B.A. in accounting from Stetson University in 1974. When asked to preach on youth day as a senior in high school, Merritt preached on "The Love of God" in his home church, the Blackshear Place Baptist Church in Gainesville, Georgia.

His first ministerial position followed, as minister of youth and activities at Blackshear Place in 1971, and then as minister of youth at First Baptist Church of Smyrna, Georgia (1972) and Piedmont Baptist Church in Marietta, Georgia (1973–1974). He knew then that the Lord had another direction for him. He was to be a pastor and a preacher.

The year 1976 was an eventful one in the life of James Merritt. Licensed on January 14, 1976, by Blackshear Place Baptist, Merritt served as associate pastor at First Baptist Church of Smyrna, Georgia, from 1974 to 1976. Within two months of his licensing, Merritt married Teresa Ovalene York on March 13, 1976, in Cornelia, Georgia. Within ten years the Merritts would have three sons: James Gregory Jr. (1979), Jonathan Michael (1982), and Joshua Lee (1985).

Sensing God's call to continue Merritt's education, the family moved to Southern Baptist Theological Seminary in Louisville, Kentucky. While completing his master of divinity degree Merritt served as pastor of the Macedonia Baptist Church in Breckinridge County, some ninety miles from Louisville. During his studies for the doctor of philosophy degree from Southern Seminary (1979–1982), Merritt pastored the Buck Grove Baptist Church in Ekron, Kentucky.

Upon completion of his Ph.D., Merritt was called as pastor of Highland Baptist Church in Laurel, Mississippi, a county seat town. At this point Merritt was coming to some renown as a passionate soul-winner and pastor, and in October 1985, First Baptist Church of Snellville, Georgia, called him as pastor.

As a young pastor, Merritt believed firmly in learning from the elder statesmen in the ministry. Following his seminary experience, Merritt attended the Southern Baptist Convention and felt led to write a letter to Adrian Rogers, asking him ministerial questions. Merritt was thrilled to receive a letter of response from Rogers, inviting him to Memphis. Merritt recounts the meeting:

> I spent the entire day with Dr. Rogers, and I was amazed. One
> of the busiest men in the country spent his time mentoring me and

advising me. I learned more about preaching during those four or five hours than I did in seven years of seminary.[1]

This type of investment of time has come full circle in the life of Dr. Merritt, who now advises young pastors and preachers, pouring himself into their lives as Dr. Rogers did to him.

Coming to such a historic church as First Baptist Snellville, Merritt knew that the church could become a world influence if it was willing to make the sacrifices and commitments necessary for God to bring revival. Not every member of the church was happy with his coming, however. In fact, in lieu of a "honeymoon" period, Merritt faced immediate opposition from those who did not care for his strong leadership and even stronger preaching. After six months, those who opposed Merritt's theological and ministerial positions led a revolt. Over the course of two weeks, three hundred people left the church. Though it was an intensely difficult period, Merritt felt God was preparing those who remained for the greatest days in the history of the church.

Few tasks or committees in Southern Baptist life have missed the time and attention of James Merritt. He has served on the tellers committee (chairman, 1987), the resolutions committee (1989, chairman 1993), the executive committee (1991–1999), and the Pastors Conference (president, 1995). From 1998 to 1999, Merritt served as chairman of the executive committee.

With the phenomenal growth of First Baptist Church of Snellville, and the launch of the nationwide television ministry *Touching Lives*, Merritt had already evidenced a capacity for leadership when he was asked to be a candidate for the presidency of the Southern Baptist Convention in the spring of 2000.

Initially reluctant, Merritt finally agreed to be a candidate after many of his mentors joined him in prayer over the matter. The election was simply a formality. He was elected unopposed and was reelected without opposition the next year.

Merritt's vision as the new president of the SBC was clear. Having gone on multiple mission trips on regular intervals throughout his ministry, he had a desire to call Southern Baptists to a renewed vigor for missions abroad and evangelism at home.

The Southern Baptist Convention annual meetings were traditionally three-day affairs, lasting from Tuesday evening to Thursday morning. In recent years the attendance of the Thursday morning sessions had become difficult for most pastors, as they had also attended the Pastors Conference on Sunday and Monday. During Merritt's tenure the annual meeting was streamlined to a two-day meeting, ending on Wednesday afternoon. This was done without any loss of reports or presentations. In fact, during his terms as president the International and Home Mission Board reports were placed once again in "prime-time" slots, to call Southern Baptists back to the "fields white unto harvest."

In his final address as president in June 2002, Merritt lamented the onslaught of lethargy in the church, and spoke prophetically:

We face a secular culture that is becoming increasingly strident and militant in its anti-Christian, anti-truth, anti-God mentality and I fear the danger of facing this spirit with a lackadaisical heart. . . . We face a world whose heart is becoming increasingly cold, [a world] that needs to feel the hot fire of evangelism.[2]

At a Seattle, Washington meeting of the International Mission Board, Merritt casually mentioned that he was leading his church on a mission trip to one of the fifteen regions the IMB served. After the meeting one regional director asked Merritt if he could also come to his region, and then another asked him to go as well. Before Merritt knew it, he had agreed to visit all fifteen regions around the world.

Such an enterprise was almost unthinkable. *Touching Lives* was one of the leading television ministries in the nation, with salvations recorded every week, and his church was one of the largest and most active churches in the world.[3] Planning and implementing such travel over hundreds of thousands of miles would drain virtually any man. Yet Merritt completed the task without skipping a beat. Surrounding himself with capable leaders and pastors was one method of accomplishing the seemingly insurmountable task.

Sitting on the platform of the Southern Baptist Convention in St. Louis in 2002, Merritt chuckled to himself. While the world saw him as the Convention leader and national spokesman for the evangelical world, James Merritt still viewed himself as that nine-year-old boy, saved in a darkened Georgia theatre. This preacher who once baptized in subzero waters of Tick Ridge Creek had now met with President George W. Bush and had traveled the world preaching the gospel with boldness. This young man who had written an impassioned letter to Adrian Rogers asking advice was now the author of three best-selling books.[4] This once-reluctant boy who wanted to be a lawyer was now on television nationwide weekly. It was proof of the verse, "God uses earthen vessels to contain the treasure of the gospel of Jesus Christ."

52

JACK NORMAN GRAHAM

June 30, 1950 —
Elected: 2002

$\mathcal{T}$he sights and sounds of tent revival are largely lost on our present generation. Yet for the young six-year-old boy, they were the sights and smells which had eternal significance. In the small town of Conway, Arkansas, in 1956, evangelist J. Harold Smith came to lead a protracted meeting for First Baptist Church on Robinson Road, outdoors in a tent, complete with sawdust and tall tent poles. Years later that young boy would explain:

> To this day, I can smell the sawdust floor and sense the air of expectancy that beat in my heart. I can picture the big black box that the evangelist used to explain his Gospel presentation. We couldn't wait to see what was in that mysterious box. I can still hear the evangelist describing "sin," and out of that box he pulled one toy stuffed black cat after another. On each cat was pinned a piece of paper which had a "sin" written on it. There was one for lying, cheating, stealing, and so forth. As he pulled each toy cat out of the box my heart became heavier. I felt as if he was talking straight to me! After the last cat was out of the box, the most wonderful thing happened; he explained to everyone how we could be forgiven of our sins by the power and love of Jesus. That vivid explanation was the greatest thing anyone has ever imparted to me. That truth changed the course of my life and my eternity. When the invitation was given, I was the first one down the aisle. I chose to follow Christ who had given His perfect life for me on the cross. I made a decision, which would set in motion all the paths to come. I made a commitment to follow Christ forever.[1]

There, under the brush arbor in the open air, that young boy would surrender to Christ and submit to his leadership. Forty-five years later he would be pastor of one of the largest churches in the Southern Baptist Convention, with over twenty thousand members on 140 acres in north Dallas, and president of the Southern Baptist Convention. In the distance of four hundred miles from that north central Arkansas town and four decades of ministry, Dr. Jack Graham would see God honor such a humble and faithful beginning.

Born in Conway, Arkansas, on June 30, 1950, Graham was raised in a Christian home under the influence of godly parents and grandparents. He noted in an interview:

> For six years my heart was prepared, my childlike mind sharpened and my life molded. Hour after hour I spent sitting on my maternal grandfather's lap while he read to me out of *Stories from the Bible.*
> I reveled in the great adventures of David, Samson, Joseph, and Moses. Most of all, I was introduced to Jesus Christ, the one who lived, died and rose again so that I could know God.[2]

When his family moved to Fort Worth, Texas, during his childhood, young Jack continued in his discipleship. When Jack was in the ninth grade, he became enthralled with the youth ministry at Sagamore Hill Baptist Church. Dr. W. Fred Swank, pastor at Sagamore Hill for forty-three years, had built an amazing family-oriented church, and the entire Graham family was soon active in the church. "Brother Swank," as he was affectionately known, was to become a mentor and father in the ministry to Graham, as well as to a myriad of young ministers.

In those high school years, Graham's growth was affected by a variety of ministries. Attending the Latham Springs Baptist Camp north of Austin, Graham found an illustration for life:

> At camp, there was a bell and very few people were allowed to ring it. So, it was always a temptation to see who could get away with ringing it. One night at about 2 A.M., the bell began to ring and then stop. By the time it started ringing again many of the counselors including Brother Swank, camp pastor, were coming out of the cabins. They stood around the bell tower shining flashlights and calling out, "Get down from there, we know you are in there." No one came down, so they examined the tree nearby. Still no one. They eventually walked away only to have it begin ringing again and no one could be found. Eventually, everyone went back to the cabins and the mystery remained. . . . Until the next morning when it was discovered that attached to the bell were hundreds of yards of fishing line and it was stretched past the softball field, beyond the cabins, . . . and into the trees. We also, even though we are spread out around the world, need to ring the bell of the Gospel to places out of reach and draw people to the resounding message of truth and forgiveness for salvation.[3]

As Graham grew through discipleship and mentoring, he began to sense that God was calling him into the gospel ministry. In high school and college, Jack excelled at baseball. Through athletics God both confirmed his call and enabled Graham to pursue it. As a varsity baseball player, he was especially valuable during the softball games every summer. One morning at the worship service, he struggled with his surrender to the gospel ministry. He left the service still laboring over God's perfect will. He walked to the prayer garden and continued to pray until he realized that he was late for the championship game. Meeting Brother Swank on the way to the field, Graham was near tears as he shared with his pastor about his struggle and his call. Swank looked at the high school sophomore and said, "That is fine son, and if you are called to preach, you will still be called after the game. Let's play ball!"[4]

The point was made. If God was calling Graham, his call was for the long term and would take a lifetime of commitment. Further confirming his call, Graham's brother was both an example and a guide. Robert A. Graham, older than Jack by thirteen years, would pastor churches throughout Texas, most notably the Field Street Baptist Church in Cleburne.

The fall of that year, Jack Graham surrendered to the ministry publicly at Sagamore Hill Baptist Church. Baseball was also a factor in Jack's first sermon. As a sixteen-year-old boy, Graham had a number of opportunities to speak in youth services, but in late 1966, Frank Minton, the pastor of the Southcliffe Baptist Church, called Rev. Swank, asking for a young preacher to speak in an evening service. As a former pitcher in the Brooklyn Dodgers system, Minton wanted an athlete. Swank knew he had two athletic preacher boys: Graham and his friend, Otis S. Hawkins. Hawkins, known to his friends as "O.S.," was an avid roller skater. Swank told Minton, "I have a baseball player and a roller skater. I'll send over the baseball player."

In 1968, Graham entered Hardin-Simmons College in Abilene, Texas, on a baseball scholarship and began his undergraduate degree in biblical studies. While at the college, Jack fell in love with a classmate, Deborah Sue Peters, and on May 22, 1970, they were married. That same year Jack accepted his first pastorate, East Side Baptist Church in Cross Plains, Texas.

East Side, which had begun as a mission of First Baptist Church of Cross Plains, was a weekend church with thirteen people in attendance. The Grahams drove to the church on Saturdays, visited in the community, and then Jack would preach on Sunday mornings and evenings. Even during this embryonic pastorate, Jack would develop ministerial principles that would guide his life. The Grahams drove a Ford Pinto in those days and used it to pick up children around the town for church. As the church began to grow, the Grahams joked that they did not have a bus ministry; they had a Pinto ministry.

Even though they often slept on the church pews on Sunday afternoons, their time at Cross Plains was invaluable in their ministerial development. When the church finally topped forty in Sunday school, Graham noted, he was as excited as he would later be when Prestonwood Baptist increased by thousands.[5]

Graduating from Hardin-Simmons in 1972, he accepted the call to become assistant pastor of Sagamore Hill, his home church. "In large measure," said Graham, "the position entailed driving Brother Swank around in pastoral visitation. It was a wonderful part of the job. Brother Swank was older and had cataracts. He could not see, so I drove. It was the highest form of ministerial training."[6] While there the Grahams were blessed with the birth of their first son, Jason Matthew. By 1983, they had two more children, Kelly Susanne (1977) and Joshua Grant (1983). Before leaving Sagamore Hill, Graham completed his master of divinity degree from Southwestern Baptist Theological Seminary in 1976, and in 1980, he completed his doctor of ministry, writing on "Church and Proclamation."

Between 1975 and 1981, Graham moved to Oklahoma to pastor the First Baptist churches of Hobart (1975–1978) and Duncan (1978–1981).[7] These were pivotal years for Graham. First Baptist Church of Duncan was running around five hundred and fifty in Sunday school when Graham arrived in 1978, and the church was primed for growth. Graham believed deeply in training the laity for evangelism, and at Duncan, the devotion to that biblical principle bore fruit. In a town of approximately 25,000, the church baptized 240 in one year. He had similar experiences during his entire tenure.

At every juncture of Graham's ministry, one common element has remained: his lifelong friendship with O. S. Hawkins. They were young ministers in the same youth group at Sagamore Hills. Though Hawkins was three years older, they would often preach together at the Union Gospel Mission in downtown Fort Worth. They double-dated. They preached their first revival together, alternating preaching and leading music. They were ordained on the same night at Sagamore Hill in 1970. Hawkins even preceded Graham at First Baptist Hobart, leaving in 1975 to become pastor of First Baptist Church of Ada, Oklahoma.

When Graham received the call to become the pastor of First Baptist Church of West Palm Beach, Florida, in 1981, he was once again in the same state as Hawkins, who was pastor of First Baptist Church of Fort Lauderdale. It would be an amazing period of growth for both churches.

In 1981, at the age of thirty-one, Graham was called as pastor of First Baptist Church of West Palm Beach, Florida. It marked a period of astonishing growth for the church and a raised prominence for the Arkansas native. During this time Graham also served on the executive committee of the Florida Baptist Convention and on the board of trustees of Palm Beach Atlantic College. He also served in his first official capacity for the Southern Baptist Convention, serving on the committee on committees during the presidency of Dr. Jimmy Draper.

It was, in Graham's estimation, one of the greatest periods of time in their lives. They were young and full of vision for what God could do, and First Baptist West Palm Beach was ready. When Graham moved to the church in 1981, worship attendance was about nine hundred. By 1989, the church was in three morning worship services and regularly having between twenty-eight hundred and three thousand in worship attendance. Few things could derail such an idyllic match between pastor and people. Few things except God.

In 1989, Prestonwood Baptist Church in Plano, Texas, was without a pastor and struggling. As a church of national prominence, the loss of their pastor led the church to near crisis. Across the Southern Baptist Convention, many were speculating about the demise of the innovative church and its future. It would be an extremely risky venture for any pastor to take over the pastorate of Prestonwood. It would be risky even for Dr. Jack Graham.

Graham had no intention of moving to Prestonwood. But the search committee of the church, chaired by Ron Murff, was absolutely convinced that the thirty-eight-year-old Graham was the man God was leading them to call. "They were so hungry to follow God," Graham noted, "and so convinced that God was calling me there, that they literally prayed me to Prestonwood." Coming to a church running approximately thirty-five hundred, Graham and the people sought God's leadership in reaching the north Dallas region.

Thirteen years later Prestonwood Baptist Church is more than a regional church; it is an international church. The growth, which has come from a laity-led evangelism program and innovative worship, has grown by two thousand members annually. In 1999, the church, burgeoning beyond its capacity at Arapaho Road and Hillcrest Avenue in Dallas, moved to their new location on one hundred and forty acres on Midway Road in Plano. On May 2, 1999, the church had its first worship service in the new seventy-five-hundred-seat auditorium.

In the midst of such growth, Graham also found time to invest himself in the Southern Baptist Convention. Serving in a myriad of capacities, Graham was president of the SBC Pastors Conference in 1992, elected the preacher of the annual Convention sermon in 1993, and in 2000 coauthored (with Dr. Daniel L. Akin) a defense of the *Baptist Faith and Message*,[8] to go along with his four books.[9]

In 2002, Dr. Johnny Hunt, pastor of the First Baptist Church of Woodstock, Georgia, nominated Graham for president, and he won by acclamation. The profile and prominence of the young boy who was led to Christ at a J. Harold Smith tent revival over forty years ago has risen exponentially, but some things remain the same. When Dr. O. S. Hawkins became the president of the Annuity Board of the Southern Baptist Convention, he joined Prestonwood Baptist Church. "I am his pastor now, after thirty years of ministry together," Graham sighed. "It is a tough job, but someone has to do it."

Endnotes

Foreword

1. Henry M. Robert, *Robert's Rules of Order* (New York: Jove Books, 1967 [1893]), 21.
2. James L. Sullivan, *Baptist Polity: As I See It* (Nashville: Broadman Press, 1983), 152.
3. Cited in Stephen Scibelli, "Presidential Power and the Modern Presidents," 1; http://web.syr.edu/~skscibel/5.html.
4. Paul M. Harrison, *Authority and Power in the Free Church Tradition* (Carbondale, Ill.: Southern Illinois University Press, 1959), 14.

Preface

1. *Annual of the 2002 Southern Baptist Convention* (Nashville: Executive Committee, 2002), 38.
2. Ibid., 85.
3. Herschel H. Hobbs, *My Faith and Message* (Nashville: Broadman & Holman, 1993), 226.
4. Dr. T. T. Eaton was forever making this a clear distinction. At the 1907 meeting in Richmond, he made himself a perceived nuisance, repeatedly taking the floor to make exactly that point, and had Article III of the adopted constitution changed from "delegates" to "messengers." See Joe W. Burton, *Road to Augusta* (Nashville: Broadman, 1976), 112.

1. William Bullein Johnson

1. Hortense Woodson, *Giant in the Land: A Biography of William Bullein Johnson* (Nashville: Broadman Press, 1950), 157. This remains the definitive biography of Johnson.
2. Ibid., 1.
3. Raymond John Legendre Jr., "William Bullein Johnson: Pastor, Educator, and Missions Promoter" (Ph.D. thesis: New Orleans Baptist Theological Seminary, 1995), 11.
4. Ibid., 12.
5. Woodson, 24.
6. Legendre, 17–24.
7. Woodson, 49.
8. Legendre, 81.
9. Woodson, 160.

2. Robert Boyte Crawford Howell

1. See J. J. Burnett, *Sketches of Tennessee's Pioneer Baptist Preachers* (Nashville, Tenn.: Marshall & Bruce, 1919), 246–52. Also note http://howellresearch.com/RobertBCHowell-bio.htm. Accessed on 17 August 2002.
2. Homer L. Grice, "Robert Boyte Crawford Howell," in *Encyclopedia of Southern Baptists* (Nashville: Broadman, 1958), 1:656.
3. Porter Routh, *Chosen for Leadership* (Nashville: Broadman, 1976), 11.

4. Grice, 656.

5. Ibid.

6. Tom Nettles, "A Biographical Sketch of R. B. C. Howell: Benign Controversialist." http://www.founders.org/library/sermons/bio_howell.html. Accessed 22 September 2002.

7. Grice, 657.

8. Union University credits Howell as indispensable to its founding:

"R. B. C. Howell, the esteemed pastor of the First Baptist Church of Nashville, Tenn., sought to expand the outreach of the church not only by starting other churches in the state, but by establishing a college which would develop and strengthen the minds of young people. Howell's passion for education and training was evident with his strong pulpit appeals for careful thought, planning and action for the continuing Christian education of the young. . . . So keen was his focus in this area that one of his highly acclaimed pupils and objects of his mentoring, Joseph Haywood Eaton, later became the first President of Union."

http://www.uu.edu/unionite/winter99/chlife.htm. Accessed on 12 August 2002.

9. Grice, 657.

10. Routh, 12.

11. The cholera outbreak caused a shift in the number of meetings of the Southern Baptist Convention. Originally, the Convention was structured as a triennial body, in the pattern of the 1814 gathering. The need for more frequent meetings, and the threat of substantial change between meetings, caused the SBC to rethink this policy. At the 1849 session, the messengers adopted a resolution by a vote of 42–17 to amend the constitution to arrange for biennial meetings. See Robert Baker, *Southern Baptist Convention and Its People* (Nashville: Broadman, 1974), 201.

12. This event took place in 1835 and served as a touchstone for many Landmarkers. By 1851, the Landmark movement was a full-blown and highly organized constituency. Ibid., 209.

13. For a full, albeit biased, treatment of the controversy, see Joe W. Burton, *Road to Augusta* (Nashville: Broadman, 1976).

14. As recorded in the family archives: http://howellresearch.com/RobertBCHowell-bio.htm. Accessed on 17 August 2002.

3. Richard Fuller

1. J. H. Cuthbert, *Life of Richard Fuller* (New York: Sheldon and Company, 1878), 74.

2. Ibid., 42.

3. Ibid., 61.

4. Ibid., 69.

5. Ibid., 93.

6. Richard Fuller, *Baptism, and the Terms of Communion* (Baltimore: Cushing and Brother, 1850), 169–74.

4. Patrick Hues Mell

1. The definitive biography of Dr. Patrick Hues Mell was written by his son, Patrick Hues Mell Jr., *Life of Patrick Hues Mell, By His Son* (Louisville, Ken.: Baptist Book Concern, 1895). All biographies of Mell, to varying degrees, depend on this biography.

2. Howard Giddens, "Patrick Hues Mell," in *Encyclopedia of Baptists*, 2:845.

3. Letter from Cynthia Mell, 13 October 1828, in Patrick Hues Mell Jr., *Life of Patrick Hues Mell, By His Son*.

4. Ibid.

5. February 14, 1839, letter from Dr. Few, president of Emory College, at Oxford, Georgia, in Mell, *Life of Patrick Hues Mell, By His Son.*

6. Ibid.

7. Giddens lists nine children, but one died at birth. Giddens, 846.

8. As was often the case, many churches in the South were half-time churches, and pastors were often able to serve two churches simultaneously. Such was the case for Mell. In 1848, he accepted the pastorate of the Baptist church in Bairdstown (Greene County, Georgia) and served both churches until 1852, when he took the church in Antioch (Oglethorpe County).

9. In a letter written to the board of trustees of Mercer University, President Dagg notes that Mell was actually dismissed, but the point is moot.

10. This list is added to other institutions that pursued Mell, including the Southern Baptist Publication Society in 1851 and the Wake Forest College in 1854.

11. He also began teaching metaphysics and ethics in 1860.

12. Giddens, 845.

13. Mell's two wives were cousins, and both were granddaughters of Rev. Wilson Conner, a Baptist missionary and pioneer in Florida and Georgia. See *Articles of Old Jacksonville, Georgia,* No. 98.

14. Cited in Porter Routh, *Chosen for Leadership,* 16.

15. Mell, 156.

16. Ibid., 255.

5. James Peligru Boyce

1. John A. Broadus, *Memoir of James Petigru Boyce* (Nashville: Sunday School Board of the Southern Baptist Convention, 1927), 222–23.

2. Ibid., 69.

3. Timothy George and David S. Dockery, eds., *Theologians of the Baptist Tradition* (Nashville: Broadman & Holman Publishers, 2001), 78.

4. Broadus, 298.

5. James P. Boyce, *A Brief Catechism of Bible Doctrine* (Greenville: Sunday School Board of the Southern Baptist Convention, 1867), 5.

6. Broadus, 309.

7. Ibid., 423.

6. Jonathan Haralson

1. Pertinent biographical information comes from Garnett E. Puckett, "Jonathan Haralson," in *Encyclopedia of Southern Baptists,* 1:597–98.

2. Basil Manly Sr. served as president of the University of Alabama from 1837 to 1855. While most Southern Baptists are aware of the ministry of his son, Basil Manly Jr., president of Georgetown College and professor at Southern Baptist Theological Seminary, his father was one of "the outstanding men of his day." See Mrs. Henry Lyon, "Basil Manly Sr.," in *Encyclopedia of Southern Baptists* (Nashville: Broadman, 1958), 2:818.

3. J. Hugh LeBaron, *Sketches from the Life of Charles Crow 1770–1845,* n.p.

4. Puckett, 1:597.

5. Ibid., 1:598.

6. Porter Routh, *Chosen for Leadership,* 19.

7. James L. Sullivan, "James Marion Frost," in *Encyclopedia of Southern Baptists* (Nashville: Broadman, 1958), 1:512.

8. Jerry Henry, "Jonathan Haralson," *The Alabama Baptist Historian,* July 2001, 113.

9. Ibid., 20. Also see *Our Time in History: First Baptist Selma* (Selma, Ala.: First Baptist Church, 1992), 15.

7. William Jonathan Northen

1. "Sea Islands Hurricanes of 1893." http://www.redcross.org/museum/vmuseum/seaislands.html. Accessed on September 19, 2002.

2. John E. White, "Address at the Funeral of Ex-Governor William J. Northen," *The Christian Index,* 3 April 1913, 6.

3. Ibid.

4. Leon McBeth, *A Sourcebook for Baptist Heritage* (Nashville: Broadman Press, 1990), 290.

5. White, 6.

8. James Phillip Eagle

1. *LDS Church Record.* TempleReady. LDS Family History Library. While basic biographical information on Governor Eagle can be found in any number of official documents, information on his family is sketchy. The most reliable information on his parents comes from the genealogical records of the Church of Jesus Christ of Latter Day Saints (Mormons). As is their custom, Mormons use genealogical information to "baptize for the dead" in private Mormon ceremonies. Such is the case with Governor James Phillip Eagle. On April 2, 1992, a Mormon was baptized in his stead in the Las Vegas, Nevada, LDS temple. This may distinguish Governor Eagle as the only former Southern Baptist president to be vicariously baptized in a Mormon Temple.

2. Porter Routh, *Chosen for Leadership,* 23.

3. Routh sets the date at 1857 (Routh, 23), but this must be a typographical error, since he also notes that Eagle's conversion took place after the Civil War ended.

4. Edwin E. Dunaway, "James Phillip Eagle," in *Encyclopedia of Southern Baptists,* 1:382.

5. Hubert Howe Bancroft, *The Book of the Fair* (Chicago: Bancroft, 1893).

6. Routh, 24.

7. W. P. Fletcher, "Organization of the Lonoke Baptist Church" read at the dedication of the new church building on Sunday, 6 April 1924. http://www.rootsweb.com/~arlonoke/lonokebaptist.htm. Accessed on 3 September 2002.

8. Ibid.

9. Edwin William Stephens

1. J. C. Maple, *Missouri Baptist Centennial 1906* (Columbia, Mo.: E. W. Stephens Publishing Company, 1907), 236.

2. B. J. W. Graham, ed., *Baptist Biography,* vol. 3 (Atlanta: Index Printing Company, 1923), 424–25.

3. Porter Routh, *Chosen for Leadership,* 26.

4. Ibid., 26–27.

5. Graham, 423.

6. R. S. Douglas, *History of Missouri Baptists* (Kansas City: Western Baptist Publishing Company, 1934), 394–95.

7. Maple, 242.

10. Joshua Levering

1. Stanley L. Jones, *The Presidential Election of 1896* (Madison: University, 1964). Also see *Great Leaders and National Issues of 1896: Lives and Portraits of Our Political Leaders and the Platforms of All the Great Parties* (Philadelphia: Winston, 1896).

2. Porter Routh, *Chosen for Leadership*, 28.

3. Ibid.

4. Roy L. Swift, "Eugene Levering, Jr." in *Encyclopedia of Southern Baptists*, 2:784. Levering Hall on the old Johns Hopkins University was dedicated in his honor.

5. Fuller, who served as the third president of the Southern Baptist Convention, also baptized Annie Armstrong and James Petigru Boyce. This would make him the only Southern Baptist president to baptize two subsequent SBC presidents.

6. W. L. Allen, "Joshua Levering" in *Dictionary of Baptists in America*, ed. Bill J. Leonard (Downer's Grove: Invervarsity, 1994), 172.

7. The amendment was repealed in 1933.

8. See W. Loyd Allen, *You Are a Great People: Maryland/Delaware Baptists 1742–1998* (Franklin, Tenn.: Providence House, 2000).

9. His gifts made possible the dedication of the Levering Gym on the Southern Seminary campus. Routh, 29.

10. Swift, 2:784.

11. The laymen SBC presidents include Judge Jonathan Haralson, W. J. Northen, J. P. Eagle, Levering, Brooks Hays, and Owen Cooper.

11. Edwin Charles Dargan

1. Edwin Charles Dargan, *The Bible Our Heritage* (Nashville: Sunday School Board of the Southern Baptist Convention, 1924), 127–28.

2. Edwin Charles Dargan, *Ecclesiology: A Study of the Churches*, 2nd ed. (Louisville: Charles T. Dearing, 1905), 677.

3. Ibid., 678.

4. Porter Routh, *Chosen for Leadership*, 30.

5. Edwin Charles Dargan, *The Changeless Christ* (New York: Fleming H. Revell Company, 1918), 44.

6. Edwin Charles Dargan, *The Doctrines of Our Faith* (Nashville: Sunday School Board of the Southern Baptist Convention, 1920), 186.

12. John Lansing Burrows

1. J. L. Rosser, "John Lansing Burrows," in *Encyclopedia of Southern Baptists*, 1:210.

2. Ibid.

3. Edwin S. Davis, "Lansing Burrows," in *Encyclopedia of Southern Baptists* (Nashville: Broadman, 1958), 1:211.

4. Ibid. In 1871 he received a D.D. from Madison (later Colgate) University in 1871, a D.D. from Bethel College in Russellville, Kentucky in 1882, and an LL.D. from Union University in 1896.

5. History of the church from the records of the First Baptist Church of Bordertown, New Jersey. A brief synopsis can be found at http://www.bordentownbaptist.com. Accessed 30 August 2002. First Baptist Church of Bordertown is now an American Baptist Church.

6. Porter Routh, *Chosen for Leadership*, 33.

7. Ibid., 34.

8. Anna Olive Jones Bannister, "History of First Baptist Church of Augusta, Georgia," recorded on October 14, 1997. This report may be viewed in First Augusta's historical archives, or at http://www.fbcaugusta.org/history.cfm. Accessed on 28 June 2002.

9. The First Baptist Church of Nashville, Tennessee, *Church History Committee Report, 1998.*

10. Routh, *Chosen for Leadership,* 34.

11. Leon McBeth, *A Sourcebook for Baptist Heritage* (Nashville: Broadman, 1990), 302.

13. James Bruton Gambrell

1. E. C. Routh, *Life Story of Dr. J. B. Gambrell* (Oklahoma City: Routh, 1929), 1. As Gambrell's longtime friend and compatriot, Routh wrote the definitive biography of Gambrell, and most biographical data in subsequent works depend to some extent on his insights. Routh interviewed Gambrell's children, friends, and family and collected an oral memoir that is a tremendous insight into the life of Gambrell.

2. Porter Routh, *Chosen for Leadership,* 36.

3. E. C. Routh, *Life Story of Dr. J. B. Gambrell,* 5.

4. James's brother, Ira, was also a scout for General Lee and was killed on an expedition.

5. E. C. Routh, "James Bruton Gambrell," in *Encyclopedia of Southern Baptists,* 1:524.

6. E. C. Routh, *Life Story,* 26.

7. *Minutes of the 1891 Southern Baptist Convention, Birmingham, Alabama.* Even this final paragraph was a negotiation. Frost wrote the paragraph, Gambrell wrote the final sentence, and Frost was allowed to add one final sentence. Apparently, the Board's arbitration was successful, for in 1913, Gambrell wrote articles calling Baptists to implement the Graded Lessons Series.

8. E. C. Routh, *Life Story,* 61.

9. Ibid., 62.

10. Ibid., 72.

11. Ibid., 128.

12. Ibid., 173.

14. Edgar Young Mullins

1. Isla May Mullins, *Edgar Young Mullins: An Intimate Biography* (Nashville: Sunday School Board of the Southern Baptist Convention, 1929), 63.

2. Fisher Humphreys, "Edgar Young Mullins," in Timothy George and David S. Dockery, eds., *Theologians of the Baptist Tradition,* 182.

3. Mullins, *Edgar Young Mullins,* 82–83.

4. Ibid., 83.

5. Edgar Young Mullins, "Address to 1923 Southern Baptist Convention," at *http://www.sbc.net/aboutus/heritage/mullins.asp*; accessed 4 October 2002.

6. Isla May Mullins, *Edgar Young Mullins,* 211.

15. George White McDaniel

1. Douglass Scarborough McDaniel, *George White McDaniel* (Nashville: Sunday School Board of the Southern Baptist Convention, 1928), 159.

2. George W. McDaniel, *The People Called Baptists* (Nashville: Sunday School Board of the Southern Baptist Convention, 1925), 7–8.

3. Douglass McDaniel, *George White McDaniel,* 37.

4. Ibid., 64. Presumably, the "traffic" in question was the sale of alcohol.

5. Ibid., 206.

6. Ibid., 210.

7. Ibid., 138.

16. George Washington Truett

1. This story, retold dramatically through the years, is included in Powhatan W. James, *George W. Truett: A Biography* (New York: Macmillan, 1940), 38–40. The book has gone through six editions, including a final 1953 edition by Broadman. The biography has a special authority, as James was Truett's son-in-law, marrying Jessie Truett, the eldest daughter. Other biographies include Joe Burton, *Prince of the Pulpit* (Grand Rapids: Zondervan, 1946); J. M. Price, *Ten Men from Baylor* (Kansas City, Kan.: Central Seminary, 1945); and W. A. Criswell, *Fifty Years of Preaching at the Palace by W. A. Criswell and George W. Truett* (Grand Rapids, Zondervan, 1969).

2. Ibid., 40.

3. Ibid., 23–26.

4. The tuition for the private school was one dollar a month. Ibid.,31.

5. See Louis Devotie Newton, "Fernando Coello McConnell," in *Encyclopedia of Southern Baptists*, 2:839. One of McConnell's sons, F. C. McConnell Jr., Truett's second cousin, would become pastor of First Baptist Church of Jacksonville, Florida. Truett-McConnell College in Cleveland, Georgia, is named in honor of the two Baptist cousins.

6. Ibid., 44.

7. Certainly the present controversy over Baptist churches holding Saturday evening services neglects frontier Baptist history, when morning services were difficult for the farming families with abiding chore and tasks. Saturday evenings were a popular time for services, often negating a traditional Sunday morning service. The logic was, the Sabbath (or Lord's Day) began at sunset the day previous and continued to sunset of the present day. A Sunday evening service would therefore be considered a Monday meeting to the biblical mind.

8. Ibid., 48–49. Italics added.

9. Carroll would remain a mentor to Truett until his death in 1914. Often Truett would study at Carroll's home library, and Carroll would test the knowledge of the young man for hours on end. This was an education in itself, as Truett often noted.

10. James, *Biography*, 79.

11. For an early history of the blessings at First Baptist Dallas, see W. L. Williams, *Golden Years: An Autobiography* (Dallas: Baptist Standard, 1921), for which Truett wrote the introduction.

12. The entire story is told with grace in James, *Biography*, 85–90. These paragraphs are adapted from that telling.

13. Powhatan W. James, "George Washington Truett," in *Encyclopedia of Southern Baptists*, 2:1,429.

14. George W. Truett, *The Leaf and the Life* (Philadelphia: American Baptist, 1902).

15. George W. Truett, *We Would See Jesus* (New York: Fleming H. Revell, 1915).

16. George W. Truett, *Christian Education* (Birmingham: Education Board SBC, 1926).

17. Powhatan W. James spent fifteen years following Truett's death compiling and editing Truett's sermons for publication. These books began with *Some Vital Questions* (Nashville: Broadman, 1946.)

18. James, *Encyclopedia*, 2:1,430.

19. Truett had addressed the Convention prior to this occasion, in 1899 in Louisville.

20. The address was compiled in a number of publications, including *Baptists and Religious Liberty* (Nashville: BSSB, 1920) and *God's Call to America* (Philadelphia: Judson, 1923).

21. James, *Biography*, 276–77.

17. William Joseph McGlothlin

1. E. Y. Mullins, *Presidential Address*, Southern Baptist Convention, May 1923.

2. Ibid.

3. Published in Germany in 1902.

4. Published in Kentucky: s.n., 1900.

5. Whitsitt's books prior to the controversy included *The History of the Rise of Infant Baptism* (1898) and *A Question in Baptist History* (1896).

6. In 1905, Carroll would become professor of theology at Baylor Theological Seminary, which was chartered as Southwestern Baptist Theological Seminary in 1908. In 1910, the seminary moved to Fort Worth, and Carroll became president until his death in 1914. See Bill Leonard, "Benjah Harvey Carroll," in *Dictionary of Baptists in America* (Downers Grove, Ill.: IVP, 1994), 76.

7. William Estep, "William Heth Whitsitt," in *Dictionary of Baptists in America* (Downers Grove, Ill.: IVP, 1994), 287.

8. McGlothlin's position prior to becoming the full professor of church history at Southern is somewhat in question. Though his daughter lists his inception at Southern Seminary as 1894, Routh purports that he did not come to Southern until 1899. Further complicating matters, the seminary has archived McGlothlin's "inaugural sermon" at Southern on October 2, 1896. The term "inaugural" may refer to the beginning of the new school year, or it may refer to his first chapel address, as speaking in chapel was not often the task of young professors. In any case his daughter's record in the *Encyclopedia* seems to be the most authoritative. See W. J. McGlothlin, (William Joseph), 1867–1933. *The Contribution of the Monuments to Old Testament History*: inaugural address, Southern Baptist Theological Seminary, 2 October 1896; Porter Routh, *Chosen for Leadership*, 44–45; and Kathryn McGlothlin Odell, "William Joseph McGlothlin" in *Encyclopedia of Southern Baptists*, 2:841–42.

9. J. B. Cranfill, "A Denunciation of Chicago University," in *Views from the Watchtower*, 28. 19, 1 October 1907.

10. W. J. McGlothlin, *Kentucky Baptists, the Seminary and Alien Immersion* (Louisville: n.p., 1908).

11. W. J. McGlothlin, *A Guide to the Study of Church History* (Louisville: Baptist World, 1908).

12. W. J. McGlothlin, *What Hinders the Union of Baptists and Disciples* (Nashville: BSSB, 1911).

13. The translation was published by W. J. McGlothlin in *Baptist Confessions of Faith* (Philadelphia: American Baptist Publication Society, 1910), and was one of the first English translations given to the Baptist world.

14. W. J. McGlothlin, *Practical Hints on Preaching: Nine Lectures on Sermon Building* (Birmingham: Strickland, 1917).

15. W. J. McGlothlin, *A Vital Ministry, the Pastor of Today in the Service of Man* (New York: Macmillan, 1913).

16. *The Christian School, The War and the Future*: an address delivered by W. J. McGlothlin at the Southern Baptist Convention, Hot Springs, Arkansas, 13 May 1918. The

sermon is archived at the Southern Baptist Theological Seminary. This may have been a special address and not the actual Convention sermon, as SBC records list the preacher as W. H. Geistweit of Missouri.

17. Here again we have a discrepancy with Routh. In *Chosen for Leadership*, Routh marks McGlothlin's election to Furman at 1914, but Odell marks the date as 1919, and Furman lists Edwin McNeil Poteat as president from 1903 to 1918. See Routh, 45.

18. As recorded in Routh, *Chosen for Leadership*, 45.

18. Fred Fernando Brown

1. In comparison, on March 12, 1928, 3,875,910 shares had been traded. To quadruple this amount meant that traders were in a frenzy, trying to recover lost money and profits in formerly safe stock portfolios. See E. N. White, "When the Ticker Ran Late: The Stock Market Boom and Crash of 1929," in E. N. White, ed., *Crises and Panics: The Lessons of History,* 1990.

2. Charles A. Trentham, "Fred Fernando Brown," in *Encyclopedia of Southern Baptists,* 3:1,625.

3. Fred F. Brown, "Her Central Message," in *Southern Baptist Preaching Yesterday,* ed. R. Earl Allen and Joel Gregory (Nashville: Broadman, 1991), 70–71. Originally preached on *The Baptist Hour.*

4. "A Brief History of the First Baptist Church of Knoxville, Tennessee," http://www.fbc-knox.org/history/Default.htm. Accessed 9 September 2002. Also see Nancy J. Siler, *First Baptist Church, Knoxville, Tennessee, 1843–1993* (Knoxville: First Baptist Church, 1992). In 1965, the church dedicated the Fred F. Brown Chapel.

5. Ibid.

6. Trentham, "Fred Fernando Brown," 3:1625.

7. Porter Routh, *Chosen for Leadership,* 47.

8. Ibid.

9. Robert E. Naylor, *A Messenger's Memoirs* (Franklin, Tenn.: Providence House, 1995), 18.

10. Ibid., 19.

19. Monroe Elmon Dodd

1. C. L. Culpepper, "Shantung Province Revival," at *http://www.u-b-c.org/sermons/revival.html*; accessed 5 October 2002.

2. Austin B. Tucker, "Monroe Elmon Dodd and His Preaching," Th.D. thesis: Southwestern Baptist Theological Seminary, 1971, 6.

3. Ibid., 16.

4. M. E. Dodd, *Missions Our Mission* (Nashville: Sunday School Board of the Southern Baptist Convention, 1930), 92.

5. Ibid., 5.

6. Tucker, "Monroe Elmon Dodd and His Preaching," 2.

7. Ibid.

20. John Richard Sampey

1. John R. Sampey, *Memoirs* (Nashville: Broadman Press, 1947), 6.

2. Ibid., 7.

3. Ibid., 17.

4. Ibid., 63.

5. Ibid., 79.

6. Ibid., 154.

7. Ibid., 168.

8. Ibid., 277.

21. Lee Rutland Scarborough

1. Personal account of Scarborough, cited in many places, most notably W. W. Barnes, *The Southern Baptist Convention, 1845–1953* (Nashville: Broadman, 1954), 209.

2. Franklin M. Segler, "Lee Rutland Scarborough," in *Encyclopedia of Southern Baptists*, 2:1,186.

3. Herein lies a discrepancy. Segler states that in 1896, the family moved to west Texas where Lee spent his youth attending the log cabin school and working on the farm. In 1896, Scarborough would have been twenty-six years old and a graduate of two colleges. This is a typographical error, but one which is perpetuated in numerous sources. See Segler, 1,186.

4. L. R. Scarborough, introduction to *Inspiration of the Bible* by B. H. Carroll (Nashville: Broadman, 1930). The book, obviously compiled after Carroll's death, was edited by J. B. Cranfill.

5. Porter Routh, *Chosen for Leadership*, 53.

6. Ibid., 54.

7. This was not only by churches but institutions as well. In February 1908, Southern Seminary hosted Scarborough as he delivered the lecture, "The Teaching Function of the Church," in the annual course on Sunday school work. The eventual booklet from this lecture was published by the Southern Baptist Sunday School Board later that year. SBTS Archives.

8. These works, published by the Sunday School Board, included *Suggested Program for Conference of Workers on Baptist 75 Million Campaign* and *Conscience and Campaign Funds*, both in 1919.

9. His memoir of the period was published by the Sunday School Board as well, entitled *Marvels of Divine Leadership; or, The Story of the Southern Baptist 75 Million Campaign* (Nashville: Sunday School Board of the Southern Baptist Convention, 1920).

10. Robert E. Naylor, *A Messenger's Memoirs* (Franklin, Tenn.: Providence House, 1996), 38.

11. Ibid., 44.

12. Kelly Davis, "Calling Out the Called," *SBC Life*, November 2002.

22. William Wistar Hamilton

1. William Wistar Hamilton, *Highway and Hedges* (Nashville: Broadman Press, 1938), 72.

2. Ibid., 12.

3. Claude L. Howe, *Seventy-Five Years of Providence and Prayer* (New Orleans: New Orleans Baptist Theological Seminary, 193), 57.

4. Ibid., 68.

5. Ibid., 70.

23. Pat Morris Neff

1. Biographies of the former governor are numerous, but some of the more prominent ones include, J. M. Price, *Ten Men from Baylor* (Kansas City, Kan.: Central Seminary, 1945); Guy B. Harrison Jr. "Pat Morris Neff," in *Encyclopedia of Southern Baptists*; and a brief but thorough biography in R. Earl Allen and Joel Gregory, *Southern Baptist Preaching Yesterday* (Nashville: Broadman, 1991). Porter Routh, *Chosen for Leadership*, includes personal interviews which enliven his work.

2. Baylor University, www.baylor.edu/about/neff.asp. Accessed 11 June 2002.

3. He remained clerk at First Baptist Waco from 1909 to 1918. Allen and Gregory, *Southern Baptist Preaching Yesterday*, 592.

4. For a detailed account of Texas politics in the Neff era, see Norman D. Brown, *Hood, Bonnet, and Little Brown Jug: Texas Politics, 1921–1928* (College Station: Texas A&M University Press, 1984).

5. "Pat Morris Neff," *The Handbook of Texas Online*. http://www.tsha.utexas.edu/handbook/online/articles/view/NN/fne5.html. Accessed on 1 September 2002.

6. A collection of his speeches, including the myriad of Christian references by Neff, can be found in *Speeches Delivered by Pat M. Neff, Governor of Texas, Discussing Certain Phases of Contemplated Legislation* (Austin, Tex.: Von Boeckmann-Jones, 1923).

7. Pat Morris Neff, *The Battles for Peace* (Ft. Worth: Pioneer, 1925).

8. Routh, *Chosen for Leadership*, 58.

9. Ibid., 59–60.

10. Originally preached on the *Baptist Hour*, as recorded in Allen and Gregory, *Southern Baptist Preaching Yesterday*, 338–39.

24. Louie Devotie Newton

1. An example would be Robin Winston Smith, "Louie D. Newton: A Baptist Statesman of the Twentieth Century," Unpublished Ph.D. dissertation at Southern Seminary.

2. R. Earl Allen and Joel Gregory, *Southern Baptist Preaching Yesterday*, 593.

3. Ibid.

4. Porter Routh, *Chosen for Leadership*, 61.

5. Ibid., 62.

6. Louie D. Newton, "Georgia Baptist Convention," in *Encyclopedia of Southern Baptists*, 539.

7. McConnell was also a renowned Georgia Baptist in his own right and a cousin of George W. Truett. "In 1887 George W. Truett established a private Christian academy at Hiawassee, Georgia, where Fernando C. McConnell joined him in his educational endeavors which led to the creation of the public school system in Towns County, Georgia." Truett-McConnell College in Cleveland, Georgia, is named for the cousins and Baptist pioneers. http://www.truett.edu/history.htm. Accessed 16 July 2002.

8. Routh, *Chosen for Leadership*, 62.

9. Ibid., 61.

10. *Historical Highlights*, 30.2 (Fall 2000), 24, 26. It was later renamed The Georgia Council on Moral and Civic Concerns.

11. Newton's meeting with President Truman concerned the fears of Southern Baptists that the United States would maintain a permanent ambassador to the Vatican, Myron C. Taylor, after the war effort. Newton was vigorously opposed to the appointment, as a violation of the separation of church and state. See Allen and Gregory, *Southern Baptist Preaching Yesterday*, 348–49.

12. J. Frank Norris actually wrote the House on Un-American Activities volunteering to appear to expose the Southern Baptist conspiracy before the committee. Barry Hankins, *God's Rascal* (Lexington: University Press, 1996), 154.

13. Allen and Gregory, *Southern Baptist Preaching Yesterday*, 349–50.

14. Robert E. Naylor, *A Messenger's Memoirs* (Franklin, Tenn.: Providence, 1995), 59–65.

15. Louie D. Newton, *An American Churchman in the Soviet Union* (New York: American

Russian Institute, 1947); *Amazing Grace, The Life of M. N. McCall, Missionary to Cuba* (Atlanta: Home Mission Board, 1948); *Why I Am a Baptist* (New York: Thomas Nelson, 1958); *Fifty Golden Years; the Atlanta Association of Baptist Churches, 1909–1958* (Atlanta: Association, 1959).

16. The record of the banquet can be found in the Southern Seminary Archives. "Georgiawide dinner honoring Dr. and Mrs. Louie D. Newton, Atlanta Sheraton Biltmore Hotel Thursday evening, September 26, 1968, 6:30 o'clock. Bishop Arthur J. Moore, chairman, Mr. John A. Sibley, speaker."

17. Allen and Gregory, *Southern Baptist Preaching Yesterday*, 343.

25. Robert Greene Lee

1. E. Schuyler English, *Robert G. Lee, A Chosen Vessel* (Grand Rapids: Zondervan Publishing House, 1949), 99.

2. Ibid., 42.

3. Ibid., 107.

4. Ibid., 233. This and other excerpts are found in Timothy and Denise George, *Payday Someday* (Nashville: Broadman & Holman Publishers, 1995), 6–7.

5. Ibid., 268–69.

6. George and George, *Payday Someday*, 9–10.

7. Robert G. Lee, "Payday—Someday," ibid., 48–49.

26. James David Grey

1. James Cole and Robert Lee, *Saint J. D.* (Waco, Tex.: Word Books, 1969), 144. This remains the definitive biography on Grey.

2. Grey was awarded the doctor of divinity by Union University (1938), Louisiana College (1952), and Baylor University (1953).

3. Ibid., 75.

4. Ibid., 84.

5. Ibid., 86–87.

6. Ibid., 138–39.

7. Ibid., 151.

8. Ibid., 51–53.

9. Ibid., 16.

27. James Wilson Storer

1. Robert E. Naylor, *A Messenger's Memoirs* (Franklin, Tenn.: Providence House, 1995). Dr. Naylor's contribution to Baptist literature cannot be overestimated. He attended sixty-one SBC annual meetings and kept meticulous records.

2. Ibid., 95–97.

3. This story was modified from Porter Routh, *Chosen for Leadership*, 70.

4. Ibid., 71.

5. During his tenure in Tennessee, Storer served as vice president of the Tennessee Baptist Convention.

6. For a complete history of the church, see Alice Heath, *The Story of a Church* (Tulsa: FBC, 1997).

7. All books were published by Broadman Press: *Truth Enters Lowly Doors* (1938), *By-Ways to Highways* (1938), *Major Messages of the Minor Prophets* (1940), *These Historic Scriptures:*

Meditations upon the Bible Texts Used by Our Presidents, from Lincoln to Truman, at Their Inaugurations (1952), and *The Preacher: His Belief and Behavior* (1953).

8. Kendall Berry, "James Wilson Storer," in *Encyclopedia of Southern Baptists*, 3:1,992.

9. Naylor, *A Messenger's Memoirs*, 93.

10. Robert Baker, *The Southern Baptist Convention and Its People*, 438.

11. Berry, "James Wilson Storer," 1,992.

28. Casper Carl Warren

1. C. C. Warren, "Baptist Jubilee Advance" (Nashville: Southern Baptist Historical Library Archives, n.d.).

2. Porter Routh, *Chosen for Leadership*, 73.

3. W. Perry Crouch, "The Influence of a Great Christian," *Biblical Recorder*, 2 June 1973, 5.

4. Sam R. Covington, "N.C. Baptist Leader Dies After Illness," *Charlotte Observer*, 29 May 1973, 1C.

29. Brooks Hays

1. Porter Routh, *Chosen for Leadership*, 78.

2. Brooks Hays, *Politics Is My Parish* (Baton Rouge: Louisiana State University Press, 1981), 274.

3. Ibid., 4.

4. Ibid., 25.

5. Ibid., 46.

6. Bob Mccord, "Remember Alford and Hays," *Arkansas Times*, 15 December 2000.

7. Relman Morin, "Rep. Hays Fills Interpreter's Role in Parley of Faubus, Ike," *Arkansas Democrat Gazette*, 13 September 1957.

8. Hays, 184.

9. Ibid., ix.

10. Ibid., 212.

11. Ibid., 235.

12. Ibid., 259.

30. William Ramsey Pollard

1. Porter Routh, *Chosen for Leadership*, 81.

2. Though this was technically a world tour, Dr. James Merritt was the first standing president actually to travel to all fifteen regions of international mission life.

3. Ramsey Pollard, "Presidential Address," 1961 Southern Baptist Convention in St. Louis, Missouri.

4. Ibid.

5. Ramsey Pollard, Convention Address, 1962 Southern Baptist Convention.

31. Herschel Harold Hobbs

1. Herschel H. Hobbs, *My Faith and Message* (Nashville: Broadman & Holman, 1993), x–xi.

2. While the brief years following his death have not allowed many examinations of Hobbs's life, the most incisive biographer to date is Dr. David S. Dockery. Preaching the inaugural Hobbs Lectures at Oklahoma Baptist University on October 9–10, 2001, his lecture was the basis of his chapter on Hobbs in *Theologians of the Baptist Tradition* (Nashville: Broadman &

Holman, 2001), 216–31. Along with Hobbs's autobiography, Dockery's introductory section on the life of Hobbs serves, in large part, as the basis for this chapter.

3. Hobbs, *My Faith and Message*, 23.

4. He would make his commitment public, and final, at Brighton Baptist Church, where he served as deacon, Sunday school superintendent, and choir member. He was subsequently ordained at the Ensley church in June 1929. Ibid., 23–24, 27.

5. Ibid., 34.

6. As students of Baptist history and professors of Baptist distinctives, the present authors have read voluminous tomes on virtually every aspect of Baptist life. Between us, it is agreed that Dr. Hobbs's chapters on his years at Southern Seminary are some of the most vibrant, affectionate, and infectious writings on the period. One immediately becomes enthralled by the stories of the hearts of the professors and their devotion to Christ's cause. These chapters alone make Hobbs's autobiography required reading. Ibid., 61–106.

7. Ibid., 61.

8. Ibid., 82.

9. Ibid., 112.

10. Pastor and the thirty-eighth president of the SBC.

11. Eventual director of Baptist Press.

12. Professor of preaching at Southwestern Seminary.

13. Foreign missionary and professor of New Testament and Greek at New Orleans and Southeastern Seminaries.

14. Professor of philosophy and theology at New Orleans Seminary.

15. For many years the executive secretary of the South Carolina Baptist Convention.

16. Pastor and president of the Louisiana Baptist Convention, and served with Hobbs on the 1963 BFM Committee.

17. Hobbs, *My Faith and Message*, 129.

18. Ibid., 144–45.

19. Herschel H. Hobbs, *Cowards or Conquerors* (Philadelphia: Judson, 1951). His first book for Broadman was *Who Is This?* (Nashville: Broadman, 1952).

20. Hobbs, *My Faith and Message*, 223.

21. Ralph Elliott, professor of Old Testament at Midwestern Seminary, had written *The Message of Genesis*, which had stirred controversy among Southern Baptists.

22. Hobbs, *My Faith and Message*, 246.

23. Walter B. Shurden, "In Defense of the SBC: The Moderate Response to Fundamentalism," *The Theological Educator* 30 (1985), 13, as recorded in David S. Dockery, "Herschel H. Hobbs," in *Theologians of the Baptist Tradition* (Nashville: Broadman & Holman, 2001), 220–21.

32. Kenneth Owen White

1. K. Owen White, "Statement by Pastor of Houston Church," *Baptist Standard*, 19 June 1963.

2. Mona Petronella, ed., *A Church in the City Reaching the World* (Houston: First Baptist Church, Houston, Tex., 1985), 49.

3. Ibid., 48.

4. Porter Routh, *Chosen for Leadership*, 87.

5. K. Owen White, "Correspondence with Dr. Thomas H. Francis," 21 June 1963.

33. William Wayne Dehoney

1. Interview with Kathy Dehoney Evitts, 21 October 2002.
2. Porter Routh, *Chosen for Leadership*, 91.
3. Ibid., 92.
4. Union University would confer a D.D. on Dehoney in 1964.
5. Preached on 26 February 1961, 5 March 1961 and 12 March 1961, respectively, in the pulpit of First Baptist Church of Jackson, Tennessee.
6. Published in 1962, *Challenges to the Cross* was Dehoney's first book. It was a courageous indictment against cultural attacks on Christianity such as Communism, alcohol, and humanism. It became a best-seller. While at Central Birmingham, he did contribute one sermon in J. E. Lambdin's anthology, "Be Strong in the Lord" (Nashville: Broadman, 1952).
7. In January 1965, Dehoney spoke to more than six thousand on "The Holy Spirit and Total Evangelism."
8. On May 31, 1965, Dehoney addressed the SBREA on the topic of "The Cutting Edge of Advance: The Place of Religious Education in Southern Baptist Advance."
9. Presidential Address, 24 May 1966.
10. Dehoney Travel continues under the leadership of Kathy Dehoney Evitts, his daughter. www.dehoneytravel.com. Accessed 16 October 2002.
11. His extensive collection of artifacts from his travels were donated to Cumberland College in Williamsburg, Kentucky, in 1998.
12. The Dehoney's grandchildren: Morgan Richardson, Bradley Richardson, Mark Evitts, and Tonya Evitts Towles. Their great-grandchildren: Hunter Evitts and Sydney Evitts.

34. Henry Franklin Paschall

1. H. Franklin Paschall, "President's Address: Good News for Today's World" (Nashville: Southern Baptist Historical Archives, 1968), n.p.
2. Albert W. Wardin Jr., *God's Chosen Path: The Life of H. Franklin Paschall* (Nashville: Gospel Progress, Inc., 2001), 15.
3. Ibid., 31.
4. Ibid., 39.
5. Ibid., 75.
6. Ibid., 87
7. Ibid., 170.

35. Wallie Amos Criswell

1. Most notably, Gray Allison, "The Preaching of W. A. Criswell: A Critical Analysis of Selected Messages," Unpublished Th.D. dissertation. (Memphis: Mid-America Baptist Theological Seminary, 1990); Robert A. Rohm, *Dr. C: The Vision and Ministry of W. A. Criswell* (Chicago: Moody, 1990); Thomas Charlton and Rufus Spain, *Oral Memoirs of W. A. Criswell* (Waco: Baylor, 1973); Leon McBeth, *The First Baptist Church of Dallas* (Grand Rapids: Zondervan, 1973); L. Paige Patterson, "W. A. Criswell," in *Theologians of the Baptist Tradition* (Nashville: Broadman, 2001). Many others make significant contributions, but Dr. Criswell's ghostwritten autobiography, *Standing on the Promises* (Dallas: Word, 1990) is certainly the most significant. Most Criswell biographies and books fall into one of two categories: hagiography or scathing critique. As Patterson notes, the definitive biography has yet to be written. Patterson, 256. Curiously, though the *Encyclopedia of Southern Baptists* was first published in 1958 and the third volume added in 1971, at the end of his tenure as president, Criswell is not covered in the mammoth work.

2. Patterson, "W. A. Criswell," 234.

3. Porter Routh, *Chosen for Leadership*, 95.

4. Yates was listed in the Home Mission Board "Hall of Fame" memorials in 1919.

5. Interestingly, his mother moved with him each time.

6. Routh, *Chosen for Leadership*, 97.

7. "Why I Am a Premillennialist," preached at Moody Founder's Week, Moody Bible Institute, 1978. Also noted in Patterson, "W. A. Criswell," 235.

8. Ibid., 236.

9. The definitive bibliography of the writings of Criswell can be found in the article by Dr. Lamar Cooper in *The New Criswell Theological Review* (1.1). One of the most fascinating books to come from Criswell was actually co-written with Duke McCall, *Passport to the World* (Nashville: Broadman, 1951), which chronicles a global mission tour of the two seemingly incompatible friends. From a completely different genre, *Passport* is a revealing insight into Criswell's life and views.

10. Robert E. Naylor, *A Messenger's Memoirs* (Franklin, Tenn.: Providence House, 1995), 149–50.

11. W. A. Criswell, "The Two-Edged Sword," Presidential Address to the Southern Baptist Convention, New Orleans, Louisiana, 1969.

12. As an example, M. G. Toulouse, "W. A. Criswell," in *Dictionary of Baptists in America* (Downers Grove, Ill.: IVP, 1994), 98, which insists on calling Criswell a "fundamentalist" leader.

13. Dr. D. McCall Brunson, "Dr. W. A. Criswell." Delivered at the Funeral of Dr. Criswell on January 16, 2002. Transcribed by Christine Moers. Recorded in *The New Criswell Theological Review* (1.1), 11–12.

36. Carl E. Bates

1. Baptist Press, "Carl Bates, Former SBC President, Dies at 85 at his N.C. Residence," 22 December 1999.

2. See the history of First Baptist Church of Amarillo at http://www.fbc-amarillo.org. Accessed 10 October 2002. During his nine years at Amarillo, the church baptized 2,143 people, and saw a total of 6,454 new members join the church.

3. *Biblical Recorder*, 23 December 1999.

4. Carl E. Bates, "Hitherto-Henceforth," SBC Presidential Address in Philadelphia, 6 June 1972.

5. *Breaking the Communication Barriers through Preaching* (Nashville: Broadman, 1977).

6. As an example, Bates taught the SBTS faculty retreat at Clifty Falls State Park in Madison, Indiana, on August 31, 1985, along with chapel sermons every year. See the SBTS Library Archives.

7. *Houston Chronicle*, 24 December 1999, A-16.

37. Owen Cooper

1. Don McGregor, *The Thought Occurred to Me* (Nashville: Fields Communications and Publishing, 1992), 91.

2. Don McGregor, "Cooper Rotation Marks Milepost," *Baptist Record*, 2 September 1982, 1–2.

3. McGregor, *The Thought Occurred to Me*, 153.

4. Porter Routh, *Chosen for Leadership,* 101.

5. Ibid., 102.

6. Anne W. McWilliams, "Owen Cooper, Baptist Statesman, Dies at 78," 7.

38. Jaroy Weber

1. *The Baptist Standard,* 2 July 1942, 8. For those too young to remember, BTU was the discipleship study course for Southern Baptists, an acronym for Baptist Training Union. The preceding discipleship entity was called BYPU (Baptist Young Peoples Union) but had been expanded to BTU to allow for adult discipleship courses. The program eventually became known as DT (Discipleship Training).

2. Jaroy Weber, personal resume of 1958, on file at the Texas Baptist Historical Archives.

3. *The Baptist Standard,* 6 June 1961, 7.

4. *The Baptist Message,* 28 June 1960, 1.

5. William Estep, *And God Gave the Increase* (Beaumont: First Baptist Church, 1971), 191–92.

6. Personal interview with L. Paige Patterson, 18 October 2002.

7. Estep, *And God Gave the Increase,* 196.

8. Robert Naylor, *A Messenger's Memoirs* (Franklin: Providence House, 1995), 178. Weber had also served as president of the SBC Pastor's Conference.

9. Jaroy Weber, "Let the Bells Ring," Presidential Address, 10 June 1975 in Miami Beach, Florida, at the Southern Baptist Convention.

10. Naylor, *A Messenger's Memoirs,* 189.

11. Albert McClellan, *The Executive Committee of the Southern Baptist Convention, 1917–1984* (Nashville: Broadman, 1985).

39. James Lenox Sullivan

1. James L. Sullivan, *God Is My Record* (Nashville: Broadman Press, 1974), 27.

2. Ibid., 26.

3. Ibid., 28.

4. Ibid., 21.

5. Porter Routh, *Chosen for Leadership,* 109.

6. Sullivan, *God Is My Record,* 127–28.

7. Lonnie Wilkey, "James L. Sullivan Still Active at Age 90," *Baptist & Reflector,* 1 November 2000; at www.tnbaptist.org/baptistandreflector/2000BpercentR/ 11–1articles/br11–12/htm; accessed 10 October 2002.

40. Jimmy Raymond Allen

1. Jimmy Raymond Allen, "Where There Is a Vision, the People Flourish," SBC Presidential Address, 13 June 1978.

2. *In the Shadow of His Hand: The History of the First Baptist Church of San Antonio, Texas* (Austin, Tex.: Hart Graphics, 1981).

3. Dr. Allen has also received honorary doctorates from the University of Richmond, California Baptist University, Southwestern Baptist University, and Howard Payne University.

4. *The Menace of Gambling* (Nashville: Broadman, 1966).

5. *Peace, Peace* (New York: World Press, 1966).

6. "Jimmy R. Allen," http://www.bigcanoechapel.org/allen.htm. Accessed 10 November 2002.

7. "Pastors of First Baptist Church" http://www.fbcsa.rg/history4.htm. Accessed 10 November 2002.

8. Bonnie Sparrow, "Mrs. Allen: Honest, Candid," *The Baptist Standard,* June 1978, 9.

9. Ibid.

10. "Allen: Conservative, Progressive, Aggressive." *The Baptist Standard,* June 1978, 8.

11. http://www.bigcanoechapel.org/allen.htm. Accessed 10 November 2002.

12. "Allen: Conservative, Progressive, Aggressive." *The Baptist Standard,* June 1978, 8.

13. Jimmy R. Allen, *The Burden of a Secret* (New York: Random House/Moorings, 1995).

14. For more information, see *Lydia's House: A Project of Love and Action.* http://www.lydiashouse.net.

15. Charlene Terrell, "Chapel's Dr. Jimmy Allen Receives Award for Leadership and Integrity," *Smoke Signals,* October 2001, 10.

41. Adrian Pierce Rogers

1. Adrian Rogers, "The Souvenirs of Pain," Campus Crusade for Christ International, 1996, at http://www.ccci.org/gl-men/stories/rogers-a.html; accessed 18 October 2002.

2. Ibid.

3. Interview of Adrian Rogers by Emir Caner, 14 October 2002.

4. Adrian Rogers, "From the Chairman of the Committee on the Baptist Faith and Message," at http://www.sbc.net/bfm/bfmchairman.asp; accessed 19 October 2002.

42. Bailey Eugene Smith

1. Bailey Smith, "Southern Baptists' Most Serious Question," 15 June 1982.

2. Bailey Smith, "The Worth of the Work," 9 June 1981, Southern Baptist Convention.

3. Ibid. Note that Smith uses the explicit phrase found in the *Baptist Faith and Message* of 1963, which states, "There is truth without any mixture of error."

43. James T. Draper Jr.

1. Written correspondence of James Draper with the author, Emir F. Caner, 6 September 2002. A follow-up interview was also conducted on 10 October 2002.

2. Ibid.

3. Ibid. Twenty years later, Draper returned to Bryan to preach a revival at a neighboring church. Demonstrating their love for their former pastor, forty-five people from Sleepy Hollow attended the services on Sunday evening.

4. Mombasa is known by many as the headquarters for Islamic theology in East Africa and is home to numerous Muslim seminaries.

5. Jerry Sutton, *The Baptist Reformation* (Nashville: Broadman & Holman, 2000), 125–26.

6. Not surprisingly, Draper has teams that go to Kenya on a regular basis.

44. Charles F. Stanley

1. Interview of Charles Stanley with Emir Caner, 14 October 2002.

2. Paul Pressler, *A Hill on Which to Die* (Nashville: Broadman & Holman, 1999), 130. The quote is a blend between Pressler's book and the personal interview with Emir Caner.

3. Jerry Sutton, *The Baptist Reformation,* 143.

4. Charles Stanley, www.intouch.org/inside/about_us/biography_76833.html; accessed 7 October 2002.

45. Charles Jerry Vines

1. Interview with the authors, 6 September 2002.

2. The bachelor of divinity degree, standard in Southern Baptist seminaries, was later changed to the master of divinity, as it always followed a prior undergraduate degree.

3. Jerry Vines, *A Guide to Effective Sermon Delivery* (Chicago: Moody, 1986) and *A Practical Guide to Sermon Preparation* (Chicago: Moody, 1985) have been combined into one volume by Jerry Vines and Jim Shaddix, *Power in the Pulpit* (Chicago: Moody, 1999).

4. Interview with the authors, 6 September 2002.

5. Carl L. Kell and L. Raymond Camp, *In the Name of the Father* (Carbondale, Ill.: Southern Illinois University, 1999), 144–45.

6. Ibid., 56.

46. Morris Hines Chapman

1. Interview with authors, 15 October 2002.

2. Correspondence with the author, 30 August 2002.

3. Morris Chapman, *Youth Affirm: The Doctrine of Christ* (Nashville: Convention Press, 1985). This was followed by *Jesus: Author and Finisher* (Nashville: Broadman, 1987); *The Wedding Collection* (Nashville: Broadman, 1991); and *Faith: Taking God at His Word* (Nashville: Broadman, 1992).

4. Correspondence with the author, 30 August 2002.

5. Ibid.

6. Interview with authors, 15 October 2002.

47. Homer Edwin Young

1. 1992 *SBC Book of Reports*, as reported in *The Founders Journal*, 11.

2. Ibid.

3. James Dotson, "Cutting Edge 21st-Century Church: Topic Draws 3,000 to Conference," in Baptist Press, 3 October 2002.

4. Interview with the authors, 20 October 2002.

5. C. Roy Angell, *Iron Shoes* (Nashville: Broadman, 1953).

6. Interview with the authors, 20 October 2002.

7. Dr. Wendell Estep, www.fbccola.com/fbcestep.htm. Accessed 11 October 2002.

8. This would be followed by degrees from The Criswell College (D.D., 1984), Southwest Baptist University (S.T.D., 1985), Mississippi College (D.D., 1987), Hannibal-LaGrange College (D.D., 1987), and Houston Baptist University (D.D., 1998).

9. Information on the history of Second Baptist can be found at www.second.org. Accessed on 12 July 2002.

10. His books include *David: After God's Own Heart* (Nashville: Broadman, 1984); *The Purpose of Suffering* (Eugene, Oreg.: Harvest House, 1985); *The Winning Walk* (Heritage, 1989); *Against All Odds* (Nashville: Thomas Nelson, 1992); *Romancing the Home* (Nashville: Broadman, 1993); *Been There, Done That, Now What?* (Nashville: Broadman, 1994); *Pure Sex* (Sisters, Oreg.: Multnomah, 1997); *Everywhere I Go* (Houston: Winning Walk, 1999), and *Everlasting Father* (Colorado Springs: Waterbrook, 2002).

48. James Bascom Henry

1. Interview of Jim Henry with the author, 10 October 2002. There was also written correspondence between Henry and the author.

2. Jerry Sutton, *The Baptist Reformation*, 226.

3. Interview, 10 October 2002.

49. Thomas David Elliff

1. J. T. Elliff would retire in 1980.

2. "On a Thursday evening in July of 1951, Tom came to repentance and faith in Christ following an outdoor crusade service sponsored by the First Baptist Church of Fordyce, Arkansas, where his father was pastor. The next fall [1952] he was baptized at Bethany Baptist Church in Kansas City, Missouri." First Southern Baptist Church of Del City, Oklahoma historical records.

3. Ouachita Baptist University, http://www.obu.edu/about/history.shtml. Accessed 14 July 2002.

4. Along with his grandfather, his father, his two brothers, and his brother-in-law, Elliff also had an uncle who was a preacher, Rev. Garland Murray.

5. Interview with the authors, 16 October 2002.

6. Interview with author, 7 October 2002.

7. Elliff has been the recipient of two honorary doctorates: doctor of sacred theology, Southwestern Baptist University; and a doctor of divinity, Midcontinent Baptist Bible College.

8. Interview with authors, 9 October 2002.

9. Dr. Elliff's books include *Praying for Others* (Nashville: Broadman, 1978); *The Pathway to God's Presence* (Nashville: Broadman, 1990); *America on the Edge* (NCM, 1992); *A Passion for Prayer* (Wheaton, Ill.: Crossway, 1998); *In Their Own Words* (Nashville: Broadman & Holman, 2003); *Letters to Lovers* (Nashville: Broadman & Holman, 2003); *The Seven Pillars of a Kingdom Family* (Nashville: Broadman & Holman, 2003), as well as contributions to *Masterlife, The Disciple's Study Bible, The Family Worship Bible*, and other discipleship materials.

10. His mission work continues, preaching crusades and conferences in Kenya, Tanzania, South Africa, Zimbabwe, South Korea, Germany, Norway, Austria, Argentina, the Caribbean, Australia, France, China, Cambodia, Cyprus, Canada, and across the United States.

11. Dr. Thomas D. Elliff, "Charting Our Course by the Unchanging Christ," presidential address, 1998 Southern Baptist Convention in Salt Lake City, Utah, 9 June 1998.

50. Leighton Paige Patterson

1. Patterson, interview with Emir Caner, 11 October 2002. Patterson also answered a written questionnaire for the interviewer.

2. Ibid.

3. Paul Pressler, *A Hill on Which to Die* (Nashville: Broadman & Holman, 1999), 60. This is perhaps the finest explanation of the Conservative Resurgence in the Southern Baptist Convention given by one who led in the reformation.

4. Ryan Hutchinson, correspondence to the faculty, 11 October 2002.

51. James Gregory Merritt

1. Interview with authors, 24 August 2002.

2. Presidential address, 11 June 2002, in St. Louis, Missouri.

3. Jeff Robinson, in a Baptist Press story, 2 Jan 2002 wrote, "Since Merritt took the pulpit in 1985, the church has undergone massive growth—numbering 7,826 baptisms and increasing in membership from 2,168 to nearly 12,000 as of February 2000."

4. James Merritt, *God's Prescription for a Happy Christian* (Victor, 1990); *Friends, Foes and Fools* (Nashville: Broadman & Holman, 1997); *How to Be a Winner and Influence Anybody* (Nashville: Broadman & Holman, 2002).

52. Jack Norman Graham

1. Clay Crosse, *I Will Follow Christ* (Nashville: J Countryman Books, 2000).

2. Tammi Reed Ledbetter, "SBC Nominee Jack Graham Rooted in Evangelism," Baptist Press, 8 June 2002.

3. Jack Graham, excerpt from sermon at Latham Springs Baptist Encampment's "75th Anniversary Celebration." Jay Raines, editor. http://www.gotelltheworld.com/illustrate/bell.htm. Accessed on 17 June 2002.

4. Graham interview with the author, 25 September 2002.

5. On 15 September 2002, Prestonwood Baptist Church established its new record for Bible study attendance with ninety-three hundred.

6. Ibid.

7. While serving in the state, Graham was a trustee of Oklahoma Baptist University.

8. Jack Graham and Daniel L. Akin, "Contending for the Faith in the 21st Century: A Survey of the 2000 Baptist Faith and Message" *The Southern Seminary Magazine,* 68.4 (November 2000), 10–12.

9. Jack Graham, *You Can Make a Difference* (Nashville: Broadman & Holman, 1992); *Diamonds in the Dark* (Nashville: Thomas Nelson,1997); *Lessons from the Heart* (Chicago: Moody, 2001); *A Hope and a Future* (Chicago: Moody, 2002). This is in addition to numerous articles and two pamphlets, which are used by churches across the nation, *New Life in Christ* and *Is the Bible Just Another Book?*

Index